Institutional Change and Economic Behaviour

This is IEA Conference Volume No. 144

Institutional Change and Economic Behaviour

Edited by

János Kornai
Harvard University, USA and the Central European University and Collegium, Budapest, Hungary

László Mátyás
Central European University, Budapest, Hungary

and

Gérard Roland
University of California, Berkeley, USA

palgrave macmillan

in association with the
International Economic Association

First published in 2008 by
PALGRAVE MACMILLAN
Houndmills, Basingstoke, Hampshire RG21 6XS and
175 Fifth Avenue, New York, N.Y. 10010
Companies and representatives throughout the world.

PALGRAVE MACMILLAN is the global academic imprint of the Palgrave Macmillan division of St. Martin's Press, LLC and of Palgrave Macmillan Ltd. Macmillan® is a registered trademark in the United States, United Kingdom and other countries. Palgrave is a registered trademark in the European Union and other countries.

ISBN-13: 978–0–230–54698–1 hardback
ISBN-10: 0–230–54698–6 hardback

This book is printed on paper suitable for recycling and made from fully managed and sustained forest sources. Logging, pulping and manufacturing processes are expected to conform to the environmental regulations of the country of origin.

A catalogue record for this book is available from the British Library.

A catalog record for this book is available from the Library of Congress.

10 9 8 7 6 5 4 3 2 1
17 16 15 14 13 12 11 10 09 08

Printed and bound in Great Britain by
CPI Antony Rowe, Chippenham and Eastbourne

Contents

List of Tables/Figures

Tables

Figures

List of Abbreviations and Acronyms

AAZ	Acemoglu–Aghion–Zilibotti
ABHV	Aghion, Boustan, Hoxby and Vandenbussche
AK	aggregate production function $Y = AK$ (constant return to capital)
BPC	beliefs, preferences and constraints
CPI	consumer price index
EU	European Union
EU-15	European Union 15 members
FDI	foreign direct investment
FOC	first-order condition
GARP	generalized axiom of revealed preferences
GDP	gross domestic product
HDI	Human Development Index
ICT	information and computing technology
OECD	Organization for Economic Cooperation and Development
NBER	National Bureau of Economic Research
MRW	Mankiw–Romer–Weil
PPP	purchasing power parity
R&D	research and development
TFP	total factor productivity
US	United States
VAM	Vandenbussche, Aghion and Meghir

List of Contributors

Philippe Aghion, Harvard University, USA

Masahiko Aoki, Stanford University, USA

Herbert Gintis, University of Massachusetts and Santa Fe Institute, USA

Geoffrey Hodgson, University of Hertfordshire Business School, UK

Thorbjørn Knudsen, University of Southern Denmark

János Kornai, Harvard University, USA, Central European University and Collegium Budapest, Hungary

Timur Kuran, Duke University, USA

Edmund S. Phelps, Cornell University, USA

Yingyi Qian, University of California, Berkeley, USA

Gérard Roland, University of California, Berkeley, USA

Jinglian Wu, Development Research Centre, Beijing, and China-Europe International Business School, Shanghai, China

The International Economic Association

A non-profit organization with purely scientific aims, the International Economic Association (IEA) was founded in 1950. It is a federation of some sixty national economic associations in all parts of the world. Its basic purpose is the development of economics as an intellectual discipline, recognizing a diversity of problems, systems and values in the world and taking note of methodological diversities.

The IEA has, since its creation, sought to fulfil that purpose by promoting mutual understanding among economists through the organization of scientific meetings and common research programmes, and by means of publications on problems of fundamental as well as of current importance. Deriving from its long concern to assure professional contacts between East and West and North and South, the IEA pays special attention to issues of economies in systemic transition and in the course of development. During its fifty years of existence, it has organized more than a hundred round-table conferences for specialists on topics ranging from fundamental theories to methods and tools of analysis and major problems of the present-day world. Participation in round tables is at the invitation of a specialist programme committee, but fourteen triennial World Congresses have regularly attracted the participation of individual economists from all over the world.

The Association is governed by a Council, composed of representatives of all member associations, and by a fifteen-member Executive Committee which is elected by the Council. The Executive Committee (2002–2005) at the time of the Marrakech Congress was:

	Professor Kotaro Suzumura, Japan
	Professor Alessandro Vercelli, Italy
Advisers:	Professor Fiorella Kostoris Padoa Schioppa, Italy
	Professor Vitor Constancio, Portugal
Secretary-General:	Professor Jean-Paul Fitoussi, France
General Editor:	Professor Michael Kaser, UK

Sir Austin Robinson was an active Adviser on the publication of IEA Conference proceedings from 1954 until his final short illness in 1993.

The Association has also been fortunate in having secured many outstanding economists to serve as President:

> Gottfried Haberler (1950–53), Howard S. Ellis (1953–56), Erik Lindahl (1956–59), E.A.G. Robinson (1959–62). Ugo Papi (1962–65), Paul A. Samuelson (1965–68), Erik Lundberg (1968–71), Fritz Machlup (1971–74), Edmund Malinvaud (1974–77), Shigeto Tsuru (1977–80), Victor L. Urquidi (1980–83), Kenneth J. Arrow (1983–86), Amartya Sen (1986–89), Anthony B. Atkinson (1989–92), Michael Bruno (1992–95), Jacques Drèze (1995–99), Robert M. Solow (1999–2002) and János Kornai (2002–05).

The activities of the Association are mainly funded from the subscriptions of members and grants from a number of organizations. Support from UNESCO since the Association was founded, and from its International Social Science Council, is gratefully acknowledged.

Acknowledgements

The Fourteenth World Congress of the International Economic Association (IEA) was held in Marrakech from 29 August to 2 September 2005. It was opened by the letter of His Majesty Mohammed VI, King of Morocco, read by M. Abdelaziz Meziane Belfkih, Advisor to the King. The IEA is deeply grateful to the patron of the Congress, to His Majesty Mohammed VI, King of Morocco, who made the event possible.

The Opening Session was addressed by Professor János Kornai, the outgoing President of the International Economic Association.

The scientific programme, comprising the Presidential Address, six Invited Lectures, nine Invited Sessions and fifty-two Contributed Papers, focused on the following main themes:

New Trends in Economics

New results in behavioural economics

New institutional economics

Pressure for and constraints on publication

Understanding the Great Changes in the World

Globalization and new developments in trade theory

Economic development

The first fifteen years of post-socialist transition

Honesty and trust

Economic Reforms in Morocco

The scientific preparation of the World Congress had been placed under the responsibility of the IEA President, János Kornai. He had been assisted by an international programme committee, co-chaired by Gérard Roland and László Mátyás, with the following members:

History of Economic Thought, Economic History:
Gerardo della Paolera (American University of Paris, France)
Econometric Theory, Applied Econometrics, Econometric Modelling:
Jaya Krishnakumar (University of Geneva, Switzerland), Timo Terasvirta (University of Stockholm, Sweden), Gábor Kézdi (Central European University, Hungary)
Economic Theory:
Andreu Mas Colell (Pompeu Fabra University, Spain)
Behavioural Economics and Experimental Economics:
Simon Gächter (University of Saint Gallen, Switzerland)
Households and Income Distribution:
Attila Ratfai (Central European University, Hungary)

Law and Economics:
Anthony Dnes (University of Hull, UK)
Macroeconomics:
Fabio Canova (Pompeu Fabra University, Spain), Eliana Cardoso (Brazil), Eduardo Engel (Chile/Yale University, USA), Robert Solow (MIT, USA), Alessandro Vercelli (University of Siena, Italy)
International Trade:
Pétér Benczúr (Hungarian National Bank)
International Economics:
Philip Lane (University of Dublin, Ireland), Jacob Frenkel (Israel/Merrill Lynch UK), Jean-Paul Fitoussi (OFCE, Paris, France)
Economic Policy (national and international):
Guillermo Calvo (University of Maryland)
Development Economics:
E. Somanathan (Indian Statistical Institute, India), Heba Handoussa (ERF, Egypt)
Public Finance and Public Economics:
Ben Lockwood (University of Warwick, UK), Kotaro Suzumura (Hitotsubashi University, Japan), Vitor Constancio (Bank of Portugal)
Health, Education, Demographics, Urban Economics:
Pierre Pestieau (CORE, Belgium), Maria Augusztinovics (Institute of Economics, Hungarian Academy of Sciences, Hungary)
Labour Economics, Gender Issues:
Bina Agarwal (Institute of Economic Growth, India), Fiorella Kostoris Padoa Schioppa (Rome, Italy)
Industrial Organization:
Patrick Rey (University of Toulouse, France)
Lessons from Economic Transition:
Stepan Jurajda (CERGE-EI, Czech Republic) Michael Kaser (University of Oxford, UK), Wu Jinglian (Peking University and Chinese Academy of Social Sciences)
Institutional Economics:
Ugo Pagano (University of Siena, Italy)
Environmental Economics:
Barry Field (University of Massachusetts, USA), Michael Hoel (University of Oslo, Norway)
Agricultural and Resource Economics:
Leo Simon (University of California, Berkeley, USA)
Computational Methods in Economics:
Felix Kubler (University of Mannheim, Germany)
North African / Moroccan Issues:
Mohamed Chafiki (Mohammed V University, Rabat, and Ministry of Finance and Privatization, Morocco)

The programme of the Congress was enriched by many memorable social events, including a dinner under the patronage of the Prime Minister of Morocco for speakers and invited guests, a guided tour in Marrakech for all Congress participants and a cultural evening. The Congress was supported by the Ministry of Finance and Privatization and other institutions in Morocco, Royal Air Maroc, Maroc Telecom, Banque Centrale Populaire and Caisse de Dépôt et de Gestion, who generously agreed to ensure most of the funding of the Congress. Generous subventions were also provided by Banca d'Italia, Bank for International Settlements, European Central Bank, Ford Foundation, Inter-American Development Bank and UNESCO through the International Social Science Council.

The IEA owes a debt of gratitude to many people personally, including those who helped the organization of the World Congress on the spot: Fathallah Oualalou, Minister of Finance and Privatization, Mohammed Chafiki, Chairman of the Local Organizing Committee, and all the other members of the Local Organizing Committee:

Omar Faraj
Naima Meziane
Mustapha Arrifi
Hakim Firadi
Mohamed Rguigue
Amina Chemlal
Hicham Zakani
Laila Essadki
Mohamed Benchekroun
Mohamed Fadel Mokhtari
Mohamed Ouchen

It is also grateful to those who carried the burden of preparations outside Morocco. We thank the IEA Secretary-General, Professor Jean-Paul Fitoussi, and also the administrative assistants, Marie David and Véronique De Labarre in Paris, Carol Smallfield in Berkeley, and Andrea Csele and Katalin Szabó in Budapest.

And finally, we are deeply indebted to all those who helped in the dissemination of the Congress outcomes. We would like to extend our sincere thanks to scholars who contributed their papers to the volumes, and also to the IEA General Editor, Professor Michael Kaser, to Maureen Hadfield, Associate Editor, and the Economics Publisher at Palgrave Macmillan, Amanda Hamilton, for their great help in shepherding the books through the production process.

Introduction

The Fourteenth World Congress of the International Economic Association took place in Marrakech between 29 August and 2 September 2005. The main themes of the Congress were 'New Trends in Economics' and 'Understanding the Great Changes in the World'. These two volumes published by Palgrave Macmillan present to the reader the presidential address by János Kornai, most of the distinguished invited lectures (by Yingyi Qian and Jinglian Wu, Timur Kuran, Edmund Phelps and Philippe Aghion) and many of the papers presented at the different invited sessions organized by Masa Aoki ('Mechanisms of Institutional Change'), Herbert Gintis ('The Implications of Experimental Economics for Economic Theory'), Mustafa Nabli ('Is Democracy a Binding Constraint for Economic Growth in the Middle East and North Africa Region?'), Susan Rose-Ackerman ('Trust and Distrust in Post-Socialist Transition'), Jan Svejnar ('15 Years of Post-Socialist Transition'), Oded Stark ('The New Economics of the Brain Drain: Analytics, Empirics, and Policy') and Claude Menard ('Institutional Design and Economic Performance').

There have been many changes both in the world and in economics these last twenty years. A fundamental change has been the end of the cold war and the post-socialist transition in Central and Eastern Europe, China and Vietnam. Countries like China and India have engaged on an impressive growth path. Globalization has continued to unravel, with goods, capital and people moving more freely around the globe. With 9/11 and the Iraq war, but also Chechnya, Kosovo, Afghanistan and the continued conflict in the Middle East, new concerns have arisen about fault-lines of conflict in the twenty-first century. Simultaneously, the spread of democracy continues throughout the world. The world in 2006 is completely different from the world in 1976 or even 1986.

Many of these important changes in the world have been concomitant to changes in economics. This is not surprising. Some of the changes in economics have been brought about by important changes in the world. The large-scale economic transition from socialism to capitalism has contributed in a significant way to put institutional economics firmly in the mainstream. The large output fall and strong variation in macroeconomic performance across countries came quite unexpected to the mainstream of the profession who thought that liberalization, stabilization and privatization should put these economies on a virtuous growth path. Economists started taking very seriously the idea that the dismal performance of the Russian economy and of most of the Former Soviet Union economies in the 1990s could be attributed to institutional failures. The transition experience convinced a large part of the economics profession of the importance of institutions as the underpinning of a successful market economy. The Marrakech Congress is a good reflection of the current strength of institutional economics, as various distinguished lectures and invited sessions related to institutional issues. Another important change in economics is the increasing success of behavioural economics. The standard model of rationality is being put into question as several of its core components are contradicted by a large body of work in psychology. Models of behavioural economics or of economics and psychology are introducing changes to the standard assumptions of *Homo Oeconomicus* and deriving new predictions about economic behaviour. More and more evidence is produced by experimental economics about individual and group behaviour, testing standard assumptions about rationality but also about game theory and the new behavioural models.

The two main themes – 'Understanding the Great Changes in the World' and 'New Trends in Economics' – are the *leitmotifs* of both volumes containing the papers of the Marrakech congress. Each paper is reflecting either one of the main themes, or both. In the present first volume under the title *Institutional Change and Economic Behaviour* we collected the papers discussing *general* topics and/or problems of *large geographical areas*. (The other volume under the title *Corruption, Development and Institutional Design* deals with more specific topics that were also discussed prominently at the Congress, such as corruption, immigration, enterprise reform and regulatory reform.)

The presidential address by János Kornai is devoted to the transition process in eight former socialist countries that became members of the EU in 2004: the Czech Republic, Estonia, Poland, Latvia, Lithuania, Hungary, Slovakia and Slovenia. More than fifteen years after the transition started, the paper reflects on the successes and disappointments of that great transformation. He compares the transformation in those countries to other great transformations in modern history such as the transformation from medieval to modern societies, West Germany's transformation after World War II or the inverse transition from capitalism to socialism. The transformation in Central Europe occurred with incredible speed, was non-violent and was not preceded by a war; it was a complete transformation both of political institutions and the economic system and went in the direction of the mainstream of historical transformations in recent history, i.e. towards democracy and capitalism. By most measures, this transformation represents an immense success story. Nevertheless, the inhabitants of those countries are not euphoric and express much dissatisfaction. Despite an undeniable general increase in the standards of living as compared to socialism, inequality has increased strongly and job security has disappeared and unemployment became part of the economic landscape. There is dissatisfaction with corruption and with existing politicians. Feelings of discontent and unhappiness are quite widespread compared to Western Europe. Kornai argues that one needs to go beyond the standard economic model to understand these disappointments and take into account phenomena studied in other social sciences such as the sociology of reference groups, cognitive flaws, etc.

The transformation in China is analysed in the paper by Yingyi Qian and Jinglian Wu. They document carefully the phenomenal growth that has been taking place in China in the last three decades. Real GDP per capita has increased by nearly 700 per cent between 1978 and 2003. At the same time, the Chinese economy has opened up tremendously, its foreign trade now representing over 60 per cent of its GDP. They document not only the spectacular increase in living standards but also the social transformations that have taken place in the most populated country on earth. Urbanization has been very fast as jobs in industry and services have increased. Poverty has declined but inequality has gone up. Corruption is still a serious problem and China ranks with Peru and Turkey in the Transparency International but better than Russia and Ukraine. Despite spectacular increases in living standards, aspirations of Chinese citizens are growing even faster. At the same time, there has been slow progress on political reform. Little has changed in the authoritarian rule of the Communist Party. They interpret the recent economic developments in China as growth maximization under the constraint of Party control. The hunger for growth is stronger than in many other nations because of China's past. For millennia, it was the most affluent country in the world. It entered the modern era a poor country and experienced tragedy after tragedy in the twentieth century, culminating in the Cultural Revolution. This policy of growth under Party control explains why economic reforms and opening up of the economy are faster than internal reforms, why the rule of law is being established before democracy and why control over firms has been abandoned. In the latter case, the growth advantage was stronger than the loss of overall control for the Party. Obviously, the tension between the economic dynamism and the absence of important change in the political sphere is a source of uncertainty. Today, most Chinese probably prefer an increase in living standards to increases in freedom. This may not always be the case.

Timur Kuran, in his distinguished lecture, gave a historical perspective on the causes of economic underdevelopment in the Middle East. He analysed, in particular, institutions that played a negative role in the development of the region: Islamic inheritance law and its form of trust, the *waqf*. Contrary to other religions, Islam has very specific prescriptions about inheritance. The Qur'an specifies that two-thirds of the estate is reserved for children, spouse and other family. The share of a female must equal half of that of a male. As a consequence, successful businesses tended to become fragmented after the death of the founder. In contrast, in European countries where no such religious prescriptions on inheritance existed, there was room for more experimentation, allowing primogeniture to emerge as a more efficient institution to prevent fragmentation of businesses. As a consequence, the

Middle East failed to adopt the organizational and institutional innovation that led to the development of the modern limited liability corporation. The *waqf* is an unincorporated trust overseen by Islamic courts. Its purpose is to provide a service allowed under Islamic law and the service must be provided in perpetuity. The establishment of a *waqf* was a way to secure assets since a *waqf* was considered sacred and rulers were reluctant to expropriate *waqfs*. The perpetuity rule made *waqfs* very rigid as the service was supposed to remain the same. The *waqf* system also had a negative effect on the development of civil society. Indeed, leaders of a *waqf* were not accountable to its beneficiaries. While these factors shed light on reasons for why the Middle East failed to catch up with the industrial revolution, they should not necessarily be seen as obstacles for the future as countries from the region have been importing modern institutions in the last two centuries.

Closer in time, the lecture by Ed Phelps, the economics Nobel laureate for 2006, analyses the large changes in the world economy since the end of World War II. In particular, he analyses the evolution of Western European economies that were catching up on the US for the thirty years after World War II but now are trailing in productivity growth. The catch-up is best explained by technology transfer. However, productivity growth started slowing down in the late 1970s and the gap with the US has been increasing since the 1990s. Phelps blames the European corporatist institutional system with big unions, big employer organizations, large banks and a large state sector. It main deficiency is its lack of dynamism and entrepreneurs. Central European countries accessing the European Union have not proven to be growth tigers as their performance pales in contrast to China. They might be in transition to the European corporatist system.

One likely factor that might be behind the disappointing performance of Europe is the weakness of its higher education system. The US devotes a twice larger share of GDP to higher education than Europe and, also, a larger proportion of the population has tertiary education. Philippe Aghion examined the link between education and growth in his lecture. The argument is that the closer one approaches the technological frontier the more important the role of higher education, because of its role for technological innovation. He sets up a model where one of the main results is that the effect of marginal increases in higher education spending becomes more important the closer one approaches the technological frontier. He reports both cross-country panel as well as cross-US-state evidence on this question. The cross-country evidence of interaction between distance to the frontier and higher education is significant but only when country fixed effects are omitted. However, the results for the US are quite convincing. Instrumenting research university education by the presence of a state representative in the House on the appropriations committee allocating funds for research universities but not other types of schools, and an additional $1000 per person in research education spending increases the state's per employee growth rate by a third of a per cent if a state is at the frontier but by less than a tenth of a per cent if it is not.

Masahiko Aoki, the president of the Association in 2008, organized a session exploring various of the themes of institutional economics. He presented a paper proposing a conceptual framework for analysing mechanisms of institutional change. This is based on the definition of an institution as the summary representation of a Nash equilibrium path held as players' shared beliefs about how to act and not to act. Institutional change happens as changes to the environment occur and strategic experimentation shows new actions to become optimal, creating momentum effects. The framework applies to the evolution of organizational forms in modern corporations; the interaction between community and market relationships and more broadly interactions between different institutions within society; and also to institutional complementarities which may facilitate momentum for institutional change. There is in general a continuum between exogenous institutions enforced by other institutions and endogenous institutions that are self-enforcing.

Gérard Roland also offers a conceptual framework to try to understand institutional change. He distinguishes between fast-moving institutions, such as political institutions that can move very fast and in a very discontinuous way, and slow-moving institutions such as culture and social norms that can only move more slowly and a continuous way. Using this framework, he proposes a Weberian view of institutions where culture which moves quite exogenously has a determinant impact on legal and political institutions. Several conclusions are derived, such as the difficulty of transplanting political and legal institutions in alien cultural environments, the recognition of institutional diversity and a tolerance towards cultural and institutional experimentation within a spirit of openness.

Herbert Gintis develops an evolutionary model where respect for private property is not related to institutions but to evolutionary forces that are also present among animal species where ownership over territory is recognized and often not contested. The model is inspired by the Hawk, Dove, Bourgeois game. It features an endowment effect whereby a resource is prized more highly by the agent possessing it than by one who does not due to loss aversion: the disutility from losing a good is higher than the utility from acquiring it.

Geoffrey Hodgson and Thorbjørn Knudsen present an agent-based model of the emergence of a traffic convention when agents are boundedly rational. The traffic example is illustrative because it is a very simple convention. They find in particular that strength of habit is an important factor in explaining the convergence towards a convention and avoiding cycling behaviour. They also examine how an individual's behaviour is influenced by the behaviour of others.

Experimental economics directly tests assumptions about human behaviour and social interaction which undoubtedly are related to institutions and institutional change. Herbert Gintis discusses in another paper from the session he organized on experimental economics some of the lessons we draw from the latter on how to think about economics. He discusses in particular the implications of the findings from experimental economics about the importance of reciprocity and gift exchange in situations of contractual incompleteness. This should be seen as a definite enrichment of the economic paradigm and more enrichment is expected with the development of neuroscience.

Other topics that were the object of invited session are published in the second Congress volume. These two volumes should be seen as a whole. All in all, we hope that the selection of papers in these volumes will give the readers a snapshot of recent trends in economics and how they reflect important changes taking place in the world.

JÁNOS KORNAI
LÁSZLÓ MÁTYÁS
GÉRARD ROLAND

1
The Great Transformation of Central Eastern Europe: Success and Disappointment*

János Kornai
Harvard University, Collegium Budapest and Central European University

1 Introduction

This chapter examines eight particular countries that became members of the European Union in 2004: the Czech Republic, Estonia, Poland, Latvia, Lithuania, Hungary, Slovakia and Slovenia. I take the liberty of referring collectively to these countries as Central Eastern Europe or the Central Eastern European region, though of course this is somewhat imprecise geographically. As I write these lines, the European Union is undergoing trying times and it is impossible to guess what the future will bring. Whatever influence the eventual fate of the European Union will exert on the eight countries under consideration is a distinct issue from the topic of this study. On the other hand, it may be worthwhile to take a look at this region separately, since the status of each country was subjected to microscopic examination by various bodies of the EU prior to accession. The memberships may be seen as certificates, which are supposed to attest to the fact that these countries boast both democratic political systems and functioning market economies.

By 1990 the Communist Party's dictatorship had come to an end in ten countries, namely in the Soviet Union and in countries that were in close military and economic alliance with it such as Bulgaria, Czechoslovakia, Poland, Hungary, Mongolia, the German Democratic Republic and Romania

*Presidential Address, delivered at the 14th World Congress of the International Economic Association in Marrakech, Morocco on August 29, 2005. I am grateful to Zdenek Kudrna, who helped my work by careful data collection and making useful comments, to Philippe Aghion, Zsuzsa Dániel, Jean-Paul Fitoussi, Stephan Haggard and Gérard Roland, who commented on the first version of the manuscript, as well as to Tamar Gendler, Noémi Peter, Katalin N. Szabó, László Szimonisz, László Tóth, István Gy. Tóth and János Varga, who assisted in the underlying research and in editing and translating the manuscript.

as well as in the former Yugoslavia and in Albania, which by then had only loose ties with the Soviet Union. I would not even dare to attempt to review this entire area in this chapter, if for no other reason than – that primarily from the standpoint of their political structures – there are huge differences among the individual countries. From this standpoint, the eight countries comprising the subject of my analysis are rather homogeneous. So although they share a number of important characteristics with this larger group, the set of countries on which I focus cannot be viewed as a 'representative sample' of this wider class. Delineating the topics of my analysis I made a deliberate choice: I wanted to focus on the region where reforms were most consistent and far-reaching. Regarding the eight new member states, I solely confine myself to the discussion of their similarities, and I do not deal with the description and the explication of the considerable differences that exist between them.

Let us return in time a couple of decades and recall the mood and expectations of the people living in this region who opposed the communist system. At that time, they felt it a hopeless daydream that within the foreseeable future their countries would become democratic market economies. Today, however, though this has become a reality, many are disappointed and bitter.

A number of analyses – both official and scholarly – have been published on this topic. They contain important statistical data revealing a great deal about the current political and economic situation of each of the countries under consideration, as well as their relative standing. Noteworthy studies have also appeared that offer causal analyses of these results.[1] I do not attempt to summarize this rich and valuable body of literature, nor is my aim to confirm or refute these prior analyses. Instead, I hope to complement them by focusing on aspects of the transformation that have not yet received sufficient attention.

In the discussion below, I take special care to separate my description of the facts from the normative judgements that I make about those facts, and from the ordering of values which underlies those judgements. Care about such matters is important both for understanding the data, and for locating properly where points of disagreement lie.

The chapter is divided into two parts: in the first, I examine the transformation historically; in the second, I consider it from the perspective of the contemporary man's everyday life.

2 In the context of world history

First, we are going to look at long historical periods. The historical units in question are relatively large – decades, even centuries. And though the focus remains on Central Eastern Europe, I examine other regions of the world for purposes of comparison. The methodology of the first section is concisely epitomized in the title of Charles Tilly's (1984) book: 'Big structures, large processes, huge comparisons.'

2.1 The main direction of economic transformation in Western civilization

During the last millennium various capitalist forms of the economy gained more and more ground in Western civilization.[2] Traces of this had already appeared in antiquity and formed important building blocks of medieval society from the very beginning. The characteristic institutions of capitalism – private property, hired labour, market-type buying and selling, a credit system, and a legal system protecting the sanctity of private property and contracts – evolved in various countries at various speeds. Institutional transformation has been inseparably associated with such profound processes as urbanization, industrialization and commercialization. All the above comprise what is known as the capitalist economy.[3]

There is no agreement among historians as to when the Middle Ages ended and when the Modern Age began.[4] Moreover, there is not even any agreement on the subject of whether any criteria could be provided to separate the end from the beginning, and if so, whether it should be sought in the economic, political, or religious–ideological–intellectual sphere. However, there is a fairly wide agreement about the fact that in what most historians refer to as the Modern Age, or modernity, it is the capitalist economy which is dominant. The economy is in a constant state of motion and transformation. Accordingly, this transformation has a characteristic *main direction*, namely, the expansion of the capitalist economic order. Expansion is accompanied by deepening of its effects.

The spread of capitalism has been slow and complicated. In some cases capitalist and pre-capitalist forms coexist in a stable fashion. In others, there is rapid acceleration followed by stagnation, even reversal. And when acceleration does occur, its causes may be numerous: political revolution, the appearance of a great statesman with a propensity for innovation, new regulations created by a political group, geographical discoveries (such as the conquest of the New World), or the introduction of great inventions (such as the steam engine, railways, or the application of electricity).

Influenced by Marx's theory, the Communist parties prior to coming into power endorsed the principle that a main direction of economic history did indeed exist. This, however, according to the Marxists, points beyond capitalism. The Communist parties considered it fundamental to create a system *superseding* capitalism. They provided explicit criteria for comparing the two systems: growth in labour productivity and its concomitants, in particular, rates of production and increases in the standard of living.

The monumental verification attempt, which eventually failed, lasted for over seventy years in the Soviet Union and for about forty years in Eastern Europe. There were moments in the race between the socialist and capitalist systems when even among the adherents of the capitalist system some became unsure. Remember that in the years following the Great Depression of 1929 most developed countries went into a deep recession while the first Five Year Plan of the Soviet Union realized spectacular results and produced a high growth rate. And remember that when the first Sputnik was successfully launched, many took this to be the dawning of an age of Soviet technical and military superiority. However, if we measure these events on the scale of long decades and look at the entire period of the existence of the socialist system, one thing is definitely a proven fact: capitalism is more productive, more innovative and with a faster growth rate that generated a greater increase in the standard of living. Table 1.1 provides a comparison between the growth of socialist and capitalist countries during the last four decades before the collapse. Socialist countries are represented by the Soviet Union, as well as by three of the new EU-members (Czechoslovakia, Poland and Hungary), whereas the capitalist economy is represented by 13 old EU-members.[5] The table clearly indicates the growing superiority of the capitalist economy.

Note that in saying this, I am certainly not claiming that we have come to the end of history, nor am I suggesting that capitalism will never be

Table 1.1 Growth rates in socialism and capitalism

	GDP per capita			Average growth rates of GDP per capita			
	(1990 Int'l dollars)		(1950 = 100)	(per cent)			
Country	**1950**	**1989**	**1990**	**1950s**	**1960s**	**1970s**	**1980s**
Czechoslovakia	3 501	8 768	250	3.9	2.9	2.1	1.2
USSR	2 841	7 098	250	3.4	3.6	2.2	0.9
Poland	2 447	5 684	232	2.4	3.2	3.4	–0.4
Hungary	2 480	6 903	278	4.0	3.8	2.1	1.0
Socialist 4	*2 819*	*7 013*	*239*	*3.3*	*3.5*	*2.3*	*0.8*
Austria	3 706	16 369	442	6.3	4.2	3.9	2.0
Belgium	5 462	16 744	307	2.4	4.2	3.3	1.9
Denmark	6 943	18 261	263	2.9	3.8	2.0	1.8
Finland	4 253	16 946	398	3.3	4.4	3.3	3.2
France	5 271	17 730	336	3.7	4.6	3.0	1.7
Greece	1 915	10 086	527	5.0	6.6	4.4	1.3
Ireland	3 453	10 880	315	1.7	4.2	3.2	2.7
Italy	3 502	15 969	456	5.6	5.4	2.9	2.3
Netherlands	5 996	16 695	278	2.8	4.0	2.5	1.3
Portugal	2 086	10 372	497	3.1	6.0	4.5	3.0
Spain	2 189	11 582	529	3.5	7.1	4.2	2.5
Sweden	6 739	17 593	261	2.5	3.8	2.0	1.8
UK	6 939	16 414	237	1.7	2.5	2.2	2.2
EU 13	*4 688*	*15 519*	*337*	*3.2*	*4.3*	*2.9*	*2.1*

Notes: Data for Luxembourg are not available. Data for Germany were excluded, because they were available only for Germany in its 1991 (unified) borders. The 1949 figure was not available for Poland to calculate growth p.c. in 1950; the 1950s average growth rate is for the 1951–59 period.

Source: OECD database accompanying Maddison (2003).

superseded at some point in the future. I do not undertake prophesy. However, it is an irrefutable fact that the *existing* (or, heretofore existing) socialism lost the race against the *existing* (or, heretofore existing) capitalism. This is not a value judgement; it is an observable, statistically accountable fact: until now, in the world of Western civilization, the main trend of history has pointed toward the direction of the expansion of capitalism.

The painful and bitter series of actions in the creation of the socialist system was a deviation from the main direction. Now, the countries of the Central Eastern European region have turned around. After backing out of the dead-end street fifteen years ago, they are now completely on the main path.

While this is a value-free statement of fact, the closely associated question of whether this is to be considered a *success* can be answered only by offering a value-based judgement. I return to this below.

Higher productivity and increased growth rates did not begin immediately: the transition to the new economic system started with a serious slowdown. By now, however, the growth has speeded up. In six out of the eight countries the growth rate during the past ten years was significantly higher than in the decade prior to 1990 (Table 1.2). During the period between 1995 and 2003, per capita GDP in the region where the eight new members are located, along with labour productivity (GDP per employee) and per capita real consumption, grew at a much higher rate than in other countries of the European Union (Table 1.3). The difference is especially impressive in labour

Table 1.2 Growth before and after 1989, and after transformational recession

	GDP/NMP index (1989 = 100)				Average annual growth rate (per cent)	
Country	**1980**	**1990**	**1995**	**2003**	**1980–1989**	**1995–2003**
Czech Republic	85	99	94	106	1.8	1.5
Estonia	75	92	66	101	3.2	5.5
Hungary	86	97	86	116	1.7	3.8
Latvia	69	103	51	79	4.2	5.6
Lithuania	65	97	56	81	4.9	4.7
Poland	91	88	99	135	1.1	4.0
Slovakia	85	98	84	117	1.8	4.2
Slovenia	99	92	89	120	0.1	3.8
CEE 8	*86*	*94*	*91*	*121*	*1.7*	*3.6*
EU 15	..	*103*	*111*	*132*	..	*2.2*

Notes: Pre-1990 growth rates for CEE 8 are based on the Net Material Product (NMP) used for growth accounting by the socialist countries. The 1980 figure for the Czech and Slovak republics is for Czechoslovakia.

Sources: Based on UN Economic Commission for Europe (UN ECE) *Economic Survey of Europe* 2001, n.1, p. 254 and UN ECE *Economic Survey of Europe* 1999, n. 1, Table A.1.; updated from UN ECE *Economic Survey of Europe* 2005, n.1, p. 117.

Table 1.3 Average growth rates for the years 1995–2003

Country	Average real GDP per capita growth	Average labour productivity growth (per cent)	Average consumption per capita growth
Czech Republic	2.2	2.6	3.0
Estonia	6.6	6.6	7.3
Hungary	4.1	3.2	4.5
Latvia	7.3	8.2	7.6
Lithuania	6.3	6.6	7.1
Poland	4.2	4.8	4.5
Slovakia	3.9	3.6	3.7
Slovenia	3.8	3.3	2.6
CEE 8	*4.0*	*4.2*	*4.3*
Austria	2.0	1.7	1.3
Belgium	1.9	1.3	1.7
Denmark	1.7	1.5	1.0
Finland	3.4	2.3	3.0
France	1.8	1.2	1.8
Germany	1.2	0.9	1.0
Greece	3.6	2.5	2.7
Ireland	6.0	3.6	4.2
Italy	1.3	0.3	1.7
Luxembourg	3.9	3.4	2.6
Netherlands	1.7	0.7	1.8
Portugal	1.8	0.2	2.1
Spain	2.8	–0.2	2.9
Sweden	2.4	2.0	2.1
UK	2.5	1.7	3.2
EU 15	*1.8*	*0.9*	*1.9*

Source: Economist Intelligence Unit – *Country Data* at <www.eiu.com>.

productivity; its pace among the new members is more than four times than that of the old members.

Let us be careful with the interpretation of these numbers. At this point in our analysis, we want to compare a *system* with another *system*, the *permanent* attributes of one system with the *permanent* attributes of the other. Applying the historical scale, only a very brief period of time has gone by. We do not know how much of the rapid growth can be traced to the new order's utilization of formerly hidden reserves not exploited by a previous inefficient system. The high rate of growth could be partially attributed to the fact that deep recessions are usually followed by rapid upswings. These obvious, easily mobilized reserves will sooner or later be depleted. It would be misleading to draw final conclusions based on the numbers of a single decade. We need a long period before the superiority of the new capitalist system could be proven unequivocally and with a fully convincing force. However, if we were to make a judgement based on past experience, we can be optimistic regarding the growth potential of the new system.

2.2 The main direction of political transformation in Western civilization

During the past few centuries the main direction of transformation in Western civilization has been felt not only in the economic but also in the political sphere. Alongside the almost unlimited monarchical power assented to by the churches could be found limited precursors of democracy, among them the various self-governing organizations and forms of representation available to the urban middle classes, and certain of the church institutions. In some countries, laws curtailing the absolute power of the monarchy were enacted and the first elements of parliamentarianism – 'enlightened' versions of the monarchy – appeared. Later, an ever-increasing range of rights were bestowed on parliament and the right to vote was extended to an ever-increasing portion of the population. Institutions of modern parliamentary democracy were gradually formed and strengthened. Over the centuries, more and more countries became democracies.

Closely tied to the changes of the political structure was the fact that an ever-increasing percentage of the population has been able to exercise their basic human rights – freedom of speech, freedom of association and the right to participate in the decision-making process. Discrimination based on various criteria such as gender, race, religious affiliation, etc. is being progressively eliminated.

A number of authors have described the 'waves' of democratization that have occurred during the second half of the 20th century.[6] The third swept Southern Europe, Latin America, and Asia from the 1970s to the 1980s; the fourth is the one we have just witnessed following the collapse of the Soviet and Eastern European communist regimes.[7]

Of course, the specific path of history differs from country to country. As I note above, progress towards democracy may come to a standstill or reverse its direction. But even an earthshaking change such as Hitler's rise to power, which led to the destruction of many millions of people and a cataclysm of immeasurable proportions, appears to have been – on a historical scale – a short-lived diversion from the main path. And the main direction eventually wins.

From the point of view of our topic, we must scrutinize the Communist Party's ascension to power. This is inextricably intertwined with the other 'deviation' just discussed, namely that in countries where the Communists came to power they derailed the economic system off its main track, and forced their socialist programme on society. That imposition was made possible by their seizure of political power and the creation of totalitarian dictatorship.

Since 1990 the Central Eastern European region has been successful in backing out of the dead end of the political sphere and moving again in the main direction, similarly to the movement in the economic sphere. Though there has been much discussion concerning the strength of the prevailing democratic order and the extent to which it satisfies various requirements, for purposes of the present analysis, it should suffice to apply the 'minimalist' criteria of democracy. A 'democratic minimum' is fulfilled if a government of a country comes into power as a result of a competition for the votes of the citizens and can be removed from office within the framework of a civilized process[8] without a palace putsch, military coup, assassination, or revolution. Elections held on the basis of political competition, together with the guarantee of other civil rights, create the procedures and mechanisms for officials to be removed and leadership to be transferred to others. This assures the elimination of tyrannical rule. It is true, however, that beyond these minimum criteria one might require the fulfilment of various additional criteria within a thriving, consolidated democracy. Let us not forget, though, that to the person who has just recently been freed from the clutches of tyranny, even the democratic minimum means a great deal. In the research presented herein, we employed the following test: the process of rising to power meets the democratic minimum if as a result of the elections that have occurred since 1989 the incumbent governments had been replaced at least twice. The CEE-region easily passes the numerical threshold established in the test: in each of the eight countries there have been at least three such elections where the incumbent government was replaced though a civilized election process that resulted in a newly and democratically elected government taking office. As Table 1.4 illustrates, 30 out of the 38 elections that concluded the competitions of the political parties resulted in the replacement of the incumbent governing political power, party or coalition.

The two categories of historical changes discussed so far are asymmetrically interconnected. The appearance of a capitalist economic system does not automatically guarantee the emergence of a democracy; there were and are countries whose economic system is capitalist, but whose political structure does not fulfil the minimum requirements for a democracy. Indeed, a capitalist economic system can be compatible with partly, or even wholly dictatorial political regimes. But this independence does not hold in the other direction: democracy can only become a permanent form of political governance where the economy operates within a capitalist system. There is no democracy without capitalism.[9]

We are now in a position to recognize the following value-free historical fact: the new political structure of the Central Eastern European region reflects the main direction of historical progress over the last two millennia. Whether this is to be lauded, and if so why, is a question we return to later.

Table 1.4 Electoral dismissals

Country	Elections 1989–2004	'Electoral dismissals'	Year(s) of dismissal(s)
Czech Republic	5	3	1990, 1992, 1998
Estonia	5	4	1990, 1995, 1999, 2003
Hungary	4	4	1990, 1994, 1998, 2002
Latvia	5	4	1990, 1995, 1998, 2002
Lithuania	5	4	1990, 1993, 1996, 2000
Poland	4	4	1991, 1993, 1997, 2001
Slovakia	5	4	1990, 1992, 1994, 1998
Slovenia	5	3	1990, 1993, 2004
CEE 8	*38*	*30*	

Note: 'Electoral dismissal' occurs when there is (i) a major rearrangement of the governing coalition following elections, including (ii) the change in the government leadership and (iii) some shift in policy priorities; see the full explanation at the following website of Zdenek Kudrna <ies.fsv.cuni.cz/~kudrna/MemoTable4.pdf>.

Source: Compiled on the basis of the Economist Intelligence Unit – *Country Reports* at <www.eiu.com>.

The idea that the large-scale political and economic changes have certain main directions is acknowledged by some schools of history and other social sciences and denied by others. I have tried to distance myself from rigid and one-sided versions of this idea; I see no evidence that some kind of simple, linear and at all times unidirectional movement takes place. I have been explicit that, regarding both the economic and the political spheres, there may be stagnation and backward movement, as well as the permanent co-existence of various economic and political systems.[10] But these acknowledgements do not undercut one of the main ideas of the current study, which is that it is possible to observe the main direction of the changes in the worlds of both economic and political institutions. The transformation that took place after the collapse of the Soviet and the Eastern European regimes provides a new and important supplement to the debate about the main directions.

2.3 Six characteristics

As a starting point for further analysis, I summarize the six most important characteristics of the transformation that has taken place in the Central Eastern European region during the past fifteen years.

1. and 2. The changes follow the *main directions* of development of Western civilization: in the economic sphere in the direction of the *capitalist economic system*, and in the political field in the direction of *democracy*.
3. There was *a complete* transformation, *parallel in all spheres*: in the economy, in the political structure, in the world of political ideology, in the legal system and in the stratification of society.

4. The transformation was *non-violent*.
5. The process of transformation took place under *peaceful* circumstances. It was not preceded by war. The changes were not forced upon society as a result of foreign military occupation.
6. The transformation took place with *incredible speed*, within a time-frame of ten to fifteen years.

This has not been the first 'great transformation' in world history, to borrow an expression from Karl Polányi.[11] He also emphasized the fact, which we already know from the study of world history, that other 'great transformations' have taken place at different times and in different regions of the world, sweeping transformations from one type of formation into another. Of the six characteristics listed above, three or four are discernible in other transformation processes as well. But *the presence of all six characteristics together is unique in world history*.

Allow me to present this conclusion in advance; I support it below by providing historical comparisons.

2.4 Historical comparisons

I compare five kinds of typical 'great transformations' with what has happened in Central Eastern Europe. It is obvious that in so doing we have not even begun to exhaust all comparative possibilities; a number of interesting and important cases have been left out. (For example, the changes taking place in Russia in the last fifteen years, the transformation of the Southern European dictatorships into democracies, or a brand new example: the changes taking place in Iraq since the fall of the regime of Saddam Hussein.) Regardless, the five transformation cases to be scrutinized present us with substantial lessons to be learned. It is not easy to follow the rhythm of these comparisons: to facilitate an understanding of this, Table 1.5 presents a comparative overview of the logical structure of the comparisons.

A. First, we examine the transformation currently being evaluated by comparing it with the preceding movement which moved in the opposite direction: the destruction of the capitalist system and the creation of a socialist system. For brevity's sake I restrict myself exclusively to Soviet history. There is similarity in characteristic No. 3: there too parallel changes transformed all spheres of society. The similarity is staggering in characteristic No. 6, the speed at which the changes took place. The Communist Party grabbed power in 1917. The 'great transformation' was completed by the end of 1932, with the collectivization of agriculture when private ownership of the means of production was basically eliminated. Only fifteen years were required to put everything in place for the creation of what we call 'classical socialism'.[12]

Table 1.5 Comparison of characteristics of system transformation

Characteristics	CEE region	A. Transformation of the Soviet Union from capitalism into socialism	B. Hungary: Horthy restoration Chile: Pinochet restoration	C. China: Transformation after Mao	D. West Germany: Transformation after WW2	E. The great historical transformation in Europe: from the Middle Ages into Modernity, from pre-capitalism into capitalism
1 In the main direction of the development of the economic system?	Yes	No	Yes	Yes	Yes	Yes
2 In the main direction of the development of the political system?	Yes	No	No	No	Yes	Yes
3 Parallel in all spheres?	Yes	Yes	Yes	No	No	Yes (with time lags)
4 Without violence?	Yes	No	No	Yes	No	No
5 Without foreign military occupation?	Yes	Yes	Yes	Yes	No	No
6 Fast?	Yes	Yes	Yes	No	Yes	No (very long period)

The striking difference lies in characteristics No. 1, No. 2 and No. 4. At the end of World War I, Russia was about to embark on the road toward establishing a Western type parliamentary democracy. A bloody revolution overthrew the earlier political authority, the tsar and his family were executed and the elite of the former regime were either killed or exiled into forced labour camps. Violence and terror imposed a new political and social order on society. This is a 180-degree opposite of the 1989–1990 velvet revolution and the non-violent nature of our current transformation.

In the remainder of my discussion, I focus only on transformations which share characteristic No. 1 with those taking place in Central Eastern Europe, in other words where the changes in the economy point to the main direction (or at least are not turning away from the main direction) of the changes in the economic sphere.

B. Characteristic No. 4, the non-violent nature of the transformation, cannot be considered to be self-evident. It is worthwhile to illustrate this with two historical examples.

After World War I, the Communists under the leadership of Béla Kun seized power in Hungary and proclaimed a Hungarian Soviet Republic. A few months later, under the leadership of Admiral Miklós Horthy, who became later Governor (i.e. head of state), the Communist rule was defeated and the former capitalist order was restored. The Red Terror was replaced by the White Terror during the initial months. Lynching, hangings and prison sentences were part and parcel of the transition and it took a few years until some sort of political consolidation was reached.

The second example is that of Chile. There Allende and his government embarked on a path which presumably could have led to the formation of a socialist system. But before it developed fully, it was destroyed by a coup headed by General Pinochet in 1973. A vindictive campaign, extra-judicial reprisals, political murders and torture were the trademarks of the attempted restoration of the pre-Allende economic system. Only after much suffering and after many years could democratic institutions develop in that country.

Let us compare these two historical episodes with what has just taken place in Central Eastern Europe. In the eight countries that are the subject of the chapter, the politicians of the former regime were neither executed nor imprisoned and there was no campaign of revenge conducted against them. In a number of countries, in preparation for a new constitution, civilized discussions were held between the leaders of the former ruling party and the new opposition leaders, who were readying themselves to take on political power. The power shift took place without bloodshed and without chaos at the highest levels of power.

As in our other cases, my aim so far has been simply to present the facts: assessment of their value will be offered in later sections.

C. The elimination of the socialist system continues to proceed in areas to the south and east of the eight countries under scrutiny. It would fit well into the logic of my analysis to take all the transformation processes one by one and make comparisons. Due to space constraints, however, I compare the changes that have taken place in the Central Eastern European region with those of only one country, China. Of course, only the future will show how far the trend of the capitalist economic development in China will reach, and how consistent will it be.

In the case of characteristic No. 1 – and this is of fundamental importance – the Chinese and Central Eastern European transformations are identical: both point in the main historical direction, toward the capitalist economic system.

The most important difference, however, can be found in the case of characteristic No. 2. Regarding the political structure, the development of the Central Eastern European countries also points in the main direction of Western civilization: it has moved away from the previous system, towards democracy and respect for human rights. By contrast, in China, the monopoly power of the Communist Party has remained intact, resulting in repression and the curtailment of human rights. While substantial changes continue to take place in virtually every sphere of society, one cannot even begin to talk about the parallelism mentioned under characteristic No. 3.

There is also a striking contrast to China's path regarding characteristic No. 4, the issue of non-violence. One cannot talk of a velvet revolution. Upon the death of the former tyrant Mao Zedong, the leadership struck those in his immediate environment with an iron fist. When the demands of the students of Beijing went too far in relation to the pace dictated by the rulers of the country, their protests were put down by military force. Those professing views displeasing to the Party are put in jail.

In terms of characteristic No. 5, there is no substantial difference between the cases: as in the CEE, China's changes are not forced by the imposition of outside military intervention. Whatever change does take place has been carried out by the imposition of internal force.

The difference is very substantial in terms of characteristic No. 6: the pace of institutional changes in China has been much slower than in CEE.

D. Finally we consider the transformation of West Germany during the period following World War II. We begin with characteristics No. 1 and No. 2. During the rule of the Nazis, the capitalist economic system basically continued to operate, but the political structure deviated fatally from the main direction. With regard to characteristic No. 3, there was no need for a complete transformation, only for a partial one. The most important differences can be found in characteristics No. 4 and No. 5. This obviously could not be a violence-free transformation. First, the power of the Nazis had to be destroyed in a war that required serious sacrifices, followed by punishment on the perpetrators of war crimes and crimes against humanity. The Allied Powers kept the country under occupation for a long period. The creation of basic democratic institutions was imposed from the outside through provision of the peace treaty enforced by the military presence of Allied troops. This became the starting point of the reforms brought about by internal forces. With regard to characteristic No. 6, the speed, measured on a historical scale, the democratization was very swift.

E. Having reached the end of these comparisons, it is time to return to the topic with which we began: the centuries-long process which led to the original formation of the capitalist economic system and democracy. In fact, several characteristics of these major transformations correspond to certain characteristics of the current (in comparison 'small') transformation taking place in the Central Eastern European region. By definition, characteristics No. 1 and No. 2 are the same, since the characterization of 'main direction' has been distilled from the major historical transformations. As for characteristic No. 3, if we look at the totality of the changes, it is clear that the economic and political transformation affected all spheres of social activity. However, if we consider these developments not in terms of centuries but instead in a much shorter time-frame, we cannot talk about the close parallelism which was observable in the Central Eastern European region during the past ten to fifteen years. In a sequence varying by country and with different time lags, events accelerated either in the political sphere, or in the religious–intellectual–ideological world, or in the economy. Considering characteristics No. 4 and No. 5 there are differences by country and period regarding how peaceful or devoid of violence the changes were, and when the changes were accelerated by bloody uprising, revolution, war and the conquest of foreign countries. Some historical schools maintain that the Modern Age began with the discovery (meaning: conquest) of America, while others date it to the outbreak of the French Revolution of 1789, which grew into a reign of terror.

The biggest divergence can be discerned, of course in characteristic No. 6, the speed of the change. It took capitalism centuries to become the prevalent economic system of an entire country. A centuries-long process preceded the realization of parliamentary democracy. By contrast, all of these have been completed with incredible speed in the Central Eastern European region now.

From the perspective of broad-scale history, the transformation of the Central Eastern European region was indeed extremely swift. But it is important to recall that there were politicians and economic experts who urged even faster changes. The countries were encouraged to compete with each other. As in a running race, odds were weighed: where will privatization come to an end first? Would the Czechs, the Hungarians, or the Poles be crossing the finish line at the end of the sixth or the ninth year? If we analyse these events from a historical perspective, we can sense the bizarre nature of such a contest.

A part of the populace also viewed the race with suspicion. In the framework of an international research project intended to measure the individual's ordering of values, citizens of a number of Central Eastern European countries were asked which they would prefer: the radical reorganization of society through a major revolutionary action, or a gradual improvement of society through reforms. Seventy-five per cent of Czechs, 82 per cent of Slovenes and 67 per cent of Lithuanians chose the latter (see Halman, 2001, p. 170).

2.5 Accelerating factors in the transformation process

The comparative analysis of all six characteristics would deserve a separate study. Here, I discuss only one – the sixth. Having observed the gradual transformation of the past ten to fifteen years to be exceptionally speedy, we may pose the question: what made this great speed possible?

1. On our first attempt we would likely offer a simple answer: it is easier to do something for the second time than to create it in the first place. We could quote from the well-known experiences of economic growth. The rebuilding of ruined economies has always been a faster process than the construction of original ones.

The 'restoration' argument however, only holds partially.

Let us start with knowledge and experience. Even those individuals who in their youth had gained some experience in the political or economic sphere before the Communists came to power were close to retirement age when the transformation began: most of those who had been active in the pre-socialist era had already passed away or retired. This type of knowledge is not genetically transmitted, and there were not many families where the accumulated economic, business or political knowledge of the pre-socialist period would have been transmitted by the parents to their offspring. In the heads and thinking of individuals there was no such thing as a 'restoration' of old knowledge, rather it was the gaining of new knowledge.

However, we can find many counterexamples. There were families during the socialist era which preserved the old values and passed them onto the younger generations. It is not unheard of that grandchildren in one way or another carry on the trade of their grandparents. The socialist system destroyed the political, economic and social institutions which had operated in the previous era. They were not instantaneously resurrected. Nevertheless, counterexamples could be exhibited here also.

Overall, it could be stated that, although the transformation has been accelerated by the fact that at many points it had been possible to return to earlier developed traditions, behaviours and institutions in order to utilize them as starting points – yet this reverting was not the strongest factor among the accelerating forces at all.

2. A significant proportion of individuals tend to instinctively take care of their own affairs, and have a spirit of entrepreneurship. The multitude of restrictions imposed by medieval society curtailed the amplification of this

spontaneous endeavour and these barriers were only gradually and slowly eliminated. The loosening and the breaking down of the restrictions of the feudal order, and the expansion of private property and market coordination are intertwined processes. The socialist economic system incorporated even more crippling constraints into the system than those of its predecessors: it virtually hamstrung the proclivity for initiative and entrepreneurship. During the post-socialist transformation period the bureaucratic prohibitions set up by the socialist centralized economic administration were not slowly and gradually dismantled but broken down at breakneck speed. For this reason, the spirit of spontaneous entrepreneurship, this unique driving force of capitalism, literally burst into the economic scene.

3. There was no strong resistance to the transformation. When capitalism and parliamentary democracy developed slowly and gradually for the first time, there were various strata, groups, and classes of society who fought against it. The new order won in the struggle against the beneficiaries of the *ancien régime*. After the victories of the new order, the adherents of the old order engaged in a political, ideological and, in some cases, armed resistance against it.

This time it was different. Six years after Gorbachev started his reforms, by the time of the collapse of the Berlin Wall, the leaders of the communist order in Central Eastern Europe had already put down their arms. There were no movements inciting against the new order, its opponents did not resort to arms, there were no guerrilla fighters or terrorists. The majority of the members of the former 'old guard' had become disillusioned with their former ideals. The more resourceful ones changed sides, they tried to become businessmen – many successfully – even active players in the democratic political arena. Others wearily retired.

4. The most significant explanation for the rapidity of the transformation can be found in the effects of the external world surrounding the Central Eastern European countries. The expression 'external world' is used in its widest possible sense to refer to various outside influences and circumstances.

One of the effects was the adoption of foreign examples. From the operational forms of corporate management and banking system to political institutions, from media programmes to advertising, from the organization of educational activities to the financing of the arts and sciences, there was hardly an area of social activity where foreign examples have not been followed.

There were numerous channels through which these examples found their way to the Central Eastern European population. People became acquainted with them during their trips abroad, some prior to 1990, many more after the changes took place. They read about them, or watched them in the cinema. Teaching about the foreign experience took place in schools, at universities, and at special seminars. Foreign consultants recommended their adoption.

I am not claiming that the adaptation of foreign models is an easy matter. It is not enough just to observe how the British Parliament or a bank in Zurich works and then expect that everything will happen in the same way at the Hungarian or at the Estonian Parliaments, in the Czech or in the Polish banks. It is easy enough to recognize the model, but it is a much more difficult task to learn how to use it, and to adapt it to the local conditions. If learning were not a difficult and contradictory process, then the realization of the bulk of the transformation would not have taken fifteen years to complete, and we would not need further cumbersome work to apply the model more effectively.

Foreign investors also exerted an extraordinary influence. Not only did they bring in capital, but – in addition to technical know-how – they brought knowledge about how to manage a company, and about what kind of legal system and behavioural norms are requirements for the operation of a capitalist economy.

The eight countries under consideration joined important international organizations – under Western leadership – such as NATO, OECD, and the WTO, and their relationships became more active with the World Bank and the IMF. The succession of various memberships culminated in their accession to the European Union. What in the language of Brussels is dubbed as the process of 'harmonization' took place not only in the realm of legislation. In every respect, Central Eastern Europe tried to assimilate Western examples. This accommodation was compelled and primarily driven by internal forces. However, it is no use denying that a certain level of external political pressure was also discernible. Characteristic No. 5 is relevant in that there was no foreign military occupation. Not a single foreign country, not even the great powers, 'pushed' the small countries of Central Eastern Europe around. However, 'conditionality' did exist. The practice started with the Washington-based financial organizations and was gradually taken up by the European Union according to which the availability of funds for loans and grants, the expansion of existing relationships and the guaranteeing of various additional rights were increasingly tied to the satisfaction of certain preconditions. It is true, however, that these preconditions were generally formulated in such a way as to serve the long-term interests of the individual countries concerned. Still, many changes were forced upon them through external pressures or, at the very least, these pressures contributed to the speedier implementation of changes.

The geographical proximity of the Western world must have contributed to the intensity of the external pressures. The quickest ones of the recent great transitions took place precisely in those counties that were located directly on the border of the developed European countries.

5. The availability of modern technology was an important accelerating factor in the process. In this context, we are not referring to any special situation enjoyed by the Central Eastern European region. The pace of the

European transformation was faster in part because nowadays *everything* changes at a faster pace. Consider, for example, the speed of transportation and communication at the end of the Middle Ages and at the beginning of the Modern Age, and compare them with the possibilities available to us today. Computers, the internet, e-mail and the mobile phone – to mention only four – exponentially accelerate the arrival of outside information for those desiring to emulate outside examples. This new technology contributed to the accelerated pace of the publication and dissemination of new regulations and norms.

Even though there was an incredible lag in the dispersion of 'high-tech' in the region before the transition, its speed of development was significantly accelerated. It is true that the spread of computers and the use of the internet is still relatively low.[13] One thing that appears to be certain, however, is that information reaches decision makers and public opinion makers quite swiftly and the media are able to disseminate it rapidly to millions of people.

2.6 The first assessment: an unparalleled success story

I am convinced that what took place in Central Eastern Europe during the past decade and a half is an unparalleled success story in history. I believe this, in spite of the fact that I am fully aware of the grief and disappointment it was associated with – an issue I address during the second half of the chapter. So, to be a bit more precise, here is my assessment: in spite of serious problems and anomalies – assessing the situation from the perspective of great historical changes – what took place in this part of the world, is a success story.

My conviction is based on a particular ordering of values. Others, basing their judgements on a different ordering of values may disagree.

On a scale of values, I accord pride of place to democracy and human rights. Perhaps this is because – together with many of my contemporaries in Central Eastern Europe – I lived through various forms of tyranny in which we experienced total deprivation of civil rights or a humiliating curtailment of human rights and in which we were subjected to brutal discrimination applied along various criteria. This is why I feel a strong aversion to arguments comparing China's performance with that of the Central Eastern European region, which put biased and one-sided emphasis on its much higher economic growth. It is true that the growth rate in the Central Eastern European region is a great deal lower than that of China, though it is still respectable, and, as I point out above, the pace is already faster than it was during the last decade of the previous regime. I am ready to resign myself to a lower rate of growth than the leaps and bounds produced by the Chinese so long as it is coupled with a respect for democracy and human rights! I acknowledge that there are those who do not see the world in this way and who believe it may be worthwhile to forgo, or postpone, democracy for an indefinite period as in order to achieve rapid economic growth.

At many times, the political institutions of democracy uncomfortably impede the concentration of the state's capacities on the promotion of growth, as well as on the forceful completion of reforms associated with greater convulsions. In my eyes, these drawbacks are far outweighed by the advantages of greater freedom rights provided by democracy. For Central Eastern Europeans, the fact that the integration with the European Union acts as a stabilizing force both in the political sphere and in the economy facilitates the creation of democracy.

I consider the transformation of the Central Eastern European region a success story because it established a capitalist economic system within a historically brief time frame, thereby placing our nations again on the course of development leading toward the main direction of history. It is not that I 'love' capitalism. It is not a very likeable system. But I hold those of its characteristics dear which are indispensable to the realization of the values I profess. In the long run, the economic advantages of capitalism will become manifest in the Central Eastern European region too: a sustainable higher growth rate of production, productivity and consumption than the one experienced under the socialist system, technical innovation, entrepreneurial spirit, and together with the above, an increasing level of prosperity for society as a whole. I also consider the values of economic growth and the increase in the standard of living it brings to be primary values. (Though, not with the finality and one-sidedness of those who would be willing to give up democracy for it.) Beyond the argument for the increase of material goods, there is another that is mentioned above: the very existence of a capitalist system is an indispensable precondition for a functioning democracy. These are those benefits that according to my ordering of values overshadow the disadvantages of capitalism. I acknowledge that there are others who subscribe to a different system for weighing the advantages and disadvantages between them.

And finally, I consider the transformation of the Central Eastern European region a success story because it took place in a peaceful manner, devoid of violence. My own life experience must have provided the formative impression for my views regarding this. I survived a World War, bloody persecutions, hard and soft dictatorships, vindictive campaigns, the execution and incarceration of friends. It was enough! For me, the fact that this time there was no bloodshed, that no one was killed or imprisoned, was an extraordinarily beneficial development. I admit that there are those who view these changes differently. They believe that changes could have happened earlier had the former regime been overthrown sooner, even by resorting to the force of arms. There are those who condemn the lack of punishment for the guilty and find the dispensing of justice wanting.

The fact that external influences played a major role among the driving forces behind these changes does not change my favourable opinion. Foreign influences, such as knowledge, experience, culture and capital flowed into the Central Eastern European countries, enabling them to be better integrated into the European Union and into a globalized world. I am aware that some people feel offended by this, as they are concerned about the preservation of national traditions. They may also be disturbed by the fact that all of this will undoubtedly result in placing limits on the political sovereignty of the individual states. I admit that here we are facing a difficult trade-off.

I have tried to openly and without circumlocution disclose the ordering of values that underlie my own judgement. I do not do this for the sake of arguing for it. There is no place here for rational argumentation, something that we economists always attempt to engage in. There are metarational ideas, beliefs and desires concealed behind these valuations – and in this regard, it is unavoidable that there will be divergences of opinion between individuals professing different worldviews. Even if – from the perspective of the great events of world history – we were to agree on what actually took place in the Central Eastern European region, we cannot count on arriving at a consensus in assessing the results.

3 From the perspective of everyday life

3.1 Problems and worries

Emotions of success and failure intermingle in everyone's life who either participated in, or was an empathetic observer of, the transformation taking place in the Central Eastern European region. Far be it from me to engage in a cheap 'success propaganda' campaign. We are not facing imaginary difficulties, nor are these problems encountered by a small portion of the populace; we are up against some very real and serious negative phenomena.

In the beginning of the new era, the real income of the majority of citizens living in the Central Eastern European region was significantly below the average for member countries of the European Union, and a considerable proportion were at the poverty level. Since that time, regardless of how much the world changed around us, the real income of a significant proportion of the population has remained unchanged, and many among the impoverished have become mired at the low level of their earlier living standard. And there are a non-negligible number of people whose standard of living has discernibly deteriorated. We cannot be certain that in every case, the degradation was attributable to the change in the political system, but it certainly took place during the period since 1990. These are those individuals who consider themselves the unequivocal victims of this era.

A dramatic restructuring has taken place in the area of the distribution of income and consumption. Though critics of the socialist system rightfully complained that a system of material privileges did indeed exist, the distribution of income and consumption generally lay within a rather narrow range. The ten to fifteen years since then has been enough to affect a marked increase in the existing levels of inequality, as shown in Tables 1.6 and 1.7.[14]

Table 1.6 Distribution of income: Gini coefficient

Country	Pre-transition 1987–1989	Mid-transition 1996–1997	Post-transition 2001–2002	Percentage change from pre- to post-transition
Czech Republic	19.8	23.9	23.4	18
Estonia	28.0	36.1	39.3	40
Hungary	22.5	25.4	26.7	19
Latvia	26.0	32.6	35.8	38
Lithuania	26.3	30.9	35.7	36
Poland	27.5	33.4	35.3	28
Slovakia	19.4	24.9	26.7	38
Slovenia	21.0	24.0	24.4	16
CEE 8	*23.8*	*28.9*	*30.9*	*29*
EU 15	*26.9*	*27.8*	*28.6*	*7*

Notes: The Gini coefficient is a measure of the degree of inequality in the distribution of income. It is equal to '0' in the case of total income equality (everyone receives the same income) and to '100' in the case of total inequality (one household receives all the income). In this table estimates are based on interpolated distributions from grouped data from various household budget surveys. Survey coverage may vary over time. Data refer to the distribution of individuals according to household per capita income. Five data points for the EU average are not available – Belgium (2), Spain (2) and Portugal (1).

Sources: CEE 8 data from various sources compiled for the UNICEF IRC *TransMONEE 2004 Database*. EU 15 data: OECD *Society at a Glance: OECD Social indicators 2005* and the World Bank *World Development Indicators 2005*.

Table 1.7 Consumption inequality

Country	Survey year	Share of income or consumption (percentages)				Richest 10% to poorest 10%	Richest 20% to poorest 20%
		Poorest 10%	Poorest 20%	Richest 20%	Richest 10%		
Czech Republic	1996	4.3	10.3	35.9	22.4	5.2	3.5
Estonia	2000	1.9	6.1	44.0	28.5	14.9	7.2
Hungary	1999	2.6	7.7	37.5	22.8	8.9	4.9
Latvia	1998	2.9	7.6	40.3	25.9	8.9	5.3
Lithuania	2000	3.2	7.9	40.0	24.9	7.9	5.1
Poland	1999	2.9	7.3	42.5	27.4	9.3	5.8
Slovakia	1996	3.1	8.8	34.8	20.9	6.7	4.0
Slovenia	1998/99	3.6	9.1	35.7	21.4	5.9	3.9
CEE 8	*1996–2000*	*3.1*	*8.1*	*39.5*	*24.9*	*8.2*	*5.0*
EU 15	*1994–2000*	*2.7*	*7.4*	*40.2*	*25.1*	*9.6*	*5.6*

Source: UN *Human Development Report 2004* database.

On one side, a heretofore unknown level of conspicuous wealth has become readily apparent, while on the other, the poverty that was less obviously manifest before, has became more deeply entrenched and much more visible. This is appalling to the sense of social justice of many individuals who were otherwise not victims of the restructuring.

The serious problems enumerated above are connected to issues of employment. Open unemployment was unknown in the socialist economy; the employment rate was very high, every worker could feel secure at his or her workplace. Indeed, an inverse disequilibrium prevailed. The socialist economy created chronic shortages, including a chronic labour shortage – at least, in the more developed and industrialized Central Eastern European countries. Whatever effect that had on efficiency, the workers enjoyed job security. This has come to an end. The employment rate has significantly declined and open unemployment has appeared. Its rate differs from country to country, but in all Central Eastern European countries the percentages are lower than the overall European average, as shown in Table 1.8. Unemployment came crashing down as a virtual trauma on society, as seen in Table 1.9.

Job security disappeared. This happened at a time when life itself became more insecure on countless fronts. In socialist societies, those who avoided risky political activity were surrounded by relatively solid and predictable conditions of livelihood. Now, all of a sudden, everything is in motion and nothing is known in advance. Formerly, a company existed forever and ever; nowadays, they are formed and go bankrupt from one day to the next. Previously, consumer prices were fixed for long periods of time, now they are in a constant state of flux. The average citizen cannot make sense of interest rates, or even rates of exchange. Though it used to be incredibly difficult to

Table 1.8 Total employment

				(1989 = 100)				
Country	**1990**	**1991**	**1992**	**1993**	**1996**	**1999**	**2002**	**2003**
Czech Republic	99.1	93.6	91.2	89.8	93.5	88.2	88.0	87.4
Estonia	98.6	96.3	90.9	83.5	74.0	69.2	70.0	71.0
Hungary	96.7	86.7	78.1	73.1	69.8	72.9	74.1	75.1
Latvia	100.1	99.3	92.1	85.7	72.4	73.9	75.4	76.8
Lithuania	97.3	99.6	97.4	93.4	87.0	85.0	82.0	83.9
Poland	95.8	90.1	86.4	84.3	88.3	90.4	85.8	85.2
Slovakia	98.2	85.9	86.9	84.6	85.5	82.3	82.1	83.6
Slovenia	96.1	88.6	83.7	81.3	78.7	80.1	82.8	82.1
CEE 8	*96.9*	*90.9*	*87.0*	*84.2*	*85.5*	*85.8*	*83.5*	*83.4*
EU 15	*101.8*	*102.3*	*101.1*	*99.6*	*100.7*	*105.2*	*109.2*	*109.5*

Source: UN ECE *Economic Survey of Europe* 2005, n. 1, p. 125.

get an apartment, once you got one, whether as a tenant or the occupant of a sublet, it was virtually impossible to be evicted. Nowadays, you can be evicted for simply not paying the rent. As the police state was being dismantled, public security was deteriorating (see Table 1.10). Everything that had been stiffened to the point of rigidity by overbearing authorities and bureaucracy became malleable, risky and insecure through the influence of market forces, competition and civil rights guaranteeing more freedom of movement.

Corruption existed during the old regime too, mostly in areas of mutual favours bestowed through political or personal contacts. Though there were

Table 1.9 Unemployment rates

			(Per cent of labour force)				
Country	**1990**	**1992**	**1993**	**1996**	**1999**	**2002**	**2003**
Czech Republic	0.7	2.6	3.5	3.5	9.4	9.8	10.3
Estonia	..	1.6	5.0	5.6	6.7	6.8	6.1
Hungary	1.7	12.3	12.1	10.5	9.6	8.0	8.4
Latvia	..	2.3	5.8	7.2	9.1	8.5	8.6
Lithuania	..	3.5	3.4	6.2	10.0	10.9	9.8
Poland	6.5	14.3	16.4	13.2	13.1	20.0	20.0
Slovakia	1.6	10.4	14.4	12.8	19.2	17.4	15.6
Slovenia	..	13.3	15.5	14.4	13.0	11.3	11.0
CEE 8	*4.4*	*10.6*	*12.4*	*10.6*	*12.1*	*15.4*	*15.3*
EU 15	*7.3*	*8.7*	*10.0*	*10.2*	*8.7*	*7.7*	*8.1*

Note: Figures for Estonia are only job seekers until 1999.

Sources: Registered unemployment rates for CEE 8 from the UN ECE *Economic Survey of Europe* 2004, no. 2, p. 85; Standardized unemployment rates for the EU-15 from UN ECE *Economic Survey of Europe* 2005, no. 1, p. 126.

Table 1.10 Crime rates

		(1989 = 100)		
Country	**1990**	**1994**	**1998**	**2002**
Czech Republic	180	309	355	313
Estonia	124	200	270	321
Hungary	153	175	272	193
Latvia	117	146	137	190
Lithuania	118	189	260	247
Poland	161	163	192	253
Slovakia	150	293	198	227
Slovenia	96	110	139	193
CEE 8	*156*	*194*	*228*	*249*

Note: Crime data cover reported and registered crime only. Crime rates are subject to varying national legislation.

Source: UNICEF IRC *TransMONEE 2004 Database*.

even incidents of bribing, these were uncommon and generally took place at the lower levels of the 'shortage' economy, to 'grease the wheels'. The majority of corrupt activities remained unseen and behind the scenes. Nowadays corruption is ubiquitous in the myriad of transactions in the political, economic and cultural sphere, in private transactions large and small, and at the highest and lowest levels of the governmental and social hierarchy. Many corruption cases become public knowledge. Everyone is angry, and – often unwillingly – many hands get dirty. It is almost impossible to avoid becoming involved in some transaction where one or another of the parties engages in certain shady transactions, and where either the client, the citizen, the seller or the buyer, would not attempt to bribe, or be involved in a phoney tax evasion scheme of some sort.

People are also upset about the disorder present in the political arena. Many view the multi-party system as not having created the preconditions for a sober political competition, but instead of having resulted in an unbridled struggle for power, lies, empty promises and the continual ranting and raving of the opposition against whoever happens to be in power. A significant proportion of the population does not place sufficient trust in their Parliament. In this respect, the difference between the 15 old and the 8 new EU members is enormous, as seen in Table 1.11. Politicians are suspected of having been involved in corruption, sometimes because they violated the law, or at the least the unwritten law of ethics, and sometimes because they are slandered by political rivals.

I have mentioned some of the most serious issues. Though I could continue, I think this much should be sufficient to demonstrate that we are not talking about trifling inconveniences, but about genuinely overwhelming and serious problems.

3.2 Social disposition

There have been numerous surveys assessing the prevailing mood and social disposition of the citizenry of the Central Eastern European countries. They point to the fact that these opinions are divided. Many more respondents in the older EU member states answered 'yes' to the (apparently) simple question 'Are you satisfied with your life?' than in the eight new member states under consideration, as shown in Table 1.12. The ratio of negative answers differs from country to country, as seen in Table 1.13. As an approximate average it appears that every third person in the region is either somewhat or very dissatisfied with his life.[15]

3.3 Cognitive problems

The intensity of people's reaction to troubles or its degree of bitterness is not merely a function of the real difficulties associated with the problem itself. When one experiences hardship, or observes the troubled with empathy, a great deal depends on how one perceives the problem at hand, and how one

Table 1.11 Confidence in Parliament and other institutions

	Parliament	**Civil Service**	**Education system**
	(percentage having confidence in)		
Czech Republic	12.2	21.8	54.6
Estonia	27.0	40.4	73.9
Hungary	34.0	49.6	64.3
Latvia	27.5	49.2	73.7
Lithuania	10.6	20.6	66.6
Poland	32.8	32.6	81.2
Slovakia	42.8	38.7	76.3
Slovenia	25.3	25.3	80.3
CEE 8	*29.3*	*33.8*	*73.7*
Austria	40.7	42.4	86.2
Belgium	39.1	46.1	77.9
Denmark	48.6	54.9	75.0
Finland	43.7	40.9	88.8
France	40.6	45.9	68.4
Germany	35.7	38.7	72.6
Greece	29.0	20.2	37.0
Ireland	31.1	59.3	86.4
Italy	34.1	33.2	53.2
Luxembourg	62.7	59.5	67.8
Netherlands	55.3	37.5	73.1
Portugal	49.2	53.6	59.8
Spain	46.4	40.5	67.6
Sweden	51.1	48.8	67.8
UK	35.5	45.9	66.3
EU 15	*39.1*	*41.1*	*66.8*

Note: The respondents were asked to answer the following question: 'tell me, for each item listed, how much confidence you have in them; is it a great deal, quite a lot, not very much, or none at all?' Those answering 'a great deal' and 'quite a lot' were counted as having confidence.

Source: Halman (2001, pp. 187 and 192).

deals with it. Let us attempt to survey some of the most important *cognitive problems* from the standpoint of our topic.

1. Prior to something happening we entertain certain hopes and expectations. After something happens we are often disappointed.[16] As the disillusionment over socialism began to take hold, expectations became more pronounced. The hope emerged that a change of the system would resolve all problems, quickly, for everyone.

Rightful hopes were intermingled with misconceptions and false illusions. Expressions like the 'West', the 'market', 'competition', and 'democracy',

Table 1.12 Lifetime satisfaction

Country	1990–1993	1995–1997	1999–2002
	(average on a scale from 1 to 10)		
Czech Republic	6.37	..	7.06
Estonia	6.00	5.00	5.93
Hungary	6.03	..	5.80
Latvia	5.70	4.90	5.27
Lithuania	6.01	4.99	5.20
Poland	6.64	6.42	6.20
Slovakia	6.15	..	6.03
Slovenia	6.29	6.46	7.23
CEE 8	*6.40*	*6.20*	*6.20*
Austria	6.51	..	8.03
Belgium	7.60	7.93	7.43
Denmark	8.16	..	8.24
Finland	7.68	7.78	7.87
France	6.78	..	7.01
Germany	7.22	7.22	7.42
Greece	..	..	6.67
Ireland	7.88	..	8.20
Italy	7.30	..	7.17
Luxembourg	..	..	7.81
Netherlands	7.77	..	7.85
Portugal	7.07	..	7.04
Spain	7.15	6.61	7.03
Sweden	7.97	7.77	7.64
UK	7.49	7.46	7.40
EU 15	*7.26*	*7.24*	*7.30*

Notes: The respondents were asked to mark their answer on a scale from 1 (most dissatisfied) to 10 (most satisfied): 'All things considered how satisfied are you with your life as a whole these days.' The typical size of the sample was about 1,000 respondents per country.

Sources: *World Values Survey and European Values Survey*; see the following website <www.worldvaluessurvey.com>. Sanfey and Teksoz (2005) use these data to study life satisfaction in post-socialist countries. The table reporting the summary data for the EU-8 countries is on p. 17 of their paper. I am grateful to Peter Sanfey and Utku Teksoz (EBRD), who provided the complementary data for the EU-15 countries and the data for region averages in direct communication.

resulted in mythical images which promised light without shade. Sobering words were few and far between, especially from the mouths of credible individuals. (When adherents of the old regime railed against capitalism, fewer and fewer people listened to them.)

The first great hopes got a cold shower with the serious transformational recession of the 1990s. The people had barely time to recover before new and unrealistic expectations were formed again, this time in regard to membership

Table 1.13 Lifetime satisfaction: distribution of responses

Country	% not at all satisfied	% not very satisfied (percentage of answers)	% fairly satisfied	% very satisfied
Czech Republic	5	26	57	10
Estonia	11	35	47	6
Hungary	11	34	45	9
Latvia	8	35	49	6
Lithuania	10	32	51	5
Poland	9	28	50	11
Slovakia	13	33	48	6
Slovenia	2	12	65	20
CEE 8	*9*	*29*	*50*	*10*
EU 15	*4*	*17*	*60*	*19*

Note: The respondents were asked the following question: 'On the whole, how are you satisfied with your life in general? Would you say you are ...?'

Source: Eurobarometer *Public Opinion in the Candidate Countries* survey conducted in October–November 2003; see the website <europe.eu.int./comm/public_opinion>.

in the European Union. These were kindled by various phrases referring to the 'convergence', and promises of multifaceted support to be supplied by the European Union. Many looked forward to the manifest and imminent benefits of accession with naïve impatience.

The problems are great. But they are magnified to even larger sizes as the result of *disillusionment.*

2. A well-known phenomenon in social psychology is that how one feels about something is dependent not only on the real circumstances, but also on *whom the individual compares himself to*. During the period of loosening of the socialist system, people living in the western periphery of the Soviet empire comforted themselves by noting that they still were better off than those living in the Soviet Union. Especially in a place such as Hungary, my home country, where experiments with market-economic reforms had been going on for some time, this self-encouragement even sounded credible. But as the borders of these countries opened, and especially now that they became member states of the European Union, the 'reference points' have generally shifted. Everyone has started to compare his own circumstances with that of Germany, France or Scandinavia. Of course, the higher one's standards of comparison, the more one will become dissatisfied with the place where one happens to live. The impatience is understandable: now that we are members of the European Union, when will we catch up with our fellow member states? But it also leads to hopeless desires. Those clinging to the Western frame of reference are likely to remain permanently bitter, impatient and disillusioned.

3. People very easily forget; both collective and individual memories are highly unreliable. Decades ago, we were flooded with complaints from individuals because certain consumer items were unavailable: one had to wait many years for a car or an apartment or a telephone line. Nowadays it seems that I, once the author of a book entitled *Economics of Shortage* (1980), will be left as the single individual in Eastern Europe who still remembers the shortage economy and feels genuine joy that it is over. Chronic shortages have been replaced by abundant supplies. Nowadays, people grumble that we are awash in an incredible number of products, that prices are prohibitively expensive and that people are tormented by the 'consumer society'.

As a result of these poorly working memories, fundamentally important achievements, material and non-material benefits are being disparaged (such as freedom of speech, association and movement, the free competition of ideas, the right to protest and so on), even though they are clearly discernible in people's everyday lives. Instead, current problems are accorded a greater relative weight.

In a 2004 survey individuals were asked to indicate on a scale ranging from –100 to 100 their evaluation of the current government as compared to that prior to the change in the political system, as seen in Table 1.14 and in its interpretation by Rose (2005). Although the incumbent governments received higher scores, it is remarkable that the ratings accorded to the previous system were not far behind. Grotesquely, all this leads to feelings of nostalgia. Many of those who muttered and hoped for changes during the Communist era find themselves thinking that the old regime was not that bad after all.

4. Finally, I would like to mention the flaws of causal analysis.

Table 1.14 Attitudes to regime: old, new and future

Country	Old regime	Current	In five years
	(percentage of positive answers)		
Czech Republic	32	69	82
Estonia	55	75	79
Hungary	58	64	81
Latvia	50	51	71
Lithuania	59	70	84
Poland	51	51	67
Slovakia	51	51	65
Slovenia	68	69	74
CEE 8	*50*	*57*	*72*

Note: The respondents were asked the following question: 'Here is a scale for ranking how our system of government works. The top, plus 100, is the best; the bottom, minus 100, the worst. Where on this scale would you put the former Communist regime / our current system of governing with free elections and many parties / our system of governing five years in the future?'

Source: Rose (2005, p. 17).

3.4 Causal analysis

There are many causes of the problems and difficulties suffered by the people of Central Eastern Europe. I only emphasize a few.

The region's level of development lags behind the West. This is not a new phenomenon; things have been this way for centuries. As one can see in Table 1.15, during the socialist period this relative gap expanded even further. There is a good chance that the relative backlog will gradually diminish, but it is highly unlikely that anything could occur in the social–economic–political arena that would fill the gap (which is more like an abyss!) in the immediate future, as shown in Table 1.16. Many of the negative phenomena, as well as the poverty, the lag in technological development, and the scarcity of available resources for health care, education and scientific research, can be explained primarily (but not exclusively) by the fact that the region is at the medium level of development, well behind the front runners.

Part of the trouble is also due to the fact that we are in transition. The structure of production had to be reorganized, since while old production

Table 1.15 Historical comparison with Austria

Country	1870	1913	1937	1950	1980	1989	2000
	Index (Austria's GDP per capita = 100)						
Czechoslovakia	62	60	91	94	58	54	43
Hungary	59	61	81	67	46	42	36
Poland	51	50	61	66	42	35	36

Note: Czechoslovakia in 2000 is a weighted average of the Czech and Slovak Republics.
Source: Calculated from the OECD database accompanying Maddison (2003).

Table 1.16 Convergence times to Western Europe

Country	To EU 14 100%	To EU 14 80%
	(years)	
Czech Republic	38	21
Estonia	60	45
Hungary	46	31
Latvia	74	59
Lithuania	68	52
Poland	72	55
Slovakia	48	33
Slovenia	30	9
CEE 8	*55*	*38*

Note: EU 14 means all old members, excluding Luxembourg. The results are based on the assumption of a real per capita GDP growth rate of 1.74 per cent in the EU 14.
Source: Wagner and Hlouskova (2005, p. 367).

lines ceased to exist, new ones did not take their place immediately. A new vacuum, new loopholes and an absence of regulation came into being in the midst of institutional transformation. While in many places the old guard was removed, the new management was still inexperienced. The fact that these difficulties are of a transitional nature is not sufficient to reassure everyone, for it is difficult to wait for them to be over with.

Other problems emanate from the very nature of the system. Like every system, capitalism has certain inborn system-specific negative characteristics. As long as capitalism is what it is, there will be unemployment, there will be income inequality, there will be economic winners and losers, and there will be excessive advertisements and so on. Wise, forward-looking and consistent governmental policies can mitigate some of the genetic faults but they cannot completely eliminate them. Serious and level-headed believers in the capitalist system accept these problems because, despite its deficiencies, they find the overall package more palatable than the socialist system.

The same thing can be said about democracy. The great multitudes of Central Eastern Europeans who are becoming disenchanted with democracy are like disillusioned lovers. They are irritated by the often barren verbal tirades taking place in parliament, by the mutual accusations levelled by various political parties at one another, by lying promises, and by seeing scandalous affairs swept under the carpet. Yet these are not anomalies associated with young democracies! Similar phenomena can be frequently observed in great democracies with a long history; they are not restricted to relative newcomers. The importance of the truth reflected in Churchill's words will not be diminished, though they have been quoted millions of times. Even given all its faults, democracy is still a better system than any form of tyranny, regardless of how wise, enlightened or clean-handed a dictator might be. Unfortunately, in the Central Eastern European countries a non-negligible proportion of the population does not think this way. Table 1.17 draws attention to disturbing phenomena.

Wrong decisions made by politicians – governments, the ruling party or the opposition, or the leadership of various advocacy groups – may create troubles, or exacerbate pre-existing difficulties brought on by extraneous circumstances. Consider the following example. It can be stated with certainty that capitalism gives birth to disparity. But tax policies favouring the rich while afflicting the impoverished, or poorly distributed state subsidies, can make matters even worse.

I have identified five different causes for the current problems (medium level of development, problems brought on by the transition, the system-specific problems of capitalism and those of democracy, and wrong decisions made by politicians); and of course there are others. One reason for the existence of a feeling of general malaise in society is in the confusion of these various causes in people's minds. In cases of multi-causal phenomena, the

Table 1.17 Endorsement of undemocratic alternatives

	Communist	Army	Dictator
	(% regarding as better)		
Czech Republic	18	1	13
Estonia	8	2	40
Hungary	17	2	17
Latvia	7	4	38
Lithuania	14	5	40
Poland	23	6	33
Slovakia	30	3	25
Slovenia	23	6	27
CEE 8	*21*	*4*	*29*

Note: The respondents were asked the following: 'Our present system of government is not the only one that this country had. Some people say that we would be better off if the country was governed differently. What do you think? We should return to Communist rule. The army should govern the country. Best to have a strong leader who can quickly decide everything.'

Source: Rose (2002, p. 10).

objective and clear identification and separation of various causes pose a difficult task, even for professional analysts. Small wonder that errors are creeping in the explanation of causes in the mind of people not specialized in the subject.

3.5 Once more about value judgements

I have tried to refrain from false generalization. So let me reiterate, as I emphasized above, that public opinion is divided: attitudes range from satisfaction with minor reservations, to grumbling and complaining, all the way to angry dissatisfaction. Allow me to make a few comments concerning the mood of those whose judgement tends to lean more towards the negative.

Among those who offer these negative judgements, there is an unfortunate mixture of half-true and half-erroneous establishment of the facts, a combination of half-substantiated and half-mistaken causal analysis, and an ordering of values that places the values of everyday life at the forefront. Those who judge from this perspective are not thinking in centuries-long historical perspective. They do not care what results the capitalist economic system and the democratic political order will produce in the distant future. They are experiencing these problems *today*, they are suffering from them now, or they are hurt by seeing others who are suffering now – and for this reason, their experience of the change that occurred in the system is a failure, rather than a success.

No one has the right to disregard the negative judgements of disappointed individuals. No one has the right to accuse them of short-sightedness, or of turning a blind eye towards the comprehension of great historical interrelationships. Every person has only one life. Someone who is, say, fifty or sixty and poor, perhaps also unemployed, will not be compensated by the promise that later generations will be better off, for he will not have the chance to enjoy it. It is even difficult to bid the younger generation to have patience, since no lost moment today can be truly compensated later with a better one.

For this reason, should I retract the statement made in the first half of the chapter, when I said that the great transformation of the Central Eastern European region could be fundamentally characterized as an unparalleled success? No, I do not want to retract this. I do not believe it to be possible, or for that matter, permissible, to compile some kind of balance sheet for the sake of a summary and comprehensive value judgement. On such a view, there are the successes (with a positive sign), and there are the failures (with a negative sign), and if the balance is positive, then the ultimate outcome should be declared a success; if negative, then it must be looked upon as a failure. I cannot accept this simple additive 'balance-sheet' approach.

I keep two accounts and not one, and do not merge them. On one account, I gladly acknowledge a great success at the level of world history: a system was created superior to the former one, without bloodshed, with incredible speed. On the other account, I have the list of good and bad experience in everyday life; much joy and much pain. I consider it both sensible and defensible to say that what has happened in this region can be simultaneously considered a success in terms of its global historical significance, *and* a failure in many important aspects because it caused pain, bitterness and disappointment for so many people.

4 On the tasks of the economic profession

I have no intention of blaming the man in the street for not having flawlessly processed his experiences and perhaps for having come to mistaken conclusions in his mind regarding these problems. But I would not accord the same dispensation to ourselves, those doing research in the field of economics. I am not addressing this only to those who happen to live in Central Eastern Europe, but to all who are concerned with this region or similar issues, wherever they may live.

Perhaps we may have gone too far in our acceptance of the famous comment by Keynes, according to which, in the long run we are all going to be dead. The type of real long-term analysis I attempted to deal with during the first half of the paper is quite rare. Nowadays in many PhD programmes economists are not even required to study history. One of the reasons for the overly negative judgement prevailing in Central Eastern European public opinion circles regarding the current great transformation is that scholars of the social sciences have neglected to analyse and evaluate the results within the requisite historical framework.

The various social science disciplines are separated not only from historical science, but also from each other. In preparing this chapter I encountered the unfortunate phenomenon that in the political-science literature which deals with the transformation from dictatorship to democracy, one finds almost no reference to studies of economists, while economists virtually ignore the works of political science. Without an interdisciplinary approach, it is impossible to understand and to evaluate the great transformations.

Mainstream economics relinquishes profound criticism of the capitalist economy to those professing radical views. Even when it accepts the fact that there may be problems, it lulls itself into believing that these problems can be reassuringly resolved by applying appropriate measures. It denies that the system may have inborn, insurmountable genetic defects.

In our profession, the careful and conscientious separation between the establishment of facts and their valuation is rather rare. It is not customary to frankly point out the ordering of values hidden behind the declaration of an economist. We consider it as self-evident that all share the implicit values accepted axiomatically by our trade: efficiency, productivity, competitiveness, growth, perhaps the principle of fair distribution of income; however, beyond these, very few pay attention to any other values.

There are academic economists who are happy to address a wider audience or the reading public. Even those who do not endeavour to do so, exert their indirect influence. Leading politicians, statesmen, businessmen, newspaper reporters and analysts who formulate public opinion pay heed to them. Not only can we make the great transformations more successful by making correct economic policy recommendations, we can also contribute to the more informed and well-balanced processing of the experiences and to helping people to find the right valuation of changes.

The great transformation in Central Eastern Europe is over. I have heard the ironic comment from my colleagues more than once: 'With this, so much for your weird science of "transitology".' I do not believe so. How is the transformation of China and Vietnam going to continue? What is going to happen in Cuba? How will the great transformation proceed in an Iraq under foreign military occupation? How will Iran be transformed? What transformation will take place in the Muslim countries?

Every transformation is different. Nevertheless, there are common elements. And we can only truly understand the unique properties of each country if we compare it with others. Not only is 'transitology' not over; its work has not even begun with the desired thorough approach. I hope that this chapter will spur a conscientious study of the accumulated body of knowledge on this subject.

Notes

1. There have been several documents commissioned by the European Union to evaluate the status of the candidate countries. Thus, for example, just before the accession, a publication entitled the *Comprehensive Monitoring Report* (European Commission, 2003) was compiled. A good insight into this topic is provided by the annual Transition Reports of the European Bank for Reconstruction and Development (see, for example, EBRD, 2002). I mention some of the recent publications of academic authors that are often cited by the experts: Campos and Coricelli (2002), Csaba (2005), Kolodko (2000), Kornai (2000), Roland (2000), Stiglitz (1999) and Svejnar (2002).
2. It is not within my present scope to offer a definition of the term 'Western civilization', to enumerate its characteristics or delineate its borders. I use the term merely suggestively. Since it does not belong to the subject of my analysis, I leave the question open, whether outside of the region that is often referred to as the 'Western civilization', the trends outlined in this study have already appeared or will appear in the future. The historical spread of the capitalist economy is primarily emphasized by the various Marxist and neo-Marxist schools (see, for example, Brenner, 1976, and the literature of the so-called 'Brenner Debate'). Other streams of historical science, such as representatives of the French *Annales* school, also recognize this tendency as important. I refer primarily to the works of Fernand Braudel (1972–1973, 1992), as well as to Immanuel Wallerstein's (1974, 1979) writings in which he combined Braudel's ideas with the findings of the neo-Marxist schools.
3. In some of my other writings, for example in *The Socialist System* (1992), I have attempted to give a more concise definition; I content myself here with a looser description of 'capitalism', one which is sufficient to encompass other characterizations and avert conceptual debate.
4. Consider the following representative publications which concern the issue of periodization – in particular, the topic of the beginning and end of the Middle Ages: Marc Bloch (1989), Jacques Le Goff (1982), Henri Pirenne (1937), and Peter Raeds (2001).

   I am grateful to Gábor Klaniczay, who assisted me in gaining insight into the discourse of historians examining this very subject; his article (2001) provides an in-depth overview of the literature written on the subject of transition from the Middle Ages to the Modern Age.

   In an interview, Peter Burke (1990), the well-known British historian stated: 'Nobody can agree as to when the early modern period begins ... ' Perhaps we as present day economists and other scholars of the social sciences are too close to the events and it is for this reason that we could so easily agree on one thing: the fall of the Berlin Wall is viewed as the start of a new period in the region. Or, perhaps there is a greater degree of homogeneity and synchronization present in the events than there was during earlier periods of history.
5. Luxembourg and West Germany were excluded from the table due to unavailability of data.
6. I would like to draw attention to a few from the rich literature: Haggard and Kaufman (2005), Huntington (1991), O'Donnell, Schmitter, and Whitehead (1988), and Przeworski (1991).
7. See, for example Offe (1996) and McFaul (2002).
8. Schumpeter (1942) introduced this criterion, which put the procedure of attaining and forfeiting power in the foreground, into the realm of political philosophy.

Following Schumpeter's interpretation, in my study (1998) of post-socialist regime change I highlighted the replacement of a government based on a parliamentary election as a practically well applicable test. In her book, Susan Rose-Ackerman (2005) very aptly dubbed the procedural approach as the so-called 'minimalist' interpretation of democracy. On the interpretation of democracy see also Dahl (1971) and Schmitter and Karl (1991).

9. On the connection between democracy and capitalism, several sharply conflicting views have developed over time. For me the most convincing argument is that according to which capitalism is a necessary, but not sufficient, condition of democracy. Among the classical writers on this topic, Hayek (1944) agreed with this statement while Schumpeter (1942) thought that democracy could evolve without capitalism. See also Rueschemeyer, Stephens and Stephens (1992), and Usher (1981) about this relationship.
10. I stress that my ideas about the main directions are restricted to 'Western civilization'. I make no attempt to apply this concept mechanically to other civilizations. Such comparative analysis lies beyond the scope of this current study.
11. This is the title of Polányi's best known work *The Great Transformation* (1962).
12. As far as characteristic No. 5 is concerned, in the Soviet Union the revolutionary transformation did not take place on the orders of foreign occupiers but was dictated by the domestic political power structure. There was a different situation in Eastern Europe, where the will of the Soviet political leadership proved to be the final authority. Nobody could refuse their orders due to the presence of Soviet military occupation forces.
13. TV and cellphones are the exception, both of which are in wide use.
14. Some Hungarian analyses show larger inequalities than the ones identified in Table 1.6 (see, for example, Tóth, 2004).
15. The data in Tables 1.12 and 1.13 are from different sources, based on different surveys. It is worth noting that despite the two kinds of approaches, the characteristic differences between the regions are quite close to each other.
16. Albert O. Hirschman (1982) pointed out that disappointment was a part of the human condition. He refers to Kant, who stated: 'Even if you were to grant man everything he wishes, all the same, at that very moment he will feel that that *everything* is not *everything*' (see Karamzin, 2003, p. 40).

    Especially the denizens of Western civilization are experiencing a state of ever present insatiability and disillusionment. In our case, this general feeling was further exacerbated by the frustration felt over the unrealized special expectations that followed the transition from socialism.
17. This list excludes references used exclusively as statistical sources for tables, unless the source is a published article or book.

References[17]

Bloch, M. (1989) [1939] *Feudal Society* (London: Routledge).

Braudel, F. (1972–1973) [1949] *The Mediterranean and the Mediterranean World in the Age of Philip II* (New York: Harper and Row).

Braudel, F. (1992) [1969–1979] *Civilization and Capitalism, 15th-18th Centuries. I-III; I. The Structures of Everyday Life; II. The Wheels of Commerce; III. The Perspective of the World* (Berkeley: University of California Press).

Brenner, R. (1976) 'Agrarian Class Structure and Economic Development in Pre-Industrial Europe', *Past and Present*, vol. 70, pp. 30–75.

Burke, P. (1990) 'Interview Conducted by Karl Vocelka and Markus Reisenleitner' http://www.univie.ac.at/Neuzeit/gburke.htm.

Campos, N. F. and F. Coricelli (2002) 'Growth in Transition: What We Know, What We Don't, and What We Should', *Journal of Economic Literature*, vol. 40(3) (September), pp. 793–836.

Csaba, L. (2005) *The New Political Economy of Emerging Europe* (Budapest: Akadémiai).

Dahl, R. A. (1971) *Polyarchy: Participation and Opposition* (New Haven: Yale University Press).

European Bank for Reconstruction and Development (2002) *Transition Report* (London: EBRD).

European Commission (2003) *Comprehensive Monitoring Report of the European Commission of 5 November 2003 on the State of Preparedness for EU Membership of the Czech Republic, Estonia, Cyprus, Latvia, Lithuania, Hungary, Malta, Poland, Slovenia and Slovakia*, 675 final (Brussels: European Union).

Haggard, S. and R. R. Kaufman (2005) *The Political Economy of Democratic Transitions* (Princeton: Princeton University Press).

Hayek, F. von (1944) *Road to Serfdom* (Chicago: University of Chicago Press).

Halman, L. (2001) *The European Values Study: a Third Wave* (Tilburg: EVS, WORC).

Hirschman, A. O. (1982) *Shifting Involvements* (Princeton: Princeton University Press).

Huntington, S. P. (1991) *The Third Wave: Democratization in the Late Twentieth Century* (Norman: University of Oklahoma Press).

Karamzin, N. M. (2003) [1789–1790] *Letters of a Russian Traveller* (Oxford: Voltaire Foundation).

Klaniczay, G. (2001) 'The Middle Ages' in Smelser, N. J. and Baltes, P. B. (eds) *International Encyclopaedia of the Social and Behavioral Sciences* (Amsterdam: Elsevier).

Kolodko, G. (2000) *From Shock to Therapy: the Political Economy of Post-socialist Transformation* (Oxford: Oxford University Press).

Kornai, J. (1980) *Economics of Shortage* (Amsterdam, New York: North-Holland).

Kornai, J. (1992) *The Socialist System* (Princeton and Oxford: Princeton University Press and Oxford University Press).

Kornai, J. (1998) *From Socialism to Capitalism: What is Meant by the 'Change of System'* (London: Social Market Foundation).

Kornai, J. (2000) 'Ten Years After "The Road to a Free Economy," The Author Self-Evaluation', in Pleskovic, B. and N. Stern (eds), *Annual World Bank Conference on Development Economics 2000* (Washington, DC: The World Bank).

Le Goff, J. (1982) [1977] *Time, Work, & Culture in the Middle Ages* (Chicago: University of Chicago Press).

Maddison, A. (2003) *The World Economy: Historical Statistics* (Paris: OECD, Development Centre Studies).

McFaul, M. (2002) 'The Fourth Wave of Democracy and Dictatorship', *World Politics*, vol. 54, pp. 212–44.

O'Donnell, G. A., P. C. Schmitter and L. Whitehead (1988) *Transitions from Authoritarian Rule: Comparative Perspectives* (Baltimore: Johns Hopkins University Press).

Offe, C. (1996) *Varieties of Transition: the East European and East German Experience* (Cambridge, MA: Polity Press).

Pirenne, H. (1937) [1933] *Economic and Social History of Medieval Europe* (New York: Harcourt, Brace and World Inc.).

Polányi, K. (1962) [1944] *The Great Transformation: the Political and Economic Origins of Our Time* (Boston: Beacon Paperback).

Przeworski, A. (1991) *Democracy and the Market* (Cambridge: Cambridge University Press).

Raeds, P. (2001) 'When Were the Middle Ages?' in Sogner, S. (ed.), *Making Sense of Global History, The 19th International Congress of the Historical Sciences Oslo 2000 Commemorative Volume* (Oslo).

Roland, G. (2000) *Transition and Economics: Politics, Markets, and Firms* (Cambridge, Mass: MIT Press).

Rose, R. (2002) *A Bottom Up Evaluation of Enlargement Countries: New Europe Barometer 1* (Glasgow: Centre for the Study of Public Policy).

Rose, R. (2005) *Insiders and Outsiders: New Europe Barometer 2004* (Glasgow: Centre for the Study of Public Policy).

Rose-Ackerman, S. (2005) *From Elections to Democracy* (Cambridge: Cambridge University Press).

Rueschemeyer, D., E. H. Stephens and J. D. Stephens (1992) *Capitalist Development and Democracy* (Cambridge: Polity Press).

Sanfey, P. and U. Teksoz (2005) 'Does Transition Make You Happy?' EBRD Working Paper no. 91 (London: European Bank for Reconstruction and Development).

Schmitter, P. C. and T. L. Karl (1991) 'What Democracy Is ... And Is Not', *Journal of Democracy*, vol. 2(3), pp. 76–88.

Schumpeter, J. (1942) *Capitalism, Socialism and Democracy* (New York: Harper and Brothers).

Stiglitz, J. (1999) 'Whither Reform?' *Annual Bank Conference on Development Economics* (Washington, DC: World Bank).

Svejnar, J. (2002) 'Transition Economies: Performance and Challenges', *Journal of Economic Perspectives*, vol. 16(1) (Winter), pp. 3–28.

Tilly, C. (1984) *Big Structures, Large Processes, Huge Comparisons* (New York: Russel Sage Foundation).

Tóth, I. Gy. (2004) 'Income Composition and Inequalities 1987–2003' in Kolosi, T., I. Gy. Tóth, and Gy. Vukovich (eds) *Social Report 2004* (Budapest: TÁRKI).

Usher, D. (1981) *The Economic Preriquisite to Democracy* (Oxford: Basil Blackwell).

Wagner, M. and Hlouskova, J. (2005) 'CEEC Growth Projections: Certainly Necessary and Necessarily Uncertain', *Economics of Transition*, vol. 13(2), pp. 341–72.

Wallerstein, I. (1974) *The Modern World-System: Capitalist Agriculture and the Origins of the European World-Economy in the Sixteenth Century* (New York: Academic Press).

Wallerstein, I. (1979) *The Capitalist World-Economy* (Cambridge: Cambridge University Press).

2

Transformation in China*

Yingyi Qian
Department of Economics
University of California, Berkeley, USA

and

Jinglian Wu
Development Research Centre (DRC), Beijing, China
China Europe International Business School (CEIBS), Shanghai, China

1 Introduction

In his Presidential Address, Professor Janos Kornai (2005a) evaluated the transformation in the eight Central Eastern European countries (CEE8) from two perspectives. From the perspective of everyday life, the transformation in the last 15 years brought much disappointment. Part of it is due to the change of the reference point – now the bar is raised to the level of the developed Europe, but part of it is real, as the evidence shows that negative sentiments among the population are strong. On the other hand, from the long-term historical perspective, the transformation is a major success: not only have both the economic and political transformations been completed in the main direction of Western society, that is, capitalism and democracy, but also its completion was fast and peaceful. The long-run gain from the transformation could be high, even though the short-run pain is not negligible. In addition, because there is an intrinsic value of the political rights that were brought about by the transformation to democracy, transformation itself has an intrinsic value.

When turning from Eastern Europe to China, we cannot fail to notice the contrast between its transformation and that in the Central Eastern European countries. From the perspective of everyday life, the transformation in China has brought significant economic benefits to a population of 1.3 billion, which is a significant success. On the other hand, from the perspective of

* The authors are grateful to Shaoqing Huang for the research assistance in compiling the tables and figures.

long-term history, it is ambiguous. In the economic sphere, much as in Central and Eastern Europe, transformation in China also moves in the same mainstream direction of the market economy. But in the political sphere, China has not yet moved in the mainstream of Western society, that is, democracy. At the time of writing, it is unclear whether China has only delayed the movement, or has not moved in that direction. Hence, China is still in the midst of a great transformation.

This simple comparison between the two transformations is instructive and serves as a starting point for our presentation which is divided into two parts. In the first part, section 2, we characterize China's transformation and assess the Chinese experiences in the last quarter of a century. In the second part, section 3, we develop a framework in order to understand some key features of the transformation. Section 4 concludes.

2 Characterizing China's transformation

In this section we first assess the economic achievement: it was a great success, but with problems. We then assess the political achievement: it had a slow pace, but with progress. Finally, we characterize the present state of China as a 'socialist market economy with Chinese characteristics', by carefully interpreting each term.

2.1 A great success in economic achievement, but with problems

The starting point is 1978. In December of that year, the Chinese Communist Party held a historic meeting that initiated a transformation known as 'reform and opening up'. It is customary for the Chinese to take the level of major economic indicators in 1978 as the benchmark. According to official Chinese statistics, during the 25 years from 1978 to 2003, China's gross domestic product (GDP) increased at the annual rate of 9.4 per cent. At that rate, the size of GDP doubles every 7.5 years. This implies that during the last 25 years, China's GDP increased by a factor of 9. By taking into account population growth, per capita GDP grew at about 8 per cent per year. At that rate, per capita income doubles every 9 years. China's per capita GDP in 2003 was 7 times the level in 1978, as Table 2.1 shows. China's high growth continued in 2004, when the rate was 9.5 per cent. During the same 25 years period per capita consumption grew annually at 7.8 per cent, matching the GDP growth, indicating that China's growth did not come at the expense of consumption.

China's high growth has an important feature: it has been closely related to China's increasing opening to the outside world. In 1978, China was one of the most closed economies in the world, with only $20 billion in total foreign trade. In 2003, foreign trade increased to over $850 billion so that the trade to GDP ratio increased to 60 per cent, as shown in Table 2.1. In 2004, the total

Table 2.1 China: growth indicators

	Real GDP* (billion yuan)	Real GDP per capita* (yuan)	Real consumption per capita * (yuan)	Total foreign trade (US$ billion)	Total foreign trade/GDP (%)
1978	658.4	684.0	334	20.64	9.80
1985	1,270.1	1,199.9	619	69.60	23.05
1990	1,854.8	1,622.3	803	115.44	29.98
1995	3,269.1	2,699.0	1,250	280.86	40.19
2000	4,864.5	3,838.1	1,847	474.29	43.19
2003	6,189.9	4,789.9	2,171	850.99	60.11
Average growth rate (%)	9.4	8.1	7.8		
2003 level (1978 = 100)	940	700	649		

* At 1990 prices.

Source: Calculated from National Bureau of Statistics, *China Statistical Yearbook* (Beijing: China Statistics Press, 2004).

foreign trade expanded further and reached a new high of $1.1 trillion. By that measure, China's economy is quite open.

Some economists suspected that China's growth rate was overstated. For example, Madison figured that China's growth rate could be overstated by one or two percentage points due to an underestimation of inflation. Even reducing China's growth rate by two percentage points, as Madison did in his calculation, 7.5 per cent (6 per cent on the per capita) is still respectable.

But it is not easy to prove with confidence that China's long-run growth rate is significantly overestimated. Although the bias for overestimation exists, so does the bias for underestimation, especially on the contributions from the private and from the service sectors. In addition, the errors are likely to be counter-cyclical. China's growth rate could be overestimated during an economic downturn; a notable example is 1998 when the official growth rate of 7.8 per cent and the real growth rate were believed to be much smaller. But during economic upturns, the growth rate tends to be underestimated. A recent example is 2003 and 2004, when the official growth rates were reported at around 9 per cent, but several international investment banks considered that they could be over 10 per cent.

We examine some other indicators in physical units and thus less subject to the errors in price information. We look at telephone lines (fixed and mobile), motor vehicles, housing, and construction of motorways, providing the type of services to which middle-income economies give heavy weight (Table 2.2). The growth of telecommunications is remarkable: by July 2005, China had over 700 million subscriptions for telephone lines, one subscription

Table 2.2 China: growth indicators in physical units

	1978	1985	1990	1995	2000	2003	2005[a]
Telephone lines (millions): Fixed	..	3.12[b]	6.85[b]	40.71[b]	171.53	271.60	337.44
Mobile	..	..	0.018[b]	3.63[b]	84.53	269.95	363.17[b]
Motor vehicles Output (millions)	0.15	0.44	0.51	1.45	2.07	4.44	5.07[b]
Stock (millions)	1.36	3.21	5.51	10.40	16.09	28.83	..
Passenger car stock (per 1,000 pop'n)	..	..	..	1.33	2.03	5.41	6.96[b]
Urban housing (m^2 per person)	6.7	10.0	13.7	16.3	20.3	23.7	..
Housing investment (as percentage of GDP)	..	..	1.97	6.41	5.51	7.73	..
Length of motorway (thousand km)	..	..	0.5	2.1	16.3	29.7	..

[a] July.
[b] CEIC database.

Source: *China Statistical Yearbook* (Beijing: China Statistics Press, 2004), Xinhua News Agency and Economist Intelligence Unit.

for every two people. China now has the largest mobile phone subscription in the world, but the explosion in growth in mobile phones is a worldwide phenomenon and not surprising. The growth in fixed line subscriptions from 3 millions in 1985 to 300 millions in 2005 looks more impressive. The motor vehicle industry grew quickly from a low base, producing less than half million in 1985, 1.45 million in 1995, and over 5 million in 2004. The number of passenger cars per thousand people is still low, but the growth rate is high, from one per thousand in 1995 to 7 per thousand in 2004. Housing construction has been a major force in the investment boom. China invested 2 per cent of GDP in real estate in 1990, but in 2003 close to 8 per cent. Urban household surveys indicate an increase in per person living space from 6.7 square metres in 1978 to 23.7 square metres in 2003, implying that on average a three-person family would have over 70 square metres living space. Another indicator is the construction of highways and motorways, an important part of national infrastructure. In 1990, China had almost no motorways, just main roads. Since then, in less than a decade and a half, China built 30,000 kilometres of motorway, next only to the United States in total length.

Table 2.3 is on social indicators. First, as a developing country, the increase in non-agriculture employment is an essential component of industrialization and the key to raising living standards. Non-agricultural employment increased from 118 million in 1978 to 358 million in 2003. On average, China created non-agricultural jobs at the rate about 10 million annually, the size of Hungary's entire population. Secondly, China also made significant progress in poverty reduction; not only did the percentage decline, but the absolute number also significantly fell while the population continued to increase (Table 2.4). On the Chinese definition of the poverty line, numbers in rural poverty were reduced from 250 million (or 31 per cent of the rural population) to 42 million (or 4.6 per cent) between 1978 and 1998. On the World Bank definition of the poverty line ($1 a day) the reduction was from 280 million in 1990 (or 31.3 per cent) to 106 million (or 11.5 per cent) in 1998. China, together with India, has contributed most to poverty reduction in the world in the last 25 years.

Table 2.3 China: social indicators

	Employment (millions)			Life expectancy (years)	Adult literacy rate(age > 15)[a] (%)
	Non-agricultural employment			In 1990	In 1990
				68.55	77.7
Year	Industry	Service	Total		
1978	69.45	48.90	118.35		
1985	103.84	55.32	159.16		
1990	138.56	83.49	222.15	In 2000	In 2002
1995	156.55	119.79	276.34	71.40	90.9
2000	162.19	168.80	330.99		
2003	160.77	198.23	359.00		

[a] *Human Development Report 2004* (New York: United Nations, 2004).
Source: *China Statistical Yearbook* (Beijing: China Statistics Press, 2004).

Table 2.4 China: population in rural areas in poverty

	Chinese national standard		World Bank standard	
Year	Population in poverty (millions)	Percentage of rural population	Population in poverty (millions)	Percentage of rural population
1978	250	30.7	–	–
1990	85	9.5	280	31.3
1993	75	8.2	266	29.1
1996	58	6.3	138	15.0
1998	42	4.6	106	11.5
2002	28	–	88	–

Source: World Bank database.

Because the poverty in these countries is the main source of world dispersion in income inequality, the world income distribution became less unequal, despite an increase of inequality within most countries.

China's adult literacy rate increased from 77.7 per cent in 1990 to 90.9 per cent in 2002, which is higher than most lower-middle-income countries. Its life expectancy has increased from 68.55 years to 71.4 years in the same time period, bringing it to equality with Estonia and Hungary and into the range of upper-middle-income countries, according to the United Nations *Human Development Report 2004*.

China's growth may be astounding, but is by no means exceptional: it corresponds to that of East Asian high-performing economies between 1960 and 1990.

China's great economic success is not without problems and we here focus on two – rising inequality and corruption – although there are others, such as environmental damage.

Several studies show that income inequality increased throughout the entire transformation period, except for the early 1980s: it increased within the urban sector, within the rural sector, as well as between the urban and rural sectors. China's overall Gini coefficient increased from 0.39 in 1988 to 0.44 in a single decade. The average income ratio of urban residents to rural residents increased to over 3 in recent years, as Table 2.5 shows. China's Gini coefficient is higher than that of Central Eastern European countries (0.30) and the United States (0.41) but lower than those of Russia (0.49), Malaysia (0.50), and most Latin American countries (in the range of 0.60). Consumption inequality also increased. Between 1991 and 2003, the ratio of consumption

Table 2.5 China: Gini coefficients and consumption inequality

	Gini coefficients*			**Consumption inequality ****			
	1988	**1995**	**2003**	**Richest 10% to lowest 10%**		**Richest 20% to lowest 20%**	
National	0.39	0.44	0.45				
Rural area	0.32	0.38	0.37				
Urban area	0.23	0.28	0.32				
Average income per capita Urban/rural	2.0	2.8	3.1	**1991**	**2003**	**1991**	**2003**
				2.42	5.66	2.02	3.95

Source: * The data for 1988 are quoted from Li Shi (2003), 'Reviews and Perspectives on the Research of Personal Income Distribution in China [Zhongguo geren shourufenpei yanjiu huigu yu zhanwang]', *Economics (Quarterly)*, Vol. 2 (2), pp. 379–403, and those of 1995 and 2003 are quoted from Li Shi and Yue Ximing (2004). 'Survey on the Income Gap between Urban and Rural Area in China [Zhongguo Chengxiang Shouru Chaju Diaocha]', *Finance* [*Caijing*], vol. 3/4, 2004.

** The National Bureau of Statistics, *China Statistical Yearbook*, Beijing: China Statistics Press, 2004, and 1992.

expenditures of the richest 20 per cent to the poorest 20 per cent increased from 2.02 to 3.95, and that of the richest 10 per cent to the poorest 10 per cent increased from 2.42 per cent to 5.66 per cent. Both values are similar to those in the EU15, and lower than in the CEE 8 (as reported by Kornai (2005a)).

Corruption is recognized as a serious problem and the Chinese press frequently reports on corruption cases. Not surprisingly, China does not score high in the Corruption Perception Index compiled by Transparency International: for China the 2004 score is 3.4 (0 is most corrupt and 10 is most clean) and is ranked 71st in the world, more corrupt than Peru (67), Thailand (64), and Mexico (64), but less corrupt than Turkey (77), Russia (90), and Ukraine (122), as Table 2.6 shows.

On the perception of ordinary people about their satisfaction with life in general, we examined several recent Gallup surveys, as shown in Table 2.7. A Gallup poll in 2004 reported that nearly two-thirds of all Chinese say they are satisfied with the way things are going in their lives (12 per cent 'very satisfied,' 51 per cent 'somewhat satisfied'). Remarkably 77 per cent also say they are satisfied with their family lives (21 per cent 'very satisfied', 56 per cent 'somewhat satisfied'), and a similar proportion express satisfaction with their

Table 2.6 Corruption perception index: international comparison

Country rank	Country/region	CPI 2004 score*
1	Finland	9.7
5	Singapore	9.3
16	Hong Kong	8.0
17	USA	7.5
24	Japan	6.9
35	Taiwan	5.6
39	Malaysia	5.0
42	Hungary	4.8
47	South Korea	4.5
51	Czech Republic	4.2
59	Brazil	3.9
64	Mexico	3.6
64	Thailand	3.6
67	Peru	3.5
71	**China**	**3.4**
77	Turkey	3.2
87	Romania	2.9
90	Russia	2.8
90	India	2.8
122	Ukraine	2.2

* CPI score relates to perceptions of the degree of corruption as seen by business people and country analysts and ranges between 10 (highly clean) and 0 (highly corrupt).

Source: Transparency International (2004), www.transparency.org.

Table 2.7 China: life satisfaction and confidence in the future

	Satisfaction score (in 2005) (%)				**Rating quality of one's personal life at different time points (10-point scale)**			
	VD	**SD**	**SS**	**VS**		**5 years ago**	**In 2005**	**5 years from now**
Your personal health	8	15	45	32	National total	3.48	4.45	6.49
Your current housing	17	27	40	15				
Your family life	6	17	56	21	Urban	4.33	4.73	6.48
Your children's education	8	14	34	11				
Your community as a place to live	13	26	46	14				
You job, or the work you do	15	25	38	10	Rural	2.92	4.26	6.49
Your household income	20	38	36	5				
The amount savings you have	34	34	24	3				
Your own education	23	32	35	8				

Note: 'VS', 'S', 'D', 'VD' stand for, respectively, 'very satisfied', 'somewhat satisfied', 'somewhat dissatisfied', 'very dissatisfied'.

Source: Compiled on the data of Gallup poll, www.Gallup.org.

personal health (32 per cent 'very satisfied', 45 per cent 'somewhat satisfied'). While family life and personal health are the areas of greatest satisfaction, household financial issues – particularly savings and income – provide the most widespread grounds for discontent. Majorities say they are dissatisfied with their own education (55 per cent), their household incomes (58 per cent), and – most dramatically – the amount of savings they have (68 per cent). This is evidence of rising aspirations for a richer life.

Another Gallup poll asked the people to rate the quality of their personal life at different time points. On the scale of 0 to 10, urban residents rated 4.73 in 2005, compared to 4.33 five years previously, while rural residents rated 4.24 in 2005, compared to 2.92 five years previously, a more significant improvement. Asked to rate the quality of life five years hence, the Chinese seem to have confidence in the future: urban residents rated 6.48 and rural residents rated 6.49. It is interesting to note that the anticipated increase in confidence for the ensuing five years is bigger than the actual increase in the previous five years.

Overall, survey results show that most Chinese are satisfied with their life and reasonably confident about their future. But their aspirations are also increasing, and they are dissatisfied with their education, income and savings.

2.2 A slow pace in political reform, with progress

China scores very poorly in all of the indices on civil and political rights and democracy compiled by Western organizations. We cite the widely used indices compiled by Freedom House (Table 2.8) which show that in the category of political rights China's score remained 7 (least free) without any change in the period covered (1990–2003) and received an aggregate 'not free' rating. In 2003, Central Eastern European countries all have scores 1 (the most free) and are rated 'free', but other Eastern European transformation countries vary. Russia's score is 5, and Ukraine's is 4, and both have

Table 2.8 Political and civil rights indicators: international comparison

Country/ region	1990			1994			2000			2003		
	PR	CL	Status	PR	CL	Status	PR	CL	Status	PR	CL	Status
China	7	7	NF	7	7	NF	7	6	NF	7	6	NF
Czech Republic	..	..	..	1	2	F	1	2	F	1	2	F
Estonia	..	..	..	3	2	F	1	2	F	1	2	F
Hungary	2	2	F	1	2	F	1	2	F	1	2	F
India	2	3	F	4	4	PF	2	3	F	2	3	F
Japan	1	1	F	2	2	F	1	2	F	1	2	F
Malaysia	5	4	PF	4	5	PF	5	5	PF	5	4	PF
Mexico	4	4	PF	4	4	PF	2	3	F	2	2	F
Peru	3	4	PF	5	4	PF	3	3	PF	2	3	F
Romania	6	5	NF	4	3	PF	2	2	F	2	2	F
Russia	..	..	..	3	4	PF	5	5	PF	5	5	PF
Singapore	4	4	PF	5	5	PF	5	5	PF	5	4	PF
South Korea	2	3	F	2	2	F	2	2	F	2	2	F
Taiwan	3	3	PF	3	3	PF	1	2	F	2	2	F
Thailand	2	3	F	3	5	PF	2	3	F	2	3	F
Turkey	2	4	PF	5	5	PF	4	5	PF	3	4	PF
Ukraine	..	..	..	3	4	PF	4	4	PF	4	4	PF

Note: 'PR' stands for 'Political rights' (1 = most free, 7 = least free); 'CL' stands for 'civil liberties' (1 = most free, 7 = least free); 'Status' is freedom status ('F', 'PF' and 'NF' respectively stand for 'free', 'partly free' and 'not free').

Source: Freedom House, www.freedomhouse.org.

'partly free' status. In East Asia, both South Korea and Taiwan score 2, 'free' status, while Singapore's score is 5, only 'partly free'. Noticeably, in the civil liberty category, China's score did improve from 7 in the 1990s to 6 after 2000. The combination of 7 in political rights and 6 in civil rights set China firmly within the overall category of 'not free'.

There is no doubt that the general pace of political liberalization is slow in China. Nevertheless, there are areas in which the country has made some progress, though not captured by the above indices. Village elections are an area that has received much attention, but their significance should not be overemphasized, because the village is not a formal tier of government under the Chinese Constitution. In discussing political progress, we mention the following three areas that deserve attention.

The first area is related to those individual rights that are directly related to the expansion of economic freedom – that freedom has expanded and is a basic reason for the economic success in China's transformation. The last column of Table 2.8 shows that China's score on the economic freedom index compiled by the Heritage Foundation is around 3.5, which represents 'mostly not free'. Ghana receives the same score but the index may underestimate the extent of China's economic freedom.

An important part of economic freedom is the freedom to move. That 120 million 'floating migrant workers' (nearly one-third of China's total non-agriculture labour force) have moved from inland provinces to work in the coastal provinces is strong evidence for such increased freedom. Table 2.9 also gives some data from the Economist Intelligence Unit (UK). It shows a dramatic increase in visits abroad by the Chinese: international departures doubled between 2000 and 2003. International capital movement is exemplified in foreign direct investment, some $45 billion annually. In the last

Table 2.9 China: economic freedom

	FDI, inward					
	Amount (US$, billion)	**% of GDP**	**Visiting abroad, departures (million)**	**Current-account restrictions (5 = 1ow)**	**Set up new business (5 = low regulation)**	**Index of economic freedom***
2000	38.4	3.55	10.5	3	2	3.40
2001	44.2	3.76	12.1	3	2	3.55
2002	49.3	3.88	16.6	3	2	3.55
2003	47.1	3.26	20.2	5	3	3.55
2005	..	..	..	..	..	3.46

Source: The data without '*' are from Economist Intelligence Unit – *Country Data* at <www.eiu.com>. Data with '*' are from Heritage Foundation at <www.heritage.org>. Index of economic freedom includes 'free' (score: 1–1.95), 'mostly free' (score: 2–2.95), 'mostly not free' (score: 3–3.95), and 'repressed' (score: 4–5).

few years, China's current account restrictions were greatly relaxed due to its accession to the WTO, so the index measuring freedom in that dimension improves from 3 to 5 (5 is the most free). Regulations on setting up a new business are also relaxed and the index measuring freedom in that dimension improves from 2 to 3 (5 is the most free).

The second area to which we draw attention is progress in establishing the rule of law, even if China is still far from being a rule of law country. Table 2.10 shows the World Bank's Governance Indicators on the rule of law for selected countries. China's score, around 50 (out of 100 maximum), is much higher than Russia and Ukraine (in the 20s) and is similar to those of Mexico and Romania. Both Mexico and Romania are richer than China and are democracies (both receive 'free' status by Freedom House as shown in Table 2.8). The conclusion is that China is progressing in the area of rule of law.

The rule of law was formally incorporated into the Chinese Constitution in March 1999 when Article 5 was amended to include the principle of 'governing the country according to law and establishing a socialist, rule of law country'. In 2004 Article 13 on the protection of private property was amended to state that 'citizens' lawful private property is inviolable' and 'the State, in accordance with the law, protects the rights of citizens to private property and to its inheritance.'

Last, but not least, we note the peaceful transfer of power during 2002–2004 from Jiang Zemin to Hu Jintao. This is significant because it is the first time in

Table 2.10 Rule of law index: international comparison

	2004	2002	2000	1998	1996
China	**40.6**	**48.5**	**48.7**	**52.4**	**37.3**
Hong Kong	90.3	84.7	90.4	90.8	90.4
Hungary	78.7	77.6	78.6	76.2	75.3
India	50.7	55.6	62.0	67.0	56.6
Japan	89.9	88.3	90.9	90.3	88.0
Malaysia	64.7	67.9	71.1	76.8	82.5
Mexico	45.9	47.4	46.0	40.0	54.2
Peru	31.9	36.7	38.5	37.3	40.4
Romania	48.3	52.0	51.9	49.7	44.0
Russia	29.5	21.4	18.7	22.7	19.9
Singapore	95.7	92.3	98.9	99.5	99.4
South Korea	68.6	76.5	73.8	76.8	81.9
Taiwan	77.8	78.6	79.1	84.9	84.3
Thailand	51.7	60.2	69.0	69.2	71.1
Turkey	54.6	53.1	59.9	65.9	58.4
Ukraine	23.2	21.4	26.2	23.2	28.3

Note: This index is a percentile rank (0–100), the higher, the better.

Source: Kaufmann D., A. Kraay, and M. Mastruzzi (2005): Governance Matters IV: Governance Indicators for 1996–2004 (www.worldbank.org).

the history of the People's Republic of China that the top leadership changed in a peaceful way. In fact, Jiang Zemin became the first Secretary General of the Chinese Communist Party to step down gracefully. His immediate predecessors, Zhao Ziyang and Hu Yaobang, were humiliated after stepping down from the post and, earlier, Party Chairman Hua Guofeng had been forced to resign in disgrace. The Gang of Four (including Mao's wife) were arrested within a month after Mao's death. The President of the country Liu Shaoqi died in prison during the Cultural Revolution. This time, not only did Jiang Zemin retire peacefully, but the entire leadership retired with him. This set up a precedent, and was an achievement, albeit that we cannot say that the procedure of peaceful succession has been institutionalized.

2.3 'A socialist market economy, with Chinese characteristics'

To assess the nature of China's transformation in the past quarter-century is difficult. Although rapid growth in China is evident, there is debate on qualitative issues such as: Is China really a market economy? Is China socialist? Is the Chinese Communist Party still a Communist Party?

It may be useful to start with the Chinese government's official slogan 'a socialist market economy with Chinese characteristics', comprising three key terms: 'market', 'socialism', and 'Chinese characteristics'. We ask three questions: 'To what extent is China a market economy?' In what sense is China socialist? And what is meant by Chinese characteristics? Our analysis here is positive, rather than normative.

The first defining term is *'market economy'*. We provide evidence to show that, after a quarter-century of reform, China has become an emerging market economy. Although it is still far from being a mature market economy based on the rule of law, by its level of development (per capita GDP $4580 in 2002 on PPP, *Human Development Report 2004*), China is a normal emerging market economy.

The first piece of evidence concerns ownership. Before the reform, private ownership of means of production was virtually zero in China. The ownership concept in China's context is more complex than in other countries, because in addition to the standard private ownership and state ownership, a third category of so-called 'collectives' also existed, albeit in rapid decline. In Chinese terminology state and collectives together are termed the public sector, and the collectives and private together are termed the non-state.

Table 2.11 shows that in 2001 the agriculture sector contributed 16 per cent of total GDP, the industrial sector accounted for 50 per cent, and the service sector, 34 per cent. Almost the entire agriculture sector (except for a small state farm sector) is *de facto* private under the household responsibility system. For the industrial and service sectors, studies have estimated the shares of state and state-controlled firms, collective firms, and truly private firms (including foreign firms). As Table 2.11 shows, the share of state ownership in total GDP declined from 48 per cent in 1990 to 38 per cent in 2001, and at

Table 2.11 China: GDP by ownership and sector

	Percentages					
	By ownership			By sector		
Year	**State**	**Collective**	**Private**	**Agriculture**	**Industry**	**Service**
1990	47.7	18.5	33.8	27.1	41.6	31.3
1995	42.1	20.2	37.7	20.5	48.8	30.7
1996	40.4	21.3	38.3	20.4	49.5	30.1
1997	38.4	22.1	39.5	19.1	50.0	30.9
1998	38.9	19.3	41.9	18.6	49.3	32.1
1999	37.4	18.4	44.2	17.6	49.4	33.0
2000	37.3	16.5	46.2	16.4	50.2	33.4
2001	37.9	14.6	47.5	15.8	50.1	34.1

* Quoted from Xu Xiaonian and Xiao Qian, 'Another New Economy [Ling yi zhong xinjingji],' *Report of the Research Department of China International Capital Corporation Limited [Zhongguo Guoji Jinrong Youxian Gongsi Yanjiubu baogao]*, 2003.

Source: *China Statistical Yearbook [Zhongguo tongji nianjian]* (Beijing: China Statistics Press), various years.

the same time, the share of private ownership increased from 34 to 48 per cent. Combining the private sector with the collective sector, which in recent years was rapidly privatized, the so-called 'non-state sector' accounted for 62 per cent of the economy.

The second piece of evidence comes from a broader measure of marketization compiled by Chinese economists. The 'marketization indicator' consists of five components: government and market relationship, the share of the non-state sector, the development of a goods market, the development of a factor market, and market organizations and institutions. Table 2.12 shows an across-the-board improvement over time, in each region, and by each component. This table also demonstrates that eastern coastal regions score higher in marketization indicators than the inland provinces. It also reveals that goods market liberalization proceeded faster than factor market liberalization.

Nobody disagrees that China's market institutions are still underdeveloped. The question is rather how China's market institutions compare with other countries, controlling for the level of income. In a simple exercise, we regress per capita income in PPP terms on the institutional index provided by EBRD for all transition economies including China (Figure 2.1). The data point of China is slightly below the regression line, indicating that the extent of institutional development is slightly above average for its given level of income.

We conclude that China is an emerging market economy. Although it is still far from a mature market economy based on the rule of law, it is not an outlier for its level of income and development.

Table 2.12 China: marketization indicators

	Aggregate indicator				Components of the indicator, national				
	National	**East**	**Middle**	**West**	**(1)**	**(2)**	**(3)**	**(4)**	**(5)**
1997	4.98	6.36	4.63	3.86	..	..	..	..	..
1998	5.15	6.5	4.78	4.06	..	..	..	..	..
1999	5.14	6.51	4.7	4.08	..	..	..	..	..
2000	5.34	6.78	4.81	4.28	6.01	5.23	7.59	3.26	4.60
2001	5.74	7.37	5.11	4.56	..	..	..	..	..
2002	5.98	7.72	5.38	4.68	6.29	6.64	7.99	3.76	5.22

Note: (1) 'relationship between government and market'; (2) 'development of non-state economy'; (3) 'cultivation of product market'; (4) 'cultivation of factor market'; and (5) 'market organizations and the institutional environment'.

Source: Compiled from data in Fan Gang and Wang Xiaolu (2001, 2004).

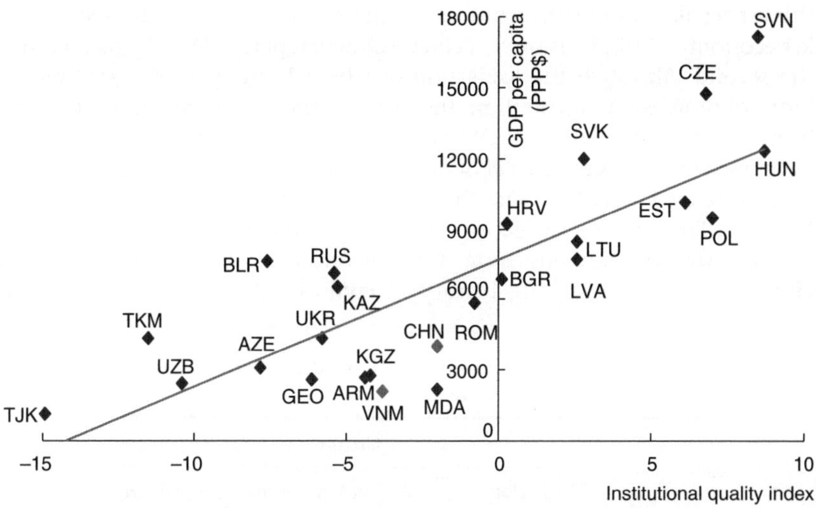

Figure 2.1 Regression of per capita income on institutional quality: transition countries

'Socialism'. The second defining term is 'socialism'. To answer in what sense China is practising socialism depends on the meaning of socialism.

Kornai (2005b) gives several definitions of socialism. The first definition is by ownership of the means of production, the definition used by Marx, Lenin and Stalin as well as Lange. With 48 per cent of the economy produced by the private sector and 62 per cent by the non-state sector, it is difficult to call China socialist on grounds of ownership.

The second definition of socialism is that used by the social democrats in Europe. Disregarding the part on democracy, socialism here means welfare state. China is not a welfare state by that definition either. The Chinese government does not support pensions, health care and education in the manner governments of welfare states do. The simple reason is China is too poor. Table 2.13 shows that government expenditure on education, health care and other types of social development as a percentage of GDP declined up to the mid-1990s before bouncing back. Even by the standards of a developing country, the state provision of primary education, health care, pensions and job security in China is not high.

The third definition of socialism is the one related to fairness in income distribution. At the beginning of the reform, Deng Xiaoping redefined socialism as having nothing to do with ownership, but also nothing to do with the resource allocation mechanism of planning or markets. His favourite slogan was 'letting some people get rich first, and gradually all the people should get rich together'. While this sounds like 'trickle down economics', it expresses a desire for getting rich together, a social goal of a fair income distribution. In this aspect alone, this concept of socialism is close to the German 'social market economy'. China has surely achieved the first part of Deng's goal, but not the second. Although the leadership of China has a goal of 'socialism' in terms of more equal distribution, the reality is that at the present time China is much less equal than most OECD countries, although it is in line with less developed countries at its level of development.

'Chinese characteristics'. The third defining key term is 'Chinese characteristics'. There are many features that make China special. China is a large country (hence different from small economies such as Singapore or Hong Kong); it has a long history of civilization (hence differing from

Table 2.13 China: government spending: social, cultural, education and health care

	China	
	% of GDP	**% of government expenditure**
1985	4.56	20.38
1990	3.98	23.92
1992	3.64	25.92
1995	3.00	25.74
1998	3.74	27.14
2000	4.90	27.59
2002	5.63	26.86
2003	5.51	26.24

Source: Compiled on the basis of the CEIC database.

recently created states); it has a Confucian culture tradition (thus differing from the Christian religion of the West); it was an agricultural, low-income country at the time of reform (thus differing from the former Central and Eastern European planned economies); and it has Hong Kong and Taiwan as springboards for foreign investment, together with a large stock of overseas Chinese (which differentiate it from many other countries).

In our view, what matters the most from the perspective of transformation, especially the political economy perspective, is the 'leadership of the Communist Party'.[1] It means the authoritarian control of the Party. There are two types of misunderstanding with regard to the role of Party control. First, by the very name of the Communist Party is often meant the Communist ideology of public ownership. However, the Chinese Communist Party is no longer a Communist Party committed to public ownership. It is also gradually moving away from being a totalitarian party in the sense of controlling everything and everybody.

While this misunderstanding is diminishing, it would be too early to conclude that the Chinese Communist Party is just an ordinary authoritarian party such as the PRI of Mexico, or a 'one-party system' country such as Singapore under Lee Kwan Yew or South Korea under Park Chung Hee. The Chinese Communist Party is still midway between a totalitarian and an authoritarian party, and is slowly evolving from of its past in ideology, and more importantly, in organization and institutions. The Communist Party in China still controls the country in many ways as in the past, but is slowly changing.

Control over propaganda and information and control over personnel are the two key components in this control. On personnel, the Party not only makes all appointments in the government, but also the executives of state-owned and controlled corporations, even though the latter are listed on the stock market and have their own boards of directors (Qian and Wu, 2003). The Party also controls the appointment of the executives in state-owned not-for-profit organizations in education, health care, media and society, which together constitute an important part of the service sector. In those organizations, the Party's control is just like before, because there are neither boards of trustees nor directors and no process of open search in the market for the most qualified people.

In summary, China has in the past quarter-century been transforming itself from a centrally planned economy with a rigid socialist ideology and the strict control of a totalitarian party. Measured by economic criteria, China has been a huge success, albeit with serious problems of increasing inequality and corruption. Measured by political criteria, China has made only slow progress. Now, China is an emerging market economy under an authoritarian rule of the Communist Party that abandoned its old ideology but is still operating in many ways as it did in the past.

3 Understanding China's transformation

Having characterized China's transformation, we now develop a framework to understand some key features of this transformation. Although the transformation is complex, we propose a simple framework to capture its essential elements.

3.1 Economic growth as the objective

There is a perception that the Chinese government is single-minded for economic growth. But why is this the case? Many governments in the world do not have that objective. Redistribution of wealth, equalization of income, democratization or civil war can be alternative objectives. Even for the Chinese government pursuing economic growth has not always been the objective, certainly not during the Mao era, for example. The Chinese aspiration for high-speed economic growth is by means an accident. We explore several explanations here. The first explanation seems obvious: China's overwhelming objective of economic modernization is due to its low initial level of income – at the inception of transformation, China was a poor, low-income country: in 1978 per capita GDP was around $600 in 2002 dollars in PPP terms. After the intense effort of a quarter of century, China's per capita GDP reached $4580 in 2002 in PPP, still the lower-middle-income level (*Human Development Report 2004*).

For Central and Eastern Europe, the starting point for the transformation was very different. These countries were already at the upper-middle-income level (per capita GDP more than $8,000 in 2002 dollars on PPP) in 1989, and their aspiration then as now is to reach the high-income level of Western Europe. It is not surprising that their preference orderings differ from those of the Chinese.

Not all low-income countries have an aspiration for economic growth as ambitious as China. The second explanation is historical. During the most of its 5000 years' history of civilization, China has been a leading economic power in the world. In AD 1000 China's per capita GDP was among the highest in the world. That was the time during China's Song dynasty. China declined after that dynasty, but according to Madison's estimates, China's total GDP due to its large population was still the largest in the world around 1820 when the Qing Dynasty Emperor Jiaqing died and his son Daoguang was crowned. China lost its lead in world GDP around the time of the first Opium War in 1840 some 160 years ago.

Chinese modern history began in the mid-19th century with the sad realization by the Chinese that China's once glorious civilization now lagged behind the West both economically and technologically. China's share in the world's GDP continued to decline for about a hundred years until the Communists took power in 1950. Ever since 1840 the Chinese have sought to revive Chinese civilization and to regain the country's economic lead. The objective of economic growth can be understood in historical perspective for it reflects the priority among most Chinese over several generations to escape from poverty and to restore China's leading economic (and national) status in the world. That status which had prevailed for most of China's 5000 years' history had been lost in the last 160 years. This Chinese sense of history reinforces their view that they should make economic development their first priority.

Indeed, China's current transformation is a continuation of the century-long effort to modernize its economy. There were several notable failed attempts in the 20th century. The Qing Emperor tried a 'new deal' in the first decade of the 20th century following the Boxer Rebellion and defeat by foreign forces in 1900, but it was interrupted by the Nationalist Revolution and the ensuing civil chaos. During the late 1920s and early 1930s, the Nationalist government oversaw some rapid economic development in the southern part of China, but it was interrupted by the Japanese invasion (1927–1937). When the Communists took power in 1949, China had a chance to develop its economy in peacetime. The economy indeed grew fast in the 1950s, but only between 1953 and 1957, when it was again interrupted – by the Great Leap Forward and the Cultural Revolution, lasting for nearly two decades until 1976. Each of the three episodes of continued development lasted for no more than 10 years before the interruption of war or chaos. In total, there were less than 25 years of economic development in the modern history of China before 1979. Historically speaking, the current wave of economic growth is the most prolonged and uninterrupted longer than the three previous episodes combined.

The third explanation is the impact of the Cultural Revolution (1966–76). The Cultural Revolution is the most immediate historic event preceding the current transformation. In the late 1950s, the Chinese leaders realized that the Soviet model of central planning was inadequate, but Mao favoured neither central planning nor the market, and did not consider economic development as a prime objective at that stage. His radical aim was to change people's minds, above everything else, even if that meant delaying economic development for some time. He launched the Cultural Revolution, which was aimed at anything but economic development.

The tragedy of the Cultural Revolution has had a huge impact on the thinking of China's current leaders. They were convinced that the great mistake of the Cultural Revolution was that the country gave up economic development as the central objective: a consensus among them emerged, that economic development should take first priority. That was embodied in the historic Party meeting in December 1978: the Party decided to shift its operational focus to economic development. But that view was shaken by the Tiananmen Square events, when some Party conservatives argued against economic reform, embracing the ideology to ignore economic development. A policy shift emerged during Deng Xiaoping's southern tour in 1992, when he formulated the ultimate objective as economic development.

He argued for the chief criterion to be 'whether it promotes the growth of the productive forces in a socialist society, whether it increases the overall strength of the socialist state, and whether it raises living standards'. These 'three tests', together with his well-known statement '[economic] development is the absolute principle', became the Party's official doctrine.

The fourth explanation is the demonstration effect from China's East Asia neighbours. After the Cultural Revolution and when China opened its windows, the Chinese were stunned by the fast economic growth in their neighbours, Japan and the 'Four Little Tigers' of Hong Kong, Taiwan, Singapore and South Korea. That type of growth was later replicated by Malaysia, Thailand and Indonesia, and was a shock to the Chinese leadership, because they had considered these countries or regions (except Japan) were not as developed as Mainland China. The contrast was eloquent between China and these economies, especially between Mainland China and Taiwan, but at the same time, the East Asian demonstration of the feasibility of fast growth gave the Chinese confidence.

That the Chinese put economic development as their first priority in their preferences, above anything else, has a direct implication on transformation. In China transformation has never been for the sake of transformation, for modernization, first and above all, of the economy. Thus most Chinese view transformation (i.e. reform and opening up) as an instrument, not an objective. It is the desire for economic growth that has brought the demand for transformation. Modernization is the ultimate drive behind transformation, neither the other way around nor independently. After the Cultural Revolution, which was transformation without growth, the Chinese can no longer accept a transformation with no, or slow, growth. Hence one observes that China's transformation accompanies its economic modernization and its rise as an economic power. In contrast, the transformation in Central and Eastern Europe may have its own intrinsic value, and economic performance may not be the only criterion.

3.2 Maximizing growth subject to the constraint of Party control

To understand specific key features of China's transformation, we propose a simple framework of a constrained maximization: the Communist Party maximizes economic growth subject to the constraint of keeping itself in power. That objective reflects the preferences of most Chinese. The constraint is what 'Chinese characteristics' are about. Transformation is seen as seeking the solution to this constrained maximization problem.

In studying how this constrained maximization might operate, there are two views on the relationship between Party control and economic growth. On a first view, economic growth and Party control are complementary: Party control promotes economic growth. Thus, Party control promotes stability and avoidance of chaos, and stability is a productive public good for economic growth; the career concerns of Party cadres ensure that they pursue economic growth as their objectives in their regions and departments. On the other hand, when the population value growth highly, rapid economic growth provides the basis of Party legitimacy. This complementarity between economic growth and Party control is enhanced in a Confucian culturalization of respect for authority and of esteem for stability (and fear of chaos) under authority. On this view, Singapore under Lee Kwan Yew is a successful example, for the economy has grown fast under authoritarian rule.

On a second view, the constraint of the Party imposes a cost on economic development because such a control restricts individual freedom and decentralized decision-making. Indeed, not all authoritarian regimes are able to promote growth: decisions under an authoritarian rule may be quick, but they may be wrong and persisting. Within the constraint of maintaining Party control, many reform strategies are not immediately feasible, and some may have to be delayed: searching for ways to reduce or minimize the cost of the constraint or to relax the constraint becomes an important part of transformation. The Chinese have demonstrated their ingenuity in pushing for high growth by loosening Party control to expand individual freedom, but at the same time without losing control. Many second-best innovations emerge in such a constrained maximization problem.

This simple framework carries several implications that are empirical features of China's transformation, some of which may seem puzzling viewed from other perspectives, or even contradictory from the experiences of other transformations. But they are logical within our framework.

Implication No. 1: Deng's strategy of 'playing two hands hard'. Deng Xiaoping's strategy of 'playing two hands hard' dominated the thinking of the Party: playing one hand forcefully to keep the Party in power, while playing the other hand vigorously to develop the economy as fast as possible. There are two rules in this strategy. The first rule is 'do not give up Party control', which sets a boundary nobody can cross, and the second rule is to embrace any means to faster economic growth.

We provide two examples in the late 1980s and early 1990s to show how violating either rule was not tolerated. Both Hu Yaobang and Zhao Ziyang were diehard followers of Deng's economic reform in the 1980s, but they were discarded because they violated the first rule. In 1987, then Party Secretary General Hu Yaobang was sympathetic to the liberal intellectuals during the campaign against them: this was viewed as violating the first rule and he was dismissed. In 1989 Zhao Ziyang, then Party Secretary General, sided with the students during the Tiananmen Square events. This also was again viewed as violating the first rule and he was immediately dismissed. On the other hand, in 1990 after the Tiananmen Square events, a group of conservatives wanted to de-prioritize economic development and reform, e.g. by abolishing the 'household responsibility system' in rural areas and returning to the commune. Deng viewed them as violating the second rule and undertook a famous tour around southern China to stress that economic development is an immutable imperative that nothing should hinder.

Implication No. 2: Ideology is endogenous and secondary. In our framework, it is natural that ideology is endogenous and secondary. Market or planning, private ownership or public ownership, are only tools for the development of the economy and for the Party to retain control. If an ideology excessively restricts economic development, and if the Party can maintain control through other means, the ideology would be changed.

We cite three examples of such ideological shift by the Communist Party. The first is the shift from central planning to the market. After Mao's death, the Party leadership was divided on how to develop the economy. Chen Yun, representing one view, advocated a more moderate approach, in which the market played a supplementary role to central planning. Deng Xiaoping represented the more radical view of greater opening to the market. However, both Chen and Deng, the two major forces of the old generation in the Party, shared the objective and they only differed in the means to reach it. In 1992 the Party decided on a 'socialist market economy' and abandoned the ideology of central planning, without any opposition by Chen Yun.

The second example is on private ownership. What distinguishes the prototype Communist Party from all other parties in the world (including socialist parties) is its ideology against private property, as was the case for the Chinese Communist Party until the 15th Party Congress in 1997, when it abandoned that ideology by pronouncing private ownership as an important component of the economy. This paved the way for the amendment of Article 11 of the Constitution in 1999, placing private businesses on an equal footing with the public sector by replacing the original clause that the private economy is a supplement to public ownership by a statement that the non-public sector, including individual and private businesses, is an important component of the socialist market economy.

The third example concerns the admission of capitalists into Party membership. Although private property facilitates economic growth, it may also undermine Party control. To prevent that, capitalists were allowed to join the Party, as was done at the 16th Party Congress in 2002. The Party claimed that it not only represented the working class but also capitalists, and welcomed the latter to join. Again, this major shift in the Party ideology was undertaken because it helped the economy and kept the Party in power.

To many outsiders, such dramatic shifts in ideology seem hard to understand. But it is very logical in our framework of constrained maximization. In Central and Eastern Europe, removing the Communist Party from power seemed to be the precondition for privatization and marketization, because the Communist parties declined to change their ideology. In China, marketization came first and privatization followed. It is the Communist Party that drives these changes.

Implication No. 3: Opening up faster than internal reforms. It is remarkable how China's economy has become so open to the outside world. Table 2.1 shows China's ratio of foreign trade to GDP is over 60 per cent, very high by the standard of a large country. For example, in neither the United States nor Japan is that ratio higher than 25 per cent. China has been the largest foreign direct investment destination for some years, and in other years still the largest after the United States. More than 400 out of the *Fortune* 500 corporations have subsidiaries or offices in China. China seems more open than Japan.

China's embracement of globalization has been comprehensive and exceptional among developing countries in the 1990s. China's negotiations to join the WTO also demonstrate its determination to open up to the global economy. Unlike many other countries, China's government policy often exhibits 'reverse discrimination' in the sense that it favours foreign firms against domestic firms. For example, foreign firms generally pay lower taxes than Chinese firms. With WTO accession, foreigners can invest in China's banking and telecommunication industries, although these industries are still unavailable to Chinese private investors.

We observe that between the two basic policies, reform and opening up, it is often the case that opening up moves faster than reform. Figure 2.2 shows the index on economic freedom in several categories compiled by the Heritage Foundation. It demonstrates that in four categories (top marginal tax rate, size of government, legal system, and regulation) China's rankings

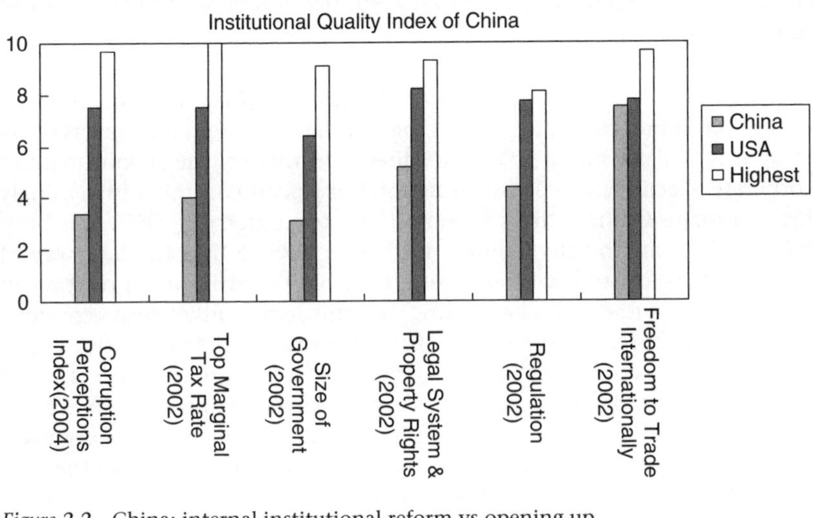

Figure 2.2 China: internal institutional reform vs opening up

are consistent and not very high, as compared to the United States and the best performer. However, one indicator stands out, that is the freedom to trade internationally. This fits our observation well, that in China opening up often moves faster than internal reform.

This is a natural implication from our framework. Opening to the outside benefits the economy enormously, but it poses few costs to Party control, because foreigners are not in the same position as the Chinese to undermine such control. On the other hand, the Party finds it easier to contain foreigners than the Chinese.

Implication No. 4: The rule of law before democracy. Our framework enables us to understand why the Chinese government has an incentive to pursue the rule of law before democracy. Table 2.8 shows that China's ranking in democracy (in terms of political rights) is the worst. But Table 2.10 demonstrates that China's ranking in the rule of law index is in the middle range. China is making steady progress on the rule of law, as the Chinese government is willing to do, but as long as it is within limits. The rule of law can bring immediate economic benefits and supports economic growth, but its impact on Party control is less immediate. Democracy's effect on economic growth is ambiguous, but its effect on Party control could be immediate and devastating, as has been shown in Central and Eastern European countries.

Barro (2004) cites cross-country regressions that the rule of law is positively correlated with economic growth, but there is no such simple correlation between democracy and growth. The relationship is instead quadratic: at low levels, more democracy helps growth, but at high levels, it retards it. If this is so, then a little bit more democracy will perhaps be seen in the Chinese transformation.

Implication No. 5: The Party gives up direct control over firms. The final implication of our framework is for something that has not been done but is likely to occur: the Party might give up its direct control over the appointment of corporate executives. The cost of maintaining such control is increasingly high as many Chinese firms become more open globally. There has been much debate among the Chinese leaders as how to find the best way of relaxing Party control without losing control. The strict interpretation of Party control is to control everything, but this may conflict with economic growth. The looser interpretation of Party control is not to control everything, but only critical matters. The Party's direct control over firms is not critically important for keeping the Party in power, and we can hence imagine that in future, the Party will no longer directly appoint top executives but only send board members according to the portion of the shares the state owns in the firm. Then, the Board of Directors, not the Party committee, would govern the firms.[2] China has not yet reached that stage, but our framework would predict this direction.

3.3 Uncertainty for the future

There is a great uncertainty for China's future, because two opposing forces are at work. On the one hand, while China's economic growth continues, its average income level rises: popular people's preferences for economic growth may shift to broader spheres, and the demand for political liberalization will likely increase. However, if the income disparity continues to expand, there may be opposite forces at work that might increase the demand for continued authoritarian rule.

A further increase in China's income inequality would make the poor and the rich, instead of the middle class, the major social forces in the society. The poor, underprivileged groups may demand an authoritarian government to protect their interests by raiding the rich. On the other hand, the wealthy, strong interest groups may also want the government to limit competition from their competitors. Both would undermine the process for political liberalization. Some Latin American countries have had this experience, and it might be China's as well.

On the other hand, China's per capita income can rise fast. In 2002, China's per capita GDP was $4580 on PPP. If China's per capita income continues to grow at the rate of at least 6 per cent annually; by 2015 (10 years from now) China's per capita GDP would cross the threshold of the upper-middle income level, the level of Russia, Mexico, and Malaysia in 2002. Although becoming richer does not guarantee a democracy, an upper-middle-income country would have a greater chance for political liberalization than a lower-middle-income country. In today's world, globalization would further increase the demand for high quality and internationally compatible institutions. Technological change increased the importance of a knowledge-based economy, which in turn emphasized the role of professionals, an important part of the middle class. Professionals often value political rights more than other members of society.

China can look to its East Asian neighbours for precedents. In the cases of Japan and Indonesia, external forces played critical roles in their political liberalization. In Japan, the United States imposed democracy after World War II. In Indonesia, democracy was introduced amid financial crisis through the external forces of the International Monetary Fund and the United States government. Singapore and Hong Kong are still not very democratic, even though their income is already at the high level: nevertheless both scored high on the rule of law and economic freedom, ranking better than the United States. The cases of Taiwan and South Korea are particularly interesting. After a long period of authoritarian rule, both experienced political liberalization starting in the late 1980s and continuing in the 1990s. At that time, their per capita income levels were about $8000 (1995 dollars). In both cases, political liberalization was peaceful, and without interruption of their economic development. Taiwan and South Korea are now functioning democracies. In both cases, former opposition leaders were elected as President at least in one of the elections.

We do see some delay to political liberalization in East Asia relative to income level. But the delay is not indefinite: East Asian peoples value democracy, but tolerate an authoritarian regime somewhat more and somewhat longer, as long as it brings in substantial economic benefits. This may be due to the Confucians' culture of respect for authority and value for stability under authority. With the strong desire among the Chinese to see China grow in economic terms, with the average level of income is still low, and with the tradition of the Confucian culture, political liberalization in China might take longer than many hoped.

3.4 Concluding remarks

As compared to Central and Eastern Europe, China's transformation has both common and unusual elements. In the economic sphere it conforms to the worldwide trend of marketization and globalization and has generated large economic benefits, but in the political sphere it has not yet moved in the same direction as Central and Eastern European countries. The future for China's transformation remains uncertain.

Professor Kornai has a frank judgement on Central European transformation, and he prefers their slower economic growth together with the completion of economic and political transformation to China's high economic growth. An ordinary Chinese might have a different value judgement, explained by two major factors. The first factor is the income level. China started its reform from a low income and even today is still a lower-middle-income country. Hungary, and Eastern Europe in general, started transformation at the upper-middle-income level. It is not surprising that preference orderings would put more weight on economic benefits in the low-income countries. The second factor is the preference difference between intellectuals and the men and women on the street. Kornai's value judgement reflects his view as an intellectual who puts more weight on non-material benefits and long-run historical impact than on immediate material benefits as compared to an ordinary person. There is a difference between intellectuals and ordinary people in preference orderings. His assessment of Eastern European transformation is clearly more optimistic than that of the population at large, as surveys show. People want more immediate material benefits, such as employment and growth, rather than transformation per se.

Therefore, in evaluating transformation, it might not be appropriate simply to judge the transformation of Eastern Europe by the standard of the Chinese, nor is appropriate to judge the transformation of China by the standard of the Europeans. On the other hand, although at the present time the preference for economic development is strong, it may change. As China's income improves and its economy develops, the preference ordering and priority might shift from growth to those broader spheres evidenced in other countries or regions, including China's neighbours. It may thus not be the case that China's political transformation will be delayed indefinitely.

Notes

1. For a general study of political economy in transition countries, see Roland (2000).
2. See Wu (2005) for details on this.

References

Barro, Robert (2004) 'Economic Growth across Countries', Chapter 9 in Marc A. Miles (ed.) *The Road to Prosperity: the 21th Century Approach to Economic Development* (New York: Heritage Books).

Human Development Report 2004 (New York: United Nations).

Kornai, Janos (2005a) 'The Great Transformation of Central Eastern Europe: Success and Disappointment', ch. 1 of this book.

Kornai, Janos (2005b) 'Market and Socialism: a Conceptual Clarification'. Paper presented at the Round Table of the International Economic Association on Market and Socialism, January, 2005.

Qian, Yingyi and Jinglian Wu (2003) 'China's Transition to a Market Economy: How Far across the River', in Nicholas C. Hope, Dennis Tao Yang, and Mu Yang Li (eds) *How Far across the River: Chinese Policy Reform at the Millennium* (Stanford, Calif.: Stanford University Press), pp. 31–63.

Roland, Gerard (2000) *Transition and Economics* (Cambridge, Mass.: MIT Press).

Wu, Jinglian (2005) *Understanding and Interpreting Chinese Economic Reform* (Mason, Ohio: Texere).

3

Institutional Causes of Economic Underdevelopment in the Middle East: a Historical Perspective*

Timur Kuran
Duke University

1 The puzzle of Middle Eastern economic underdevelopment

To anyone who knows the Middle East, broadly defined to include North Africa and the Balkans, it is a puzzle that the region became and remains economically underdeveloped. Visit any major city in the region – Cairo, Aleppo, Istanbul – and you will encounter big covered bazaars, centuries old. Istanbul's stunning Grand Bazaar, whose core was built in the 1460s, boasts more than 4000 shops. Wandering in its vaulted streets, you appreciate the major commercial centres that the region has had. Travellers and resident foreigners of the sixteenth century marvelled at the size of the markets and at the variety of commodities traded. They were also impressed by the prevailing living standards. None considered the region economically backward. Admittedly, some foreigners were critical of Islam, or of 'the Turk' who by then ruled much of the region, or of handicaps endured by visiting merchants. However, informed foreigners did not consider Islam inimical to wealth creation or the region's institutions harmful to economic activity.

Yet, subsequently the region's economic output per person failed to keep up with that of countries now categorized as 'developed'. It fell behind Western Europe, and in the late twentieth century behind parts of East Asia as well. Except for a few sparsely populated oil exporters, no predominantly Muslim country, in the Middle East or elsewhere, currently ranks among the countries generally considered developed.

* This work was supported by the USC Institute for Economic Research on Civilizations through a grant of the Templeton Foundation's Metanexus Institute.

2 Searching for historical causes

To identify the sources of the Middle East's decline in economic standing, it helps to know when the slippage began. It was in the late eighteenth century that outsiders began to hint in unison that the region was relatively poor. Impressions can mislead, but work by economic historians confirms that in this case they were empirically sound. Modern economic growth had already taken off; in the nineteenth century Western Europe grew steadily faster than the Middle East and the divergence continued into the twentieth century (Özmucur and Pamuk, 2000; Easterlin, 1996). In the late eighteenth century, as various data show, certain developments came together to make Western Europe more hospitable to growth than elsewhere.

What is unique about this period of divergence in living standards? The eighteenth and nineteenth centuries mark the Industrial Revolution, whose hallmark was mass production based on new technologies. The new technologies emerged in Western Europe, which by then had the organizational means to exploit them. England, the Low Countries, and the rest of the region could finance mass production. They could mobilize the savings of large numbers and channel them into large projects. And they could pool the labour and capital of large numbers within indefinitely living companies (North, 2005; Lal, 1998; Mokyr, 1990; Jones, 1987).

These are capabilities now taken for granted, but they posed immense challenges in some parts of the world, including the Middle East. The new physical technologies were easily transferable. One can transport a steam engine on a ship, along with the technicians and raw materials needed to make the engine productive. By contrast, the organizational vehicles of economic advancement – the institutions that enabled the West to exploit the new physical technologies – cannot be readily transferred. A viable stock market cannot be established overnight, for it requires an intricate legal system; also a range of specialized professions, including schools to train them, must support its operation.

As growth took off in the West, the Middle East lacked the organizational capabilities to use the technologies of modern industry. To make matters worse, these could not be borrowed at will. Thus the Middle East was an economic laggard during the Industrial Revolution.

Two critical institutions blocked adaptations during the Industrial Revolution: the region's law of commercial contracts and its distinct form of trust, the *waqf*. Both institutions were elements of Islamic law, the region's dominant legal system after the rise the Islam. Neither had changed significantly over the previous millennium, and in the nineteenth century both became the focus of legal reforms aimed at stimulating economic development through secularization. Accelerating the growth process required, reformers of the period thought, modifying these Islamic institutions in the light of new global realities. Indeed, to understand why the Middle East fell behind during the Industrial Revolution we must identify the static and dynamic consequences of these two institutions. We must set out, that is, the short-term outcomes they enabled and blocked, and also their long-term effects on economic modernization.

3 Commercial contract law

By the start of the second millennium, Islam had generated a law of contract that enabled the pooling of labour and capital through partnerships. Under the system enforced through Islamic courts, investors who could not, or did not want to, exert physical effort financed merchants and producers lacking the capital to undertake profit-oriented ventures (Udovitch, 1970). What is striking about the consequent partnerships is their small scale and short duration. Known as *mudaraba*, the typical partnership involved two people: a sedentary and passive investor, along with an active labourer. Their profit shares, which could be unequal or contingent, were set in advance and losses were shared up to a point. Whereas the active partner carried unlimited personal liability, the liability of the passive partner was limited. In particular, the latter risked only the capital that he placed at the partnership's disposal.

Islamic partnership contracts were enforceable over a vast area. As merchants and producers moved, they carried their law with them, helping to spread Islam. In time, it would become possible to conduct commerce under a more or less uniform legal system over a vast area stretching from Morocco and Spain to India and Indonesia. Initially at least, Islamic partnerships did not hinder Middle Eastern capabilities in exchanges with Westerners. Around the start of the second millennium, essentially the same partnerships were used throughout the Mediterranean basin. In twelfth-century Venice the institutions governing resource pooling did not differ fundamentally from those of Baghdad (Pryor, 1977; Çizakça, 1996).

Islamic law did not put any limits on the number of people who could contribute labour or capital to a commercial partnership nor restrict how long the partnership would last. It was legal for 50 people to pool labour and capital for a trading mission expected to last three years. As a matter of practice, however, the number of partners was usually two; in historical records, rarely do we encounter partnerships with more than five members. Moreover, the typical partnership was established to pursue a mission with an expected duration of at most a few months, such as a trading venture between Cairo and Aleppo.

At the end of an Islamic partnership its members could form a new partnership. In the medieval Middle East recontracting was possible and did occur. Yet, a medieval partnership was not what we now call a firm. Lacking legal standing, it had no life of its own. If a partner died before the contract had been fulfilled, the partnership ended, the assets were divided, and the deceased's share was distributed among his or her heirs. Whether the interrupted business activity was restarted depended on the prevailing inheritance system.

4 The Islamic inheritance system and its impact on modernization

After the rise of Islam, the dominant inheritance system in the region was the Islamic inheritance system. According to rules outlined in the Qur'an, two-thirds of any estate is reserved for children, parents, spouse(s), and possibly other relatives. For any category of relatives, the share of a female equals half that of a male. Thus, a daughter gets half as much as a son, and a sister half as much as a brother.

By medieval standards, this system was remarkably egalitarian. It did not allow a parent to favour one child over others. No relative entitled to a share could be disinherited (Powers, 1999). On the downside, the system made it difficult to keep property intact from one generation to the next. Although ways existed to circumvent the egalitarian provisions of the inheritance regulations (e.g. *inter vivos* gifts to minor grandchildren), they all had serious drawbacks of their own. Consequently, successful businesses tended to fragment after their founder's death.

In principle, the heirs of a successful producer or merchant could reconstitute his liquidated business. But the larger the number of heirs, the higher the reconstitution costs were. Successful businessmen – those who commanded abundant capital – were most likely to have many heirs, if only because they tended to have multiple wives. So the death of a partner was especially problematic if he was a successful businessman, in that untimely termination was especially likely to impose substantial reconstitution costs (Kuran, 2003).

If premature dissolution of partnerships was costly, their members would have tried to reduce the risks involved. These risks rose with partnership size, in that the probability of at least one death increased. The risks increased also with the duration of the partnership's business agenda. Thus, merchants, producers and investors could all minimize their risks by keeping their partnerships small and limiting their duration.

In the Middle Ages, premature dissolution could pose problems in Western Europe as well. Italian partnerships known as *commenda* became null and void if a partner died. However, inheritance practices differed between the Christian- and Muslim-dominated shores of the Mediterranean. Because the Bible does not explicitly specify an inheritance system, on matters of inheritance there was much more experimentation in Western Europe. Accordingly, inheritance practices in France, England, the Netherlands, Germany and elsewhere varied greatly over both space and time. In some places, including those that led the Industrial Revolution, a common practice was primogeniture, under which a deceased's business could fall in its entirety to his oldest son. Primogeniture greatly reduced the risks of premature partnership termination. It allowed a partner to pre-commit credibly to having a son take over in the event that he himself could not continue. It made it profitable, therefore, to form large business enterprises expected to last for years, as opposed to mere months.

Over many centuries, the consequent interregional difference in the scale and duration of business activity had a huge impact on business practices. In the West, precisely because businesses expanded and gained longevity, pressures arose to develop more advanced commercial institutions (Hunt and Murray, 1999). Thus, standardized accounting methods were developed to facilitate communication among growing numbers of business partners and changes in their ranks. Likewise, stock markets developed to provide liquidity to people who invested in long-lived enterprises. In the Middle East, such innovations did not occur until the nineteenth century, essentially because the demand for organizational change was absent. Where partnerships are ephemeral and limited to at most a few people, no pressing need arises for double-entry bookkeeping because it is relatively easy for partners to agree to a simple accounting system of their own. Likewise, there is no need to establish formal equity markets as an instrument of liquidity because shares in ephemeral enterprises are already liquid.

The persistent smallness of traditional Middle Eastern enterprises also limited the division of labour. This is evident in the stagnation of the number of distinct commercial occupations. Lists of commercial occupations compiled from court transcripts, palace records, travel accounts, advice to sultans, and other written documents show that in the Arab Middle East their number stayed statistically constant between four early Islamic centuries (8th to 11th centuries) and the subsequent four-century period (12th to 15th centuries). During the same interval, the number of occupations in the state bureaucracy and the military tripled, and the number in education, law, and religion more than quadrupled (Shatzmiller, 1994). Given that division of labour is a correlate of economic dynamism, we may infer that there was enormous dynamism in certain sectors, but also that commerce was relatively stagnant.

We can hence identify a major reason why the Middle East fell behind the West. In the course of the second millennium, the West developed the capacity to form enterprises with hundreds, eventually even thousands, of employees and shareholders. Some of these enterprises lasted for many generations and by virtue of their long histories, they came to be very widely known. Because few Middle Eastern enterprises could compete with such enterprises, commerce between the Middle East and Western Europe fell increasingly under the control of Westerners (Kuran, 2003, 2005). Moreover, as the West industrialized, the Middle East could not exploit the technologies of mass production to form modern industries.

The Middle East could not easily borrow the organizational forms that gave the West an advantage because, due to a millennium of organizational stagnation, the preconditions were lacking. Standardized bookkeeping and stock markets offer examples. Modern firms require double-entry accounting. In case of disputes, they need judges familiar with modern accounting conventions. If for no other reason, the indigenous courts were unequipped to handle financial cases involving modern firms. Likewise, the absence of stock markets made it difficult to raise the capital needed to start industrial enterprises. In sum, institutional borrowing was hindered by the lack of complementary institutions.

To sum up thus far, the Islamic inheritance system, by creating incentives to keep commercial enterprises small and short-lived, prevented the emergence of modern commercial institutions from within Islamic law. These institutions emerged initially in Western Europe, helping to make it the first region to experience modern economic growth. The Middle East could not borrow the winning institutions in piecemeal fashion. Their complementarities meant that reforms, whenever launched, would have to be wide-ranging. Hence no major reforms of direct relevance to the private economic sector were initiated until the mid-nineteenth century, by which time the Middle East was already far behind the West, as a range of economic indices demonstrated.

5 The role of attitudes

Insofar as inheritance practices mattered, the West did not leap ahead by knowingly adopting the right regime. The people who adopted inegalitarian inheritance practices such as primogeniture could not have known the institutional dynamics that would be unleashed, or the global advantages that would eventually emerge. Rather, it was greater experimentation that generated the winning combination in the West.

Nothing in the foregoing argument relies on the common claim that Islam discourages commerce. In the medieval era the Middle East was as friendly to merchants as anywhere (Rodinson, 1966/1973). Its businessmen participated heavily in, if not dominated, several of the world's major long-distance trade emporia, including the Middle East itself, and also East Africa, Central Asia, and the Indian Ocean (Ensminger, 1997; Chaudhuri, 1985). Middle Easterners were commercially so successful, in fact, that where they went in large numbers, their commercial institutions, including Islam's law of commercial contracts, went with them. Islam spread to the Far East and Africa not through the sword but primarily through trade. Vast numbers of conversions to Islam were motivated by the lure of joining Middle Eastern trade networks.

Notice also that the argument does not invoke attitudes toward innovation. The Middle East has never been opposed to innovation *per se* as a matter of general policy. Adaptations did occur as exemplified by the repeated adjustment of tax systems for reasons explicable through economic logic (Coşgel and Miceli, 2005; İnalcık, 1994). However, during the second millennium institutional changes occurred mostly outside the profit-driven private economic sector as evidenced by our data on the division of labour. The division of labour increased in state-controlled sectors, which points to their dynamism. By and large Muslim clerics went along with the state-introduced modifications – evidence that Islamic institutions are not inherently static and Muslim clerics not inherently conservative. If commercial laws and techniques remained stagnant, this is because, until quite late, private merchants, producers, and investors were unmotivated to demand fundamental changes.

In what ways has this history left its mark on the present? At the start of the twentieth century, native Middle Easterners, with the telling exception of religious minorities who purchased foreign legal protection, were unable to found or operate large companies (Kuran, 2004; Toprak, 1995). For this reason alone, domestic private capital accumulation was limited. Subsequently, modern economic institutions have taken root in the region; every major country now has growing stock markets, and each benefits from modern accounting systems. But adapting such transplanted institutions to local circumstances is taking time. It took centuries for the modern economy to develop in Western Europe. Given the recency of the first Middle Eastern steps toward economic modernization, it is not surprising that businessmen find the business climate less hospitable in, say, Egypt, than in developed countries.

There is, however, another channel by which the foregoing history has had an enduring effect. At the start of the twentieth century, partly because private capital accumulation was limited, civil society – the part of the social system outside direct state control – was weak. The resulting political vacuum allowed, even compelled, states to take the lead in economic development. State-centred development programmes have resulted in large bureaucracies and sharp limits on private economic freedoms. Even today, adaptations to global economic realities are slowed and hindered by the political weaknesses of civil society.

6 The *waqf*

The other Islamic institution that played an enormous role in the Middle East's economic evolution, accounting for stunning successes but also for some of the shortcomings of recent centuries, is the *waqf*, which is an unincorporated trust established under Islamic law and overseen by Islamic courts. The founder of a *waqf*, man or woman, is an owner of private immovable property – land or buildings. The purpose is to provide a service allowed under Islamic law. A *waqf* may be established to support a mosque, a school, an orphanage, a park, a lighthouse, a region's water supply, or a road, among other possibilities. Whatever the nature of the service, it must be provided in perpetuity.

In the pre-modern Middle East, the *waqf* permitted individuals to supply in a decentralized manner a wide variety of public goods now commonly supplied by governments. In some respects it formed an admirable system: precisely because of its lack of centralized control, it was responsive to local needs.

Over many centuries, vast resources flowed into what became the *waqf* sector. The figures are staggering. By 1700, depending on the region, *waqfs* controlled between a quarter and half of all real estate. Their income was used partly to provide social services. In 1700, when Istanbul had a population of around 700,000, 30,000 people were fed each day through *waqf*-financed soup-kitchens. Most of the centuries-old structures that tourists now admire – fountains, inns, mosques, schools, bathhouses, hospitals, even certain markets – are structures built and then operated for centuries through *waqfs*.

The *waqf* is not among Islam's original institutions. It is not mentioned in the Qur'an. The earliest evidence of its existence belongs to a century after the rise of Islam. Although the evidence is largely circumstantial, a key motivation appears to have been the quest for economic security. In the eighth and ninth centuries, when the *waqf* system took shape, private property was insecure throughout the Middle East, as elsewhere. Arbitrary taxation and outright expropriation threatened high officials, who were major landowners. These officials did what wealthy people still do: they looked creatively for a wealth shelter. The region's older civilizations, including Roman civilization from which Islam borrowed widely, had developed various forms of trust – endowments whereby a trustor set aside assets to be managed by a trustee according to his or her wishes. Early Muslims took the basic idea and developed it into a distinct and ingenious institution that achieved massive economic significance.

Why did assets become more secure when converted into the corpus of a *waqf*? Regardless of the service it provided, a *waqf* was considered sacred. Given this belief, which took root in its formative centuries, rulers were hence reluctant to tamper with *waqf* assets, lest they develop a reputation for impiety, lose legitimacy, and embolden political opposition. People endowed *waqfs* to protect their assets; in other words, to lower the probability of becoming a victim of expropriation or arbitrary taxation.

If a founder's goal was to shelter assets for his own use, what would he have gained by setting up a trust to provide a public good? Just as a *waqf* was considered sacred, so establishing a *waqf* was considered an act of piety. The founder thus obtained, in addition to inner satisfaction, social prestige. But he also achieved significant material returns (Kuran, 2001; Çizakça, 2000). The founder could appoint himself as the *mutawalli* (trustee and manager) of the *waqf* for life. In this capacity, he could set his own remuneration, appoint relatives and friends to salaried positions, and designate his successor. The last privilege allowed him to circumvent Islam's inheritance rules. In setting up a *waqf*, then, a property owner did not simply engage in charity, which is the impression one might derive from the historical literature. A portion of the secured income accrued to him and his family. The *quid pro quo* for the privilege of sheltering some wealth for personal use is that ordinarily he accepted certain social responsibilities.

There was no hard rule regarding the share of the *waqf* income that the *mutawalli* could reserve for personal use. Local social norms determined the limit. If he went beyond the customary level, he could draw objections, prompting the courts to intervene. This institution provided identifiable benefits to diverse political players, which is one reason it lasted so long. The wealthy obtained from the state a credible promise of material security. For its part, the state could collect taxes without providing much in return, other than law and order; cities would run on services provided by the wealthy. Finally, the average person benefited from various subsidized services. From his standpoint, this was a system that encouraged philanthropy and responded to local conditions. The system was bound, therefore, to generate coalitions with a stake in its continuation. Once in place, it would be preserved.

7 Static perpetuity

For all its strengths, this system had economic drawbacks, which became increasingly serious over time. The functions of a *waqf* had to be fixed in perpetuity, presumably to give credibility to the implicit deal between the state and the *waqf* founder. The static perpetuity rule kept a property owner from founding a *waqf* to provide a particular service and then, once the property had been secured, make self-serving changes to the *waqf* mission. Thus, the *waqf* was meant to be a rigid organization (Kuran, 2001; Schoenblum, 1999).

The consequent costs would have been limited in the Middle Ages, when demand patterns and opportunities were very slow to alter. As physical technologies and patterns of global comparative advantage started changing rapidly, the static perpetuity rule might have been expected to lock capital into seriously inefficient uses. Indeed, in the eighteenth and nineteenth centuries, when around the world resources were being reallocated to exploit new technologies of production, in the Middle East major *waqfs* became conspicuously dysfunctional. Their vast resources could not be transferred – at least not quickly – to new *waqfs*, or moved outside the *waqf* sector, in order to provide new public goods, or supply old ones more efficiently. Nor could existing *waqfs* be reinvented. Thus, *waqf*-funded schools generally did not modernize their curriculum, and *waqfs* meant to finance public water fountains were not merged to form a modern water system. Modern schools and water delivery systems emerged outside the *waqf* sector.

In practice, of course, the *waqf* was not totally rigid. The law allowed operational changes and asset swaps in times of dire necessity. *Waqf* deeds contained ambiguities that *mutawallis* might exploit. The judges (*kadis*) empowered to stop modifications could look the other way as rules of operation and objectives underwent modification. Nevertheless, the costs of adaptation were high. Conscious of the returns to flexibility, judges often made their approval conditional on payment of a bribe. Therefore, a school established as a *waqf* exhibited greater inertia than if it had been founded as a corporation, that is, as a self-governing organization enjoying legal personhood.

8 Absence of the corporation

To put the last observation in comparative perspective, note that *waqfs* supplied services delivered in the West largely through corporations. Whereas Islamic colleges (*madrasas*) were financed by *waqfs*, the early European universities were founded as, or quickly became, corporations. In a major Middle Eastern city urban services were supplied by thousands of *waqfs*. In a Western city, similar services were provided by a municipality that enjoyed corporate powers. Mosque complexes, which delivered a huge array of services ranging from education to charity, were organized as *waqfs*. Churches performed analogous functions under corporate structures.

Forerunners of both the *waqf* and the corporation were present in Roman law. The famous law code completed during the reign of the Byzantine emperor Justinian (r. 527–65) recognizes various forms of trust as well as rudimentary corporations. Starting in the eighth century, as the Middle East was developing the *waqf* as an antidote to predatory states and unreliable property rights, central authority was relatively weak in the West. Under the circumstances, corporations emerged to supply enforceable legal systems for associations seeking to differentiate themselves from the outside world, overcome anarchy, and exercise a measure of self-governance. Two separate institutional choices, made in response to distinct local conditions, thus set the two regions on divergent organizational paths.

The divergence continued until the nineteenth century, when corporations, including the Middle East's first municipalities, began to take over the delivery of public goods once supplied exclusively by *waqfs*. This organizational transformation occurred largely because a municipality offers dynamic advantages over a *waqf* system. As a corporation, a municipality is self-governing, so it is able to make changes denied to a traditional *waqf*. A municipality can reallocate resources quickly in response to evolving demand patterns. In contrast to a *waqf*, whose expenditure patterns must conform to the founder's stipulations, it can make its own budgets. It can also impose new fees on users, or modify existing ones. Finally, it can impose ordinances, such as building codes and rules for using public goods.

The unintended costs of the *waqf* system were not limited to rigidities in the supply of social services. If most countries of the Middle East currently have non-democratic governance systems that inhibit individual initiative and limit material security (Yousef, 2004; Arab Human Development Programme, 2002), a basic reason is that the *waqf* system hindered the development of civil society – the backbone of stable democracy. The ingredients of a strong civil society are freedom of association and organizational autonomy. In allowing property owners to choose with whom they would associate and to what ends, the *waqf* system provided a form of associational freedom. At the same time, it sharply restricted self-governance in comparison to a municipality. For one thing, the discretion of a *mutawalli* was substantially more limited than that of a mayor. For another, whereas a mayor's constituents could remove him from office, the beneficiaries of a *waqf* had no say over who would serve as *mutawalli*.

In the nineteenth and early twentieth centuries diverse reformers worked to dismantle the *waqf* system. They were motivated partly by a quest for resources to finance their modernization projects, which the *waqf* system offered in abundance. A complementary motivation was to reduce the weight of the *waqf* system, both because of its rigidities and because it was controlled largely by conservatives. In the light of this history, it may come as a surprise that the *waqf* is regaining significance in certain countries, including Turkey and Egypt. Ironically, an assorted mix of civil rights advocates and economic reformers – groups whose precursors once considered the *waqf* a source of backwardness – are behind movements to re-energize the *waqf* sector. But the contemporary *waqf* differs substantially from the traditional Islamic *waqf* (Çizakça, 2000). Whereas the founder of a traditional *waqf* had to be an individual, its modernized namesake may be formed by a consortium of natural or legal persons. A modern *waqf* is overseen by a *mutawalli* board, which delegates managerial responsibility to professionals. Most important, it is a corporation – a self-governing entity enjoying legal personality. The spread of modern *waqfs* may be expected to strengthen civil society and improve the quality of governance.

9 Implications for future reforms

Like the corporation, various other elements of a modern economy, including stock markets, double-entry bookkeeping, and courts familiar with advanced economic institutions, were transplanted to the Middle East in the nineteenth century. The fact that such institutions were borrowed almost two centuries ago now hides their foreign origins from the masses even where, as in Saudi Arabia, Islamic law remains the law of the land (Vogel, 2000). As such, these institutions are culturally acceptable even to Islamists committed to preserving or reviving structures associated with traditional Islam. Reforms to improve the transplanted institutions can proceed, therefore, without appearing to be promoting cultural alienation or opposing Islam as a religion.

If the historically problematic institutions associated with Islamic law no longer hinder development directly, does it follow that the institutional history just interpreted has lost its relevance to economic performance? The persistent weaknesses of civil society in countries of the region, and thus the enduring obstacles to reforms beneficial to economic sectors beyond the control of Middle Eastern states, are rooted in the two historical patterns discussed above: rigidities of the traditional *waqf* and the protracted stagnation of Islamic contract law. Weaknesses of civil society in the region hindered collective action to institute political checks and balances. In the process, they left political vacuums filled as the twentieth century unfolded by economically interventionist states uncommitted to the rule of law and generally fearful of political and economic liberalization.

The very logic of the foregoing historical argument provides, however, a reason for some optimism about the future. Largely through reforms that began in the nineteenth century, the factors responsible for the weaknesses of Middle Eastern civil society have been overcome. Consequently, the institutional means of a much stronger civil society are now available. Although groups with a stake in the political *status quo* will put up resistance, sooner or later, one can expect on that basis, organized private groups will voice demands for more extensive economic and political rights. In relation to even a half-century ago civil society has already made remarkable strides in Turkey and, to a lesser extent, also in Iran and in some parts of the Arab world. Should the pattern continue, the twenty-first century may become what the late twentieth century was for East Asia: a period of renewed economic vigour and leadership.

References

Chaudhuri, K. N. (1985) *Trade and Civilization in the Indian Ocean: an Economic History from the Rise of Islam to 1750* (Cambridge: Cambridge University Press).

Çizakça, M. (1996) *A Comparative Evolution of Business Partnerships: the Islamic World and Europe, with Special Reference to the Ottoman Archives* (Leiden: E. J. Brill).

Çizakça, M. (2000) *A History of Philanthropic Foundations: the Islamic World from the Seventh Century to the Present* (Istanbul: Boğaziçi University Press).

Coşgel, M. M. and T. J. Miceli (2005) 'Risk, Transaction Costs, and Tax Assignment: Government Finance in the Ottoman Empire', *Journal of Economic History*, vol. 65, no. 3, pp. 806–21.

Easterlin, Richard A. (1996) *Growth Triumphant: the Twenty-First Century in Historical Perspective* (Ann Arbor: University of Michigan Press).

Ensminger, J. (1997) 'Transaction Costs and Islam: Explaining Conversion in Africa', *Journal of Institutional and Theoretical Economics*, vol. 152, no. 1, pp. 4–29.

Hunt, E. S. and J. M. Murray (1999) *A History of Business in Medieval Europe, 1200–1550* (Cambridge: Cambridge University Press).

İnalcık, H. (1994) 'The Ottoman State: Economy and Society, 1300–1600', in H. İnalcık with D. Quataert (eds) *An Economic and Social History of the Ottoman Empire, 1300–1914* (Cambridge: Cambridge University Press), pp. 9–409.

Issawi, C. (1982) 'The Transformation of the Economic Position of the *Millets* in the Nineteenth Century', in B. Braude and B. Lewis (eds) *Christians and Jews in the Ottoman Empire*, vol. 1 (New York: Holmes and Meier), pp. 261–85.
Jones, E. L. (1987) *The European Miracle: Environments, Economies, and Geopolitics in the History of Europe and Asia*, 2nd edn (Cambridge: Cambridge University Press).
Kuran, T. (2001) 'The Provision of Public Goods under Islamic Law: Origins, Impact, and Limitations of the Waqf System', *Law and Society Review*, vol. 35, no. 4, pp. 841–97.
Kuran, T. (2003) 'The Islamic Commercial Crisis: Institutional Roots of Economic Underdevelopment in the Middle East', *Journal of Economic History*, vol. 63, no. 2, pp. 414–46.
Kuran, T. (2004) 'The Economic Ascent of the Middle East's Religious Minorities: the Role of Islamic Legal Pluralism', *Journal of Legal Studies*, vol. 33, no. 2, pp. 475–515.
Kuran, T. (2005) 'The Logic of Financial Westernization in the Middle East', *Journal of Economic Behavior and Organization*, vol. 56, no. 4, pp. 593–615.
Lal, Deepak (1998) *Unintended Consequences: the Impact of Factor Endowments, Culture, and Politics on Long-Run Economic Performance* (Cambridge, Mass.: MIT Press).
Mokyr, Joel (1990) *The Lever of Riches: Technological Creativity and Economic Progress* (New York: Oxford University Press).
North, Douglass (2005) *Understanding the Process of Economic Change* (Princeton: Princeton University Press).
Özmucur, S. and Ş. Pamuk (2000) 'Real Wages and Standards of Living in the Ottoman Empire, 1489–1914', *Journal of Economic History*, vol. 62, no. 2, pp. 293–321.
Powers, D. (1999) 'The Islamic Family Endowment (*Waqf*)', *Vanderbilt Journal of Transnational Law*, vol. 32, no. 4, pp. 1167–90.
Pryor, J. H. (1977) 'The Origins of the *Commenda* Contract', *Speculum*, vol. 52, no. 1, pp. 5–37.
Rodinson, M. (1966/1973) *Islam and Capitalism*, trans. B. Pearce (New York: Pantheon).
Schoenblum, J. (1999) 'The Role of Legal Doctrine in the Decline of the Islamic *Waqf*: a Comparison with the Trust', *Vanderbilt Journal of Transnational Law*, vol. 32, no. 4, pp. 1191–1227.
Shatzmiller, M. (1994) *Labour in the Medieval Islamic World* (Leiden: E. J. Brill).
Toprak, Z. (1995) *Milli İktisat – Milli Burjuvazi* (Istanbul: Tarih Vakfı Yurt Yayınları).
Udovitch, A. L. (1970) *Partnership and Profit in Medieval Islam* (Princeton: Princeton University Press).
United Nations Development Programme, Arab Fund for Economic and Social Development (2002) *Arab Human Development Report 2002* (New York: United Nations).
Vogel, F. E. (2000) *Islamic Law and Legal System: Studies of Saudi Arabia* (Leiden: Brill).
Yousef, T. M. (2004) 'The *Murabaha* Syndrome in Islamic Finance: Laws, Institutions and Politics', in C. M. Henry and R. Wilson (eds) *The Politics of Islamic Finance* (Edinburgh: Edinburgh University Press), pp. 63–80.

4

Understanding the Great Changes in the World: Gaining Ground and Losing Ground since World War II

*Edmund S. Phelps**
Columbia University, USA

The composer Richard Strauss would warn his conducting students 'never look at the brass – it will only encourage them'. I am afraid that the subject the organizers have looked to me to speak about – Understanding the Great Changes of the World – has given me dangerous encouragement: I have responded by analysing the great tectonic shifts in the global economy that I have witnessed and thought about since I began studying economics.

I recount three stories of *gaining ground* on the world economic leader – of 'catching up' – and one story of *losing* ground. First, there are the postwar 'economic miracles' of fast growth and high activity in western continental Europe (which I abbreviate to 'the Continent') and the fact that the miracles in Germany, France and Italy stopped short, leaving their economies constantly trailing the United States – their prosperity steadily below the United States level and their productivity steadily behind. Secondly, there is the catching-up going on in several economies of eastern Europe, though not in all of them. Thirdly, there is the extraordinary advance in technical know-how and resulting productivity made by the Chinese economy in recent decades. There is also the lost ground in western continental Europe *vis-à-vis* the United States over the past ten years – *declines* in relative productivity *level* (in Germany, Italy, Holland and Austria) and *declines* in prosperity as indicated by lower activity and investment rates (especially in Germany, Austria and Holland). Japan is another instance.

This rich historical experience can help us to get right our international macroeconomics. Both growth and business activity, I argue, are driven by opportunities for *technical progress*, not by the neoclassical concept of human capital and not the taxation of labour, on which most supply-siders are

* A grant from the Kauffman Foundation is gratefully acknowledged.

focused. To an important degree globalization has helped countries to have a higher technical potential and to progress toward it more quickly through foreign direct investments and capital inflow generally. But this technical progress does not raise all boats.

This experience can also help us to get right the political economy of economic performance – though to talk about those things requires us to make distinctions that are lost in some discussions. What I call *capitalism*, or (for emphasis) a *well-functioning* capitalism, means a well-functioning system of *free enterprise* – a system that well motivates new entrepreneurial ideas and chooses well which ones to finance; it does not mean *laissez-faire*, or 'free market' in the sense of a small public sector, minimal regulation and no social insurance, whence low tax rates.[1] Eastern European nations adopted *socialism* in the postwar period and *market socialism* in the 1980s, systems with not much freedom of enterprise and with little or no private ownership. Continental western Europe in the interwar period opted for what is known as *corporatism* (and in postwar terminology the *social market economy*) – a system that, while retaining private ownership, constricts enterprise by submitting it to demands of interest groups, reducing the rewards from innovation, and regulating start up and closings of businesses and plants.

It is necessary also to specify some notion of economic performance. For me, it is about productivity and prosperity. High productivity is to be valued by 'advanced economies' in large part because the high wages it supports enable workers to afford to take jobs offering high job satisfaction. Prosperity means high job satisfaction – jobholders developing through the change and challenge of their work – and low unemployment, thus ample access to such jobs. High performance means making the best of existing conditions. It is not reliably measured by the growth rate of anything.

Expressed in the above terminologies, I infer from the historical experience to be examined here that the *non*-capitalist economies tend not to be high-performance economies. They can – under *favourable market conditions* – grow very fast and have a high level of activity (and job satisfaction too) while doing it; but then, of course, they slow down as they 'grow out of' those initial conditions. In the end they generally fail to pull up to the *levels* of either *productivity* or *prosperity* that the well-functioning capitalist economy tends to reach, thanks to its system for well-directed innovation and its culture of enterprise. They lack the dynamism needed to *sustain* the catch-up, the high job satisfaction and thus the high employment.

Another hypothesis supported by this review is that the high performance of which capitalism is capable (under ordinary circumstances) does not hinge on the side condition of a free market – a laissez-faire social policy that leaves low-wage workers and unemployed workers without social insurance and that deprives the public of valuable services in order to keep tax rates low. The premise of corporatist Europe – that prosperity and human development and productivity are fine but not at the expense of any of the 'social partners' and certainly not at the expense of its job security – is disastrously wrongheaded. (A society should view a policy move from the viewpoint of citizens' *life* prospects rather than make the crude demand that every social partner gain from every transaction.) The economies built for job security have suffered the biggest swings in economic activity and have for two decades exhibited the highest unemployment in the OECD. The twin socialist goals of high development and high employment require the *dynamism* that only well-functioning institutions of capitalism can generate.

1 The continental economies' part-way catch-up (ca. 1953–75)

As everyone knows, when World War II came to an end western continental Europe found itself with a large setback in hourly productivity and thus income per worker relative to the level in the early 1940s.[2] On top of that, a widening gap between hourly productivity on the Continent and in the United States had developed throughout the interwar period (more precisely, from the early 1920s to the early 1940s) – something Hitler vexed over. There followed the 'economic miracles' of rapid productivity growth from the early 1950s well into the 1970s, in which Germany, then France and lastly Italy caught up *largely* but *not fully* with productivity in the United States.[3]

What caused these miracles and why did the miracle economies stop short of matching productivity and activity to the United States levels? There is more than one interpretation. In the neoclassical view, the Continent's loss of output per worker can be traced to a loss of physical capital, owing to the wartime destruction, and perhaps a loss of human capital too, as the death or retirement or flight of well-educated people was not offset during the war (and may not have been during the 1930s) by new entrants with similar education.[4] Symmetrically, the economic miracles were simply the result of rebuilding capital and when that wound down the curtain fell on the miracles. A failing of this theory, among many shortcomings, is that to the extent the Continent's catch-up was just a matter of putting the railway sleepers and bricks back together, much or most of the benefit in terms of hourly productivity would have been achieved by the mid-1950s. But in fact, the Continent's catch-up did not even begin until the early 1950s: its output per man hour *relative* to United States output per man hour was *falling* until the early 1950s.[5] Evidently the Continent had a steep mountain to climb just to come near the still-rising output per man hour in America's dynamic economy, where productivity was growing almost as fast as in the 1920s and 1930s.[6]

In the supply-siders' view, the onset of the Continent's catch-up was generated by Ludwig Erhard's 1948 injection into West Germany of tax cuts and a more pro-competition stance, a liberal economic policy (liberal in European terminology) that spread to most other countries on the Continent;

and what halted the catching-up was a return of high tax rates and barriers to competition. It is true that the activity rate in Europe (the ratio of employment to working-age population) began rising strongly *relative* to the activity rate in the United States around 1952. But that might have been the result of a recovery of the marginal productivity of labour once the bricks and railway sleepers had been put back. Also, the relative activity rate regained its 1929 level only in the mid-1950s; a far higher relative activity was reached from the mid-1950s through most or all of the 1960s; moreover, as I argue below, that was more the result of wealth falling behind wages than after-tax wages rising, thanks to a 1948 tax cut. In any case, I do not believe the reduction of tax rates in the late *1940s* can be credited with the speed-up of productivity growth that started rather abruptly in the *late 1950s* and extended over the 1960s – the high years of the economic miracles.

The correct view, to my mind, is that the fast two-decade-long climb of productivity from the mid- or late 1950s to the mid- or late 1970s (depending on the country) and the accompanying fall of unemployment to very low levels was driven by a rapid injection of new technologies – though it is a semantic issue whether we ought to call that 'innovation'. This injection of technologies was so extensive that it could not have been primarily the result of one or more original innovations on the Continent. It largely depended on *technology transfer* from overseas.

One part of this technology transfer story – the growth part – is hardwired into the brain of every economist and does not require a manual or pictures.[7] In this story, the best (and generally the latest) product or method available from supplying sector *i* of country *j* is called the *best practice* technology from that sector. In general, any economy will have one or more sectors in which even this best technology, B_{ij}, falls short of the best in the *world*, $\bar{B}_i$. A measure of the gap between the two is $1 - (B_{ij}/\bar{B}_i)$; another is $\log \bar{B}_j - \log B_{ij}$. In these terms, the key point is that, other things equal, the emergence of such a gap is an opportunity for the country to advance its best practice by 'transferring' to itself the world's best practice. The *larger* the gap, the greater will be the advance in best practice achieved by the transfer. Furthermore, the more widespread such gaps in the economy are, the wider the opportunities for such advances. This suggests a simple macroeconomic hypothesis: the *growth rate* of a country's mean best practice – its best-practice technology *as a whole* – is faster the larger is the *gap* between the country's mean best practice and the *world* level. What happened in Germany, France and Italy was that, once the war and the postwar political unrest were over and the bricks and railway sleepers were back together, the external gap between best practice at home and best-practice technologies overseas (most of them first introduced in the United States) was so wide that those countries' best practice grew faster than that in the United States. The catching-up process, which had been delayed, went into full swing.

A more general formula for the growth rate of best practice contains an induced part, just discussed, and an autonomous part. In the former, $\Psi(\cdot)$ is the coefficient of imitation and adaptation. The autonomous growth is the *innovation* of products and methods based on original, possibly indigenous ideas, rather than imitation and adaptation of overseas products and methods. An example of such a formula is

$$\frac{\dot{B}_j}{B_j} = \Psi(\bullet)\left(\frac{\bar{B} - B_j}{\bar{B}}\right) + \frac{I_j(1, \bar{B}/B_j, B_j/A_j, \ldots)}{B_j}. \tag{1}$$

There is a little more to it than that. Productivity and employment too are largely influenced by *average* practice, not best practice. Average practice is driven by best practice yet the dynamics may be quite slow and several factors intervene in determining how close average practice comes to best practice. In the model by Nelson and Phelps, the rate at which the best-practice technology in a country is diffused over the economy is a function of the internal productivity gap between best practice, B_j, and average practice, A_j, as well as the speed with which the best-practice technology travels across the economy (Nelson and Phelps, 1966). Let $\Phi(\cdot)$ denote the coefficient of diffusion, which measures the speed with which a new best-practice technology spreads through the economy. Then the familiar equation is

$$\frac{\dot{A}_j}{A_j} = \Phi(\bullet)\left(\frac{B_j - A_j}{B_j}\right). \tag{2}$$

It is now obvious that when best practice suddenly grows faster, average practice does not at first respond; only gradually does its growth rate rise to the growth rate of mean best practice.[8]

The *other* part of the story about the miracle period – the period of very fast growth from the late 1950s through the 1960s and into the early 1970s – is about employment. What were the employment effects of the prolonged rapid growth of average technical progress? Let me use a version of one of my models of the natural unemployment rate – a turnover-training model of a small open economy having a single good traded in a perfect global market (so the exchange rate is a constant).[9] In this model and not only in that one, country's *j*'s technical progress rate, λ_j, influences the unemployment rate through two channels, one the fast-working asset-value channel and the other the slow-working wealth-supply channel. (I think of this pseudo-parameter as measuring the growth rates of both best practice and average practice, which are equal and constant over the medium term.)

In the former channel, *ex ante* λ_j is subtracted from the *ex ante* real interest rate in the equation giving the demand wage relative to productivity – the wage that employers can pay and still earn a normal return on their investments in their employees (hence a zero pure profit). The logic is that the expected growth of the technology, in causing the expected opportunity cost of training to trend upwards, is a reason to advance some future training outlays into the present, just as the interest rate is a reason for deferring some present training outlays into the future.[10] A sudden *increase* of λ_j unaccompanied by a coincidental increase of the overseas real interest rate, r^*, causes an immediate speculative jump in the value per unit placed on the business asset, which is the job-ready employee, just as a sudden *decrease* of the interest rate would do; the effect of that, taken alone, is an immediate jump in the hiring rate and thus an expansion of employment. With unemployment falling and the quit rate rising, the asset price will be rising but not keeping up with productivity, and the ratio of the asset price to productivity will gradually subside back to its normal level.

In the other channel, the *ex post* λ_j is subtracted from the *ex post* real interest rate in the equation that determines the population's steady-growth income from wealth relative to productivity. A sudden increase of λ_j, unaccompanied by an equal increase of the overseas interest rate, generates a *gradual decline* of income-from-wealth relative to productivity, just as a fall of the interest rate would do; the effect, taken alone, is a decline in quit rates, which in turn causes a slow increase of employment – and a slow decline of unemployment.

This model presents in one respect a classical picture of the catch-up process in a single country or region of a larger world. With the step-increase in λ_j, consumption jumps up more than wage income jumps, thus forcing the current account from balance into deficit for a time. Ultimately, the Continent's wealth slips back *relative* to the now faster-growing output and thus also *relative* to the corresponding valuation of domestic firms, so that some of the Continental firms' capital (in the form of employees with firm-specific know-how!) must be financed through debt or shares sold overseas. I would comment that this structural view of the Continent's mounting net debtor position is at 180 degrees to the monetary view held at the time. (Milton Friedman, 1953, expressly denied that the 'dollar shortage' was a 'fundamental structural' phenomenon.)

To get a sense of the size of this effect note that between 1955 and 1965 the United States current account was always in surplus and the cumulative surplus in the period mounted up to about 8 per cent of 1960 national income.[11] (The previous decade's total was half that amount; in the following 15 years there was a rough cumulative balance.)

How did this phenomenal Continental speed-up impact on the rest of the world? I finally worked out an answer from an extension of the model to a theoretical world of just two regions, say, the Continent and the United States. The starting point is that the speed-up, in turning the United States into a net creditor nation, creates a *wedge* between the wealth owned by nationals and the capital in the United States economy – more precisely, a *positive excess* of national wealth over domestic capital, which is counterbalanced by the opposite difference on the Continent. This fall of domestic capital relative to national wealth in the United States translates into to a fall of output per worker and the *wage* relative to *national wealth*; the effect in turn is a *decrease* of employment.

A brief remark may help – as may the Appendix (pp. 93–6). If the Continent were the only region in the world and experienced a speed-up, the model would predict an immediate increase of the real interest rate exactly equal to the increase in the rate of technical progress – at least if the workers' utility function is logarithmic in current consumption; and, as a consequence, there would have been no boost to employment on the Continent. With the Continent only a part of the world, the speed-up *still drives up the world interest rate*, though not by as much as the increase in the rate of technical progress on the Continent. Clearly it is precisely through this rise of the world real interest that the United States is induced to save more and invest less, leading to its net creditor position (or increase in that position). Incidentally, data confirm that the world long-term interest rate was elevated from 1955 to 1970 compared with the 1970s and the present decade.[12]

This sheds light on an interesting way in which the globalized market-place works. Although the economic policies of governments may be designed for economic justice, the private market-place is not designed to be just – and in fact it is neither systematically just nor unjust. It did *not* direct some private capital to the Continent because the Continent was poorer or less advantaged; it sent capital there only because the Continent's technical progress rate soared above the United States rate, which pulled up the world interest rate and sucked capital out of the United States economy into the Continent, which it would have done even if the Continent had initially possessed superior technologies – as long as the expected and actual growth rate of that technology became faster than the United States growth rate. Nevertheless, it usually happens that when a nation or region suffers a catastrophe, such as wartime destruction, global private capital tends to flow to the affected area – if the area takes steps aimed at reconstruction and catching-up. The global market-place can therefore be said to be humanitarian. The foreign aid of the Marshall Plan was small next to the private capital that helped fuel the Continent's catch-up miracles.

Two final comments on the Continent's catch-up. First, the major *slowdowns* that struck first Germany, then France, and later Italy in the 1970s provide a test of the model. The model predicts that the fall of the expected rate of productivity growth had an *immediate* negative effect on employment through its impact on the *net* interest rate (net of the rate of technical progress) and a *gradual* effect through the resulting rise of wealth relative to capital, productivity and the wage. In fact there was an enormous climb of unemployment rates between 1975 and 1985 and in France and Italy a further upward trend from 1985 to 1995.[13]

The other point is that the slower growth rates of productivity were nearly down to the United States rate. The productivity gaps in Germany, France and Italy contracted a little further until the early 1990s yet did not go any lower after that. The Solow–Bailey (2001) computations put hourly productivity in 1992 at 92 per cent of the United States level in France and Germany. OECD data put men in the labour force in 1996 at about 75 per cent of working-age population in France and Italy as against 87 per cent in the United States.[14] (This is before any adjustment for demographic differences.) The unemployment disparities are well-known.

If my view is right, the Continent's leading economies were thus revealed in their true colours. The Continent's economies were not conducive to low unemployment and not suitable for reaching world-class productivity levels. The shortcoming of the system was the Continent's corporatist economic system (or systems), a system constructed of big unions, big employer confederations and big banks, all mediated by a big public sector – a system that had been built up starting in the 1920s on the belief that it would be better than capitalism, better for employment and productivity. That system had *seemed* in the catch-up years to prove itself a good system because it was not understood in those years that unemployment would go on being extraordinarily low only as long as growth would be extraordinarily rapid; and not understood that the growth rate differential between the Continent and the United States was sheer catch-up, so it had to end when the catch-up could not go further.

My research suggests that the root of the problem is the system's deficiency of dynamism, not the rule of law or high tax rates or poor schooling. I suspect there is no single institution whose replacement or repair would make the corporatist system dynamic. The Nelson–Phelps model points to the dearth of higher education on the Continent; Amar Bhidé (2005) extends that model to say that there will be no entrepreneur or financier to demand innovations in an economy where there is no expectation of potential users with the willingness or capability to pioneer their adoption. Acemoglu, Aghion and Zilibotti say the rarity of higher education also impacts negatively on a would-be innovator's ability to develop an innovation (Acemoglu, Aghion and Zilibotti, 2002). Furthermore, as I have theorized (Phelps, 2002), the Continent's corporatist system – its capital markets, its corporate governance and labour union powers, its employment laws such as job protection legislation, and the state's and the public's corporatist attitudes toward enterprise – are important too and critically so. (Phelps and Zoega, 2004, have looked at some of these indictments of corporatist institutions.)

Was it instead the case that the Continent's economic system had been better – perhaps superior to the capitalist systems – in the early postwar years, before the rot set in, as argued by Mancur Olson, by Enzo Tarantelli and by Michael Bruno and Jeffrey Sachs? Or, at the other extreme, was the system poor from the start of the postwar period as well as the prewar period, which Herbert Giersch and (more recently) I have supposed? It is an engaging historical issue, but there is no space to take it up here.

2 Catching-up in eastern European economies (ca. 1995–2005)

For me there are two salient features of eastern Europe's 'transition' since the early or mid-990s. One is that the countries where productivity growth has been pretty fast – since 1995, say – are primarily those that had enjoyed a relatively high productivity level before their economies were converted to communism. The percentage growth rate of labour productivity (per employee) since 1996 has averaged 5.4 in Poland, 4.0 in the Slovak Republic, 3.0 in Hungary and 2.8 in the Czech Republic. The other fact is that activity rates are quite depressed even in that fortunate group which had been relatively advanced before their communization. The activity rate – employment as percentage of working-age population – is about 52 in Poland (the unemployment rate about 19 per cent), 57 in the Slovak Republic (unemployment about 18 per cent), 56 in Hungary (unemployment about 6 per cent) and 65 in the Czech Republic (unemployment 8 per cent).[15]

It should not be surprising that these four countries have had better productivity growth than some other parts of eastern Europe. During the communist decades, there must have been a lot of levelling down, so the lifting of communism from the region gave the above four countries, whose economies had once excelled, the prospect of regaining their relatively high productivity through good investments and adoption of foreign technologies. Accordingly, the global capital market awarded these countries large capital inflows, which served to boost their investment rates and thus their growth rates, presumably on the same principle that we inferred above in looking at the catch-up on the western Continent: capital inflow is attracted to economies whose *potential* levels of productivity are high relative to *actual* levels, so that their expected productivity growth rates are relatively high. Yes, capital markets equalize expected rates of return to investing of all kinds, but they achieve equalization by awarding an extra investment rate to the economies with the best growth prospects (otherwise expected rates of return would not be equal). OECD data confirm that since 1996 the four countries have run significant current account deficits while Russia and Ukraine have not.[16]

I would observe about these growth rates that they are certainly not eye-popping. In the high years of the western economic miracles, say, from 1960 to 1968, the percentage growth rates of GDP per employee were in Spain 6.8, Italy 6.3, France 4.9 and West Germany 4.3; Japan's growth rate was 8.9 (OECD, 1983).

I observe also that the four eastern European leaders have low activity – in Poland and Slovakia it reflects huge unemployment – right in the midst of their economic miracles. With activity so low during the catch-up years, what will happen to activity and unemployment rates when the miracles end? If the model I set out earlier applies well enough to these four eastern countries, either because it is literally rather descriptive or there are other models having analogous implications (e.g. the customer model), the inevitable slowing of productivity in these nations – down, say, to the United States' productivity growth rate – will add greatly to their unemployment. Hoon and Phelps (1997, Fig. 2) found that a two-percentage-point slowdown of productivity in Germany and France was followed by a near-doubling of the unemployment rate. Certainly such a slowdown might push unemployment well over 20 per cent in Poland and Slovakia.

When I worked at the European Bank for Reconstruction and Development in the early 1990s we used to wonder: what sort of economic system will the economies of eastern Europe make a 'transition' to? Will it be something like the corporatist systems on the western Continent – big banks, big enterprises, big bureaucracies and maybe big unions, with plenty of barriers to entry, state influence over financing, poor corporate governance and so forth – or something more like a well-functioning capitalist system? When around 2000 Vaclav Klaus came to Columbia, I asked him whether the Czech Republic was transiting to capitalism or to corporatism. He was cordial but he did not answer the question.

Each of these four countries made decisions that may have contributed to the disappointing growth and low activity rates (and in some cases high unemployment). In Poland, there is the overhang of its substantial state-enterprise sector, though perhaps that is compensated by its receptivity to new, small private enterprises. Outside Poland, there are the flawed privatizations, which left many enterprises under the managerial control of the old guard without any redress for shareholders and left some industries with not even the oligopolistic competition that Schumpeter came to admire in his 1941 book *Capitalism, Socialism and Democracy*. Evidence supporting these and other charges has been gathered and examined in papers by Roman Frydman, Janos Kornai, Andrei Shleifer and others.[17] Part of the problem may be that these nations are so small that there is a tendency toward high concentration and toward interventionism and cronyism. The United States has the exceptional advantage that it is very big and even its larger cities are very big. (I recall John Reed's saying after years as CEO of Citibank, 'I've never met the mayor. I don't want to – I might like him.')

Whatever the faults of the eastern countries' economic system, the macro evidence I have reviewed – the unspectacular growth despite a yawning productivity gap and the generally low activity rates – suggests to me that even the four relatively successful eastern countries have not managed so far to 'transit' to a good economic system: they are simply pulled forward by the huge productivity gap *vis-à-vis* the West.

3 China's rapid catch-up (ca. 1990–2005)

I am eager to discuss the remarkable catching-up going on in China, since Amar Bhidé and I have recently set out an interpretation of China's growth strategy and China's resulting relationship with the West (Bhidé and Phelps, 2005, 2005a).

A great many of the facts about this phenomenon are well known – the very rapid growth rate of productivity, especially since 1990 (though also in the previous decade), and a very high rate of saving. A recent World Bank paper digs deeper: a large public-sector fiscal surplus contributes a significant segment of current national saving. Business saving, that is, retained earnings (after interest), is an even larger contributor – the companies pay negligible dividends (Kuijs, 2005). Of course, households might be imagined to step up their consumption by an offsetting amount on the calculation that that they will enjoy capital gains as a result of the retained earnings. But the household sector is also a somewhat high saver compared to the personal saving in comparator countries. Share owners, it seems, are not expecting high rates of return on the extant investment opportunities or they worry that business investments will be badly allocated over the opportunities. The financial sector thus faces a business sector making poor allocations of saving and creating investment risks with little accounting transparency and without good corporate governance. In these and some other respects China is not yet one of the advanced economies.

In view of how underdeveloped its institutions were in 1980 or even 1990, though, it is clear that China has made progress with its economic institutions. It is also clear that more decades of rapid growth will require further fundamental development on the institutional front. China is a highly practical and flexible country and the economy it has fashioned is highly entrepreneurial. There are myriad private entrepreneurs who submit projects to banks and municipal bodies for approval and backing; and there are public entrepreneurs, so to speak, operating in municipal councils and other governmental structures. The challenge now is to improve radically the quality of the entrepreneurship in China and the quality of the financiership that serves (or tries) to separate worthy investments from unworthy ones.

It is all the more remarkable, therefore, that China's economic strategy has succeeded in driving its growth through the acquisition and assimilation of advanced technologies – and this in a country in which large areas were fairly primitive not long ago and some still are. When the 'east Asian tigers' embarked on their stage of rapid productivity growth, some students of the process characterized the increase in productivity as more a function of increased physical capital than of improved technologies – not that technologies did not improve (they did) but simply that the increase of physical capital was enormous and was presumed to account for the lion's share of the productivity increase. This is done through technological 'transfers' by means of joint ventures, inward foreign direct investment (FDI), licensing and even purchase of foreign companies or parts of companies. All this is something qualitatively new. Some observers have suggested that new technologies can be imported more easily than in the past thanks to the digitalization of some methods of production. Technologies may also be more public than they were a century ago and many of them are easily accessed through the internet – such as the method for building a bomb. (Moreover, in Shanghai technological research centres are springing up that aim to be world-class.)

Observers in the West, however, have been fascinated by another element of the Chinese miracle – the extraordinary excess of saving over investment and thus a current account surplus. This was the impetus for the Bhidé and Phelps (2005) puzzle of the huge trade surpluses that China is running with the West, especially with the United States; this is all the more puzzling in the context of rapid catch-up growth, which, as the review of the western Continental catch-up and the eastern European catch-up suggests, has generally been associated with current account *deficits* in the past. Some media commentators have termed the chronic trade surplus 'mercantilist', though without offering a rationale for it or even admitting the possibility of a rationale. Academics taking the classical static view have regarded the trade surpluses as simply a policy error.

Bhidé and Phelps set out a rudimentary model in which an early trade surplus is central to an optimal growth trajectory. The novelty derives from two features of underdevelopment shaping trade between backward economies such as China and advanced economies such as the United States. First, the initial comparative disadvantages in China are an artefact of the uneven technical advances made by the United States, so China should be able to erase those disadvantages through technological transfers bought with surpluses of exports over imports in goods and services.[18] Furthermore, China may want to squirrel away precautionary balances in order to have the money to take advantage of big-ticket opportunities to buy technologies or whole companies that may present themselves in the future.

Second, the diffusion of new products requires learning, which takes time. The principle is Nelson–Phelps again, but Bhidé–Phelps applies it to consumer goods new to the Chinese. The initial dearth of familiarity in China with a wide range of western consumer goods operates as a drag on import demand for them. Clearly this may also tip the trade balances into surplus. In older terminology, deciding to adopt the novel and learning to master it takes time and may pose other 'frictional' costs; such 'investing' in the novel may even hit absorptive capacity. The fact that consuming the novel is damped by this consideration is not necessarily a reason to fill in with increased consumption of the familiar; the optimum rate of saving may be quite high as long as it can be stored in overseas assets until such time as the reserves can be profitably invested. There will come a time when investment will exceed saving. We find no irrationality in this strategy.

One could imagine that the rest of the world, especially the United States, would write China a note thanking it for entrusting with us an excess of their saving over their investment, which permits us to invest more than we save. The reason so many in the West are ungrateful is that they think they live in a Keynesian world in which China's restraint in expanding consumption demand is an outgoing tide that lowers all boats. You might think it is some kind of paranoia to believe that Keynesianism lives today, when every schoolboy knows that Milton Friedman and Ned Phelps, with their natural rate, killed off the Phillips Curve and the whole Keynesian apparatus for purposes of any medium- or long-term analysis decades ago (Robert Lucas attacked that apparatus even for short-term analysis). In fact, though, this Keynesian view is frequently expounded even in some of the most prominent and admired financial newspapers.

In the two-region version of my model of the natural rate, however, a decision by the other country – now China – drives down the world real interest rate, which induces our country to invest more and, in view of the reduced rate of return, to save less. This pulls up employment and the real wage as well, as we are pulled up our 'wage curve'. Although the real interest rate on our saving will be reduced, the other side of the coin is an increase in the real wage per hour worked. A formal analysis would show that the Chinese shock operates to drive a beneficial *wedge* between the wealth of our country and the capital invested in our country – a wedge that has the effect of reducing propensities to quit and shirk and of lengthening the hours that we are willing to work, thanks to the rise of the wage relative to wealth (and the income therefrom). So Americans ought to thank China for playing a positive and significant role in the generation of generally high asset prices and thus high investment and high employment by historical standards over the past ten years.

4 Recent economic declines in Continental Western Europe (1995–)

It must be hard for Europeans to see the *rest* of the world economy enjoying the stimulus of the ICT revolution – having healthy investment, rapid growth and rather low unemployment (even five years after the boom's peak). Since at least 1998 (if not 1996), most of western continental Europe has been gripped by a new slowdown, one that has brought the productivity growth rate *far below* the rate enjoyed by Americans and most others in the world's population – those in China, India, South Korea, Scandinavia, central Europe and Ireland, to name most of the buoyed up populations. In the eurozone the growth rate of hourly productivity in the business sector grew at 2.1 per cent per annum from 1988 to 1997, precisely as in 1978 to 1987; but grew at 0.9 per cent since 1998. Although this slowdown is nothing next to the shuddering slowdown from the mid-1970s the early 1980s, it is understandable that Europeans consider it far more dire than the earlier one. The question is the cause of that new slowdown – and how to make up the lost ground.

I started arguing in the year 2000 that the Continent – I was focused on the western part – had lacked the vibrancy and flexibility to latch on to the investment boom of the second half of the 1990s, which had been driven by the novel opportunities opening up for commercial development of the internet. In some recent papers I laid that failure to the undersupply of higher education, the underdevelopment of the stock market, the bureaucratic red tape impeding or discouraging entrepreneurs from starting up firms and entrepreneurs generally for creating new plants or outlets – in short, several features of the western Continent's corporatist system (Phelps and Zoega, 2001, 2004). I had supposed that the present decade – the '00s – would be a good decade for the Continental economies, as they undertook the necessary R&D to imitate and adapt what they found promising overseas, made the plant and equipment investments needed to produce, built the required distribution systems and did the marketing to create demand. When several economies on the Continent – one after the other – went into a slowdown in the waning years of the '90s and the present decade (the '00s), I was puzzled, since those economies had not experienced the boom and speed-up that came to the United States, the United Kingdom, Australia and Ireland in the mid-1990s. It was only when forced to come up with an answer to this puzzle at a conference organized by Willi Semmler at the New School (formerly the New School for Social Research) in 2003 that a hypothesis came to me (Phelps, 2005, pp. 16–19).

My thought was that the Continent had let too much time go by while several other nations had made the new investments to develop the internet. The result, I suggested, was that the Continent's share of investment activity in the world would now be depressed for several years. I had in mind the capture of customers and also the cost advantage that first movers are apt to acquire. There must be few pieces of the internet remaining whose development has not long been underway and captured by one or more of the world's economic players – from Samsung to Nokia. (That would further account for the low real interest rates of the past few years.) This would account for the inability at this point for the Continent to get into the game.[19] Much the same hypothesis of first-mover advantage is stated by Reati and Toporowski (2004, p. 404):

> In the uneven process of structural change that characterizes [long waves], the winners are the countries that adapt ... more rapidly to the new techno-economic paradigm. The countries that do not succeed in [changing] are excluded from the benefits of the paradigm ...

While such an Anti-Gershenkron Effect – followers discouraged when the leader leaps forward so the catch-up is attenuated – might eventuate, the theory of it appears to be ambiguous. It may be that the farther ahead the world leader goes in some sector(s), the *smaller the probability* that the laggards making a given research effort would 'catch on' to the new technology over a given period; that, *taken alone*, does argue for their deciding to *reduce* their R&D effort. But the increased *size* of the gap and hence of the magnitude of the catch-up if researchers succeed, *taken alone*, warrants *stepping up* R&D efforts at imitation (or improvement) of the foreign technology. (My interpretation of the Continent's economic miracle from the mid-1950s into the 1970s need only assume that its research effort at imitating/adapting/improving the superior foreign technologies was positive, however larger or smaller it *would have been* in the absence of the huge gap *vis-à-vis* the United States; the crux of the thesis is that this effort was extraordinarily productive because of the size of the gap.) The facts appear to be mildly supportive of the Anti-Gershenkron Effect, though perhaps not persuasively so. The Continent's R&D and its investment outlays have *not increased* as a share of output since advent of the ICT boom in the second half of the 1990s and have *decreased* in Germany and France. Productivity growth has shown no sign of picking up since its abrupt drop around 1998.

A less demanding, less radical answer to the puzzle of the severe Continental slowdown (variously dated at 1996 or 1998) is my earlier hypothesis that average practice on the Continent responds far more slowly to a given increase in best practice than does average practice in the United States owing to a range of burdens and barriers present on the Continent, such as a far narrower base of higher education on the Continent than in the United States. The dearth of higher education in causing entrepreneurs a long wait to break even is a drag on the *demand* for advances in best practice, as proposed by Bhidé and the present writer (Bhidé, 2005; Phelps, 2002). (The same dearth, in raising the cost of knowledgeable personnel, is also a drag on the *supply* of such advances, as argued by Aghion and Howitt, 2005.) Some of the European firms that *are* innovative prefer to market their new products in the United States. This hypothesis helps to explain why, ten years after the start of the boom, the Continent had not yet shown the pick-up of productivity growth that the United States did in the second half of the 1990s and more strikingly in the first half of the present decade. This same hypothesis may even help to explain why productivity *decelerated* on the Continent (a fleeting slowdown in 1996 and a sustained one since 1998) while the United States economy saw its productivity *accelerate* (in the mid-1990s and then again in 2002). It may be that the Continental consumers and firms on which an innovator in the Continent would have to depend for the adoption of new products were little equipped to cope with the novelty and unfamiliarity of the goods made possible by the ICT revolution; so the flow of new goods and techniques to Continental consumers and firms may have diminished as a result. In this view, the Continent will begin a long, belated catch-up sooner or later. (The Continent's economic miracles did not begin until the 1950s and many of the technological advances taken from the United States were not technologically novel and not even very new.)

Another answer to the puzzle of the Continent's productivity slowdown is that the entrepreneurs' prospects of large productivity advances in the

United States as well as eastern Europe and some other regions, in bringing about high United States investment rates relative to saving rates, diverted capital investment from the Continent to the United States. (Some of the Continent's firms not only launch their innovations in the United States but often find it convenient to conceptualize them, develop them and produce them there as well.) This is acute in Germany, where 'crowding in' has redirected an appreciable part of national saving into a huge current account surplus – more exporting and less importing. But more exports do not translate into growth.

The absence of a pick-up of productivity growth (or even the deceleration) has deprived the Continent of a lift of entrepreneurial expectations that would boost a range of investment activities and thus lift economic activity. Furthermore, the strong investment expenditure in the United States, now boosted by the 'honorary investment' in the form of a huge budgetary deficit, in tending to decrease investment and increase saving on the Continent, has also operated to decrease the Continent's economic activity, according to my theory. In fact, we do see higher unemployment rates in Germany, Switzerland, Austria and Luxembourg (and Japan too) than prevailed before the ICT boom started in 1996, while in the United States the unemployment rate is significantly reduced. (Yet the data on economic activity are complicated. Employment as a ratio to working age population has risen more strongly on the Continent than in the United States since 1996.[20])

It is not certain how this will end for the Continent. One would think that after the Internet is fully 'deployed' and investment activity in the rest of the world has subsided as a result, the Continent would recover to its former productivity growth rate. But these growth rates are rather meandering. In another decade or two another technological revolution may break out and – unless the Continent reforms itself – the Continent will again miss the boom and may have hurdles to pass in catching up.

To conclude: Opportunities to make up lost ground, as arose in postwar Europe, or increased capacities to gain ground, as in China, lead to faster growth and higher employment for a time. But, even if the growth and jobs are stimulating and gratifying, they do not signify a capability to reach high productivity and sustain high employment. Episodes of fast growth and high employment are no evidence that a nation's economic institutions and economic culture enable high performance. The Continent's slow growth now is no evidence that its institutions and culture perform worse than we thought. Indeed, it is reasonable to expect that the productivity *growth* rate and, with it, the unemployment rate will soon return to their zone over most of the 1990s. And it is plausible to think that the Continent will ultimately gain back some of the cumulative lost ground.

Yet a comparison of mean unemployment rates and mean productivity levels in the past three decades suggests relatively poor economic performance on the Continent – not unlucky market forces. The Continent's meagre response to the investment chances of the 1990s suggests the main cause: it is an insufficiency of dynamism for high productivity, prosperity and job satisfaction – not too much welfare. Yet few in the public see it and many of them are averse to change. This situation is a danger to the world.

Appendix

This appendix studies the equations of the open-economy version of the turnover-training model specialized to an approximately *steady-growth state* in which the unemployment rate and normalized wealth are treated as constants: first, the zero pure profit condition gives an equation in the wage, v, as a ratio to the productivity, Λ, of employees on the production line,

$$v/\Lambda = 1 - \beta\,[\zeta(1-u,\, y_h^w/v) + \theta + r - \lambda], \tag{A1}$$

where the quit rate $\zeta(.)$ is increasing in employment per unit labour force, $1 - u$, and in the household's income from wealth, y_h^w. Second, incentive wage analysis gives another equation in v/Λ, the equation of the 'wage curve':

$$v/\Lambda = \beta\,[(1-u)\zeta_1(1-u,\, y_h^w/v) + (y_h^w/v)\zeta_2(1-u,\, y_h^w/v)] \equiv \mathrm{V}(y_h^w/v,\, 1-u)\,, \tag{A2}$$

where the right-hand side – the V function – is increasing in $1 - u$ and in y_h^w. The pair (A1) and (A2) implicitly determine $1 - u$ as a decreasing function of y_h^w/v. (In this model, wealth is the root of all evil.) Third, defining y_h^w as spendable non-wage income, that is, $(r + \theta - \lambda)W$, where W denotes wealth, we derive from the Blanchard-Yaari-Euler equation the steady-state rate of interest:

$$r = \rho + \lambda + [1 + (v/y_h^w)(1-u)]^{-1}\,\theta. \tag{A3}$$

This makes y_h^w/v increasing in $1 - u$ and in $r - \lambda$:

$$\begin{aligned} y_h^w/v &= \{(r+\theta-\rho)/[\theta-(r+\theta-\rho)]\}(1-u) \\ &\equiv \Omega(r-\lambda,\, 1-u;\, \rho,\, \theta),\ \Omega_1>0,\ \Omega_2>0. \end{aligned} \tag{A3$'$}$$

For the *small* open economy the model may be closed by equating the (constant) real interest rate to the world real interest rate, r^*:

$$r = r^* \tag{A4S}$$

To see the implications of that simple system first substitute (A4S) and (A3′) into (A1) and (A2). Then equate the demand wage given by the right-hand side of (A1) to the 'incentive wage' given by the right-hand side of (A2). The resulting equation determines $1 - u$ as a function of r^* and λ:

$$1 - \beta[\zeta(1-u,\, \Omega(r^* - \lambda,\, 1-u)) + \theta + r^* - \lambda]$$
$$= \beta[(1-u)\zeta_1(1-u,\, \Omega(r^* - \lambda,\, 1-u)) + \Omega(\cdot)\, \zeta_2(1-u,\, \Omega(r^* - \lambda,\, 1-u))] \quad \text{(A5S)}$$

It follows that an increase in the country's λ alone, given the overseas interest rate, r^*, and growth rate, λ^*, has two effects, both expansionary. It shifts up the demand wage on the left-hand side *directly* by decreasing the *net* interest rate and *indirectly* by reducing non-wage income relative to the wage rate (which impacts on quitting); it shifts down the incentive-wage curve on the right-hand side through its effect on the non-wage-income ratio. An increase in r^* has precisely the opposite effects throughout.

What are the associated effects on the country's net foreign assets? To begin, define spendable non-wage income earned from domestic business assets (firms' 'capital') per worker, y^w_f, as $(r + \theta - \lambda)\beta\Lambda(1 - u)$ including actuarial dividends. Then, by (A1), this income is given by domestic output net of wage and turnover cost:

$$y^w_f = [\Lambda - \beta\Lambda\zeta(1-u,\, y^w_h/v) - v](1-u)$$
$$\equiv Z(r - \rho - \lambda,\, 1-u;\, \beta\Lambda, \theta),\; Z_1 < 0,\; Z_2 > 0. \quad \text{(A1')}$$

The income from nationals' wealth in (A3) equals the income from domestic capital in (A1') *plus* their income from net foreign assets, or capital export, to be denoted by x. Using (A3') and, upon dividing by v/Λ, (A1') gives

$$[1 - \beta\zeta(1-u, \Omega(.)) - 1](1-u)/V(\Omega(.),\, 1-u) + x$$
$$= \{(r + \theta - \rho)/[\theta - (r + \theta - \rho)]\}\,(1-u) \quad \text{(A6S)}$$

The curve of this equation in the $(1 - u,\, r)$ plane is analogous to the Keynes-Hicks LM curve. This wealth-capital curve solves for the Wicksellian natural interest rate, which is the rate that 'equilibrates' the asset market at given employment. If $x \approx 0$, the two *direct* effects of increasing $1 - u$, being equal, are counterbalancing, so the curve is flat in this respect: the required interest rate is independent of $1 - u$. Yet there are *indirect* effects, however weak, coming from increased quitting and (to the extent the domestic capital is owned by nationals) the increased y^w_h/v, both of which decrease the income from domestic capital, which in turn require a *decrease* in the Wicksellian r to get y^w_h/v back down. (If $x > 0$, the left-hand side will be less sensitive to an increase of $1 - u$ than is the right-hand side; hence, when $1 - u$ is increased the required r is decreased on this account as well.) For all x, an increase in x will at any given $1 - u$ shift *up* the required r, since the right-hand side is the more sensitive to r. The intuition is that an increase in the stock of net foreign assets drives up the interest rate required for asset market equilibrium just as a helicopter drop of public debt would.

This alternate framework can be closed by adopting the counterpart of (A5S):

$$1 - \beta[\zeta(1-u, \Omega(r-\lambda, 1-u)) + \theta + r - \lambda]$$
$$= \beta[(1-u)\zeta_1(1-u, \Omega(r-\lambda, 1-u)) + \Omega(\bullet)\, \zeta_2(1-u, \Omega(r-\lambda, 1-u))]. \quad \text{(A5')}$$

The curve of this equation in the same Hicksian plane is analogous to the Keynes-Hicks IS curve. It solves for the employment level consistent with 'equilibrium' in the labour market. An increase in r, in increasing the income from wealth, impacts negatively on the left-hand side (thus shifting down the demand wage in the Marshallian plane) and, on standard assumptions, impacts positively on the right-hand side, thus shifting up the 'wage curve'. So $1 - u$ must increase to satisfy the equation. The curve slopes downward.

Let us suppose that the latter curve is steeper than the former, which I believe is the 'realistic' case. Then a given increase of x raises the required r and thus contracts $1 - u$. Hence, an externally caused increase of r^*, if it is to drive up r to match in the small open economy, must do so by inducing an increase of x; that, in turn, forces a decline of $1 - u$. If the inequality between the slopes of the two curves were the reverse, the implied increase of r would required a *decrease* of x, which does not fit observation.

For the *large* open economy it is necessary to add more structure. Suppose there are two large and broadly similar countries. It appears helpful to invert (A3) to express $r - \lambda$ as a function of the wealth variable rather than the other way around, writing

$$r - \lambda = \rho + [1 + (v/y_h^w)(1-u)]^{-1}\theta \equiv R(y_h^w/v, 1-u; \rho, \theta). \quad \text{(A3L)}$$

Then, using (A3L), we may replace (A5S) with

$$1 - \beta[\zeta(1-u, y_h^w/v) + \theta + R(y_h^w/v, 1-u; \rho, \theta)]$$
$$= \beta[(1-u)\zeta_1(1-u, y_h^w/v) + (y_h^w/v)\zeta_2(1-u, y_h^w/v)] \quad \text{(A5L)}$$

In place of the previous (A4S) we use the steady-growth implication of the interest parity condition making the interest rate in the other country, r^*, which our country is large enough to affect, equal to our r:

$$\rho + \lambda + [1 + (v/y_h^w)(1-u)]^{-1}\theta$$
$$= \rho^* + \lambda^* + [1 + (v/y_h^w)^*(1 - u^*)]^{-1}\theta^* \quad \text{(A4L)}$$

Defining y_f^w as the non-wage income *originating in domestic firms* and using it to rewrite (A1) gives the new structural equation

$$y_f^w/\Lambda = (1-u)\{1 - \beta[\zeta(1-u, y_h^w/v) + \theta] - (v/\Lambda)\}. \quad \text{(A6L)}$$

Upon dividing by ν/Λ and using (A2) to substitute the incentive-wage function V for ν/Λ,

$$y_f^w/\nu = (1-u)\{1-\beta[\zeta(1-u,\ y_h^w/\nu)+\theta] - V(1-u,\ y_h^w/\nu;\ \beta)\}/V(.). \qquad \text{(A7L)}$$

There is also the balance equation,

$$(y_h^w/\nu) - (y_f^w/\nu) = [(y_f^{w*}/\nu^*) - (y_h^{w*}/\nu^*)](\nu^*/\nu), \qquad \text{(A8L)}$$

where V*(.) can be substituted for ν^* just as V(.) can be substituted for ν. Besides (A5L) and (A7L) there are the counterpart equations (A5L*) and (A7L*) describing the other country together with the linkages in (A4L) and (A8L). This is a six-equation system in the six variables u, u^*, y_h^w/ν, y_f^w/ν, y_f^w/ν^*, and $y_h^w{}^*/\nu^*$.

A graphical analysis shows that if λ^* increases without an increase of the home country's λ (think of the Continent's speed-up in the 1950s–1960s), $y_h^w{}^*/\nu^*$ falls, which pushes up $1 - u^*$ and creates a positive wedge between capital and wealth, that is; $y_f^{w*}/\nu^* > y_h^w{}^*/\nu^*$; the opposite wedge in the US causes y_h^w/ν to rise, which contracts $1 - u$.

Finally, it should be noted that the two countries modelled here can only come *close* (and only in transient fashion) to constant unemployment rates and balanced growth, each growing at its respective rate of technical progress, since net foreign assets (and the income therefrom) cannot be growing simultaneously at the two disparate rates. A proper dynamic analysis would be greatly impeded by the high dimensionality of such a model. I hope readers will nevertheless view the above mathematical analysis as providing significant support for the propositions in the text regarding the international transmission mechanism in non-monetary models of the structuralist kind.

Notes

1. So I do not regard the anarchism of the Wild West as a species of capitalism. Similarly, a corporatist system mired in state corruption might not exemplify a well-functioning corporatism.
2. GDP *per capita* in Germany fell from 71.4 per cent of the US level in 1941 to 44.7 per cent in 1950 according to data from Angus Maddison (1995).
3. EU-15 GDP per hour worked went on catching up with the United States in the next 15 or 20 years, rising from about 70 per cent of the US level in the mid-1970s to nearly 90 per cent by the mid-1990s. But this gain represents catch-up by other economies (such as Greece, Spain, Portugal and Ireland) more than further catch-up by Germany, France and Italy. See *Eurostat Structural Indicators*, 2004.
4. I do not know of a written neoclassical account of the Continent's catch-up. I am simply applying the framework to produce one for discussion.
5. See the charts and discussion in Gordon (2004).
6. The stunning resilience of productivity growth – indeed, a significant acceleration of productivity – through the 1930s Depression (right to 1941) is studied in Field (2003).

7. Gershenkron is cited in this context. Recent work includes Nelson (2004), Aghion and Howitt (2005) and Zoega (2005).
8. This might explain the finding (which if I am right is an exaggeration) by Peter Temin that *best* practice on the Continent caught up to the US by the mid-1950s (see Temin, 2002).
9. Three non-monetary models are built and studied in Phelps (1994).
10. This effect was first derived in Pissarides (1990); the second edition treats the subject in an entirely non-monetary framework. Phelps (1994) looked for a growth effect only in a closed-economy context and then with a model (the 2-sector) lacking a valuation effect.
11. *Economic Report of the President*, February 2003, Tables B-103 and Table B-27. The trade surplus includes paid and unrequited exports but the calculation of the current account surplus subtracts an item that includes exports donated through foreign aid. The current account surplus would have been twice as large had there been no aid so that Europe had to pay for all the exports sent to it by the United States.
12. See the chart on p. 320 of Phelps (1994).
13. The proportionate increase of the unemployment rate is highly correlated with the magnitude of the slowdown of total factor productivity among the G7 economies. See Hoon and Phelps (1997), Fig. 2, p. 556. Evidence from wealth-income ratios is discussed in Phelps (2000).
14. See Table 3 in Phelps and Zoega (2004).
15. The 2001 male activity percentage rates are 59 in Poland, 62 in the Slovak Republic, 64 in Hungary and 74 in the Czech Republic. Western rates are much higher: Italy 69, France 69, Germany 73, Spain 74, Austria 76, Sweden 77, Holland 83 and Switzerland 88 (OECD, 2002).
16. OECD, 2005 and EBRD, 1999. The euro area is in current account surplus. (I suppose special factors are behind the huge current account deficits in Armenia and Azerbaijan.)
17. Evidence from surveys is shown in Roman Frydman, Marek Hessel and Andrzej Rapaczynsky (1998; 1999).
18. Inward FDI *can* finance domestic investment financed by an increase of imports or decrease of exports, thus possibly creating a trade *deficit*. But subsequent repatriation of future earnings requires a trade surplus. And much FDI inflow may be 'sterilized' through purchase of offsetting assets overseas.
19. Reati and Toporowski (2004), which surveys the literature on the 'long wave' and the latest wave, arises from new computerization and information technologies.
20. Perhaps the decrease of labour force participation in the United States reflects the enormous rise of real-estate and stock-market wealth there. Part of the Continent's increase reflects surely labour-market and welfare reforms on the Continent.

References

Acemoglu, Daron, Philippe Aghion and F. Zilibotti (2002) 'Distance to Frontier, Selection and Economic Growth', NBER Working Paper no. 9066.

Aghion, Philippe, and Peter Howitt (2005) 'Growth with Quality-Improving Innovations' in P. Aghion and S. N. Durlauf (eds), *Handbook of Economic Growth* (Amsterdam: Elsevier).

Bhidé, Amar (2005) 'Non-destructive Creation: How Entrepreneurship Sustains Development', in G. T. Vinig and R. van der Voort (eds), *The Emergence of Entrepreneurial Economics* (Amsterdam: Elsevier Science).

Bhidé, Amar, and Edmund Phelps (2005a) 'A Dynamic Theory of US–China Trade: Making Sense of the Imbalances', CCS Working Paper no. 4 (July).
Bhidé, Amar, and Edmund Phelps (2005b) 'Classical Theory vs the Real World', *Wall Street Journal,* 25 July.
EBRD (1999) *Transition Report 1999: Ten Years of Transition* (London: EBRD).
Field, Alexander (2003) 'The Most Technologically Progressive Decade of the Century', *American Economic Review,* vol. 93(4), pp. 1399–414.
Friedman, Milton (1953) 'Why the Dollar Shortage?' *The Freeman,* vol. 4(6), 13 December, reprinted in M. Friedman, *Dollars and Deficits* (Englewood Cliffs NJ: Prentice Hall), pp. 211–17.
Frydman, Roman, Marek Hessel and Andrzej Rapaczynski (1998) 'Why Ownership Matters', *C. V. Starr Report,* no. 98–22, April.
Frydman, Roman, Marek Hessel and Andrzej Rapaczynski (1999) 'When Does Privatization Matter?' *Quarterly Journal of Economics,* vol. 114(4), pp. 1153–91, November.
Gordon, Robert J. (2004) 'Two Centuries of Economic Growth: Europe Chasing the American Frontier', NBER Working Paper no. 10662, August.
Hoon, Hian Teck and Edmund Phelps (1997) 'Growth, Wealth and the Natural Rate: Is Europe's Jobs Crisis a Growth Crisis?' *European Economic Review,* vol. 41(5), pp. 549–57.
Kuijs, Louis (2005) 'Investment and Saving in China', World Bank Policy Research Paper no. 3633, June.
Maddison, Angus (1995) *The World Economy in the 20th Century* (Paris: OECD).
Nelson, Richard (2004) 'A Program of Study of the Processes Involved in Technological and Economic Catch-Up', mimeo. Earth Institute, Columbia University.
Nelson, Richard, and Edmund Phelps (1966) 'Investment in Humans, Technological Diffusion and Economic Growth', *American Economic Review,* vol. 61(2), pp. 69–75.
OECD (1983) *Historical Statistics 1960–1981* (Paris: OECD).
OECD (2002) *Labour Force Statistics 1981–2001* (Paris: OECD), Part III.
OECD (2005) *Economic Outlook,* no. 77, June.
Phelps, Edmund (1994) *Structural Slumps* (Cambridge, Mass.: Harvard University Press).
Phelps, Edmund (2000) 'Lessons in Natural-Rate Dynamics', *Oxford Economic Papers,* vol. 52(3), January, pp. 51–71.
Phelps, Edmund (2002) 'The Continent's High Unemployment Rate: Possible Institutional Causes', mimeo. Center on Capitalism and Society, Earth Institute, Columbia University.
Phelps, Edmund (2005) 'Some Notes on Monetary Policy and Unemployment', in Willi Semmler (ed.), *Monetary Policy and Unemployment* (London: Routledge), pp. 16–19.
Phelps, Edmund, and Gylfi Zoega (2001) 'Structural Booms', *Economic Policy,* no. 25, April.
Phelps, Edmund, and Gylfi Zoega (2004) 'The Search for Routes to Better Economic Performance', *CESifo Forum,* Spring, pp. 3–11.
Pissarides, Christopher (1990) *Equilibrium Unemployment Theory* (Oxford: Blackwell).
Reati, Angelo, and Jan Toporowski (2004) 'An Economic Policy for the Fifth Long Wave', *Banca Nazionale del Lavoro,* vol. 57(231), December, pp. 395–437.
Solow, Robert M. and Martin N. Bailey (2001) 'International Productivity Comparisons Built from the Firm Level', *Journal of Economic Perspectives,* vol. 15.
Temin, Peter (2002) 'The Golden Age of European Growth Reconsidered', *European Review of Economic History,* vol. 6, pp. 3–22.
Zoega, Gylfi (2005) 'Notes on Institutions, Innovation and Economic Performance', mimeo, Earth Institute, Columbia University (July).

5
The Schumpeterian Approach to Education and Growth

Philippe Aghion
Harvard University, USA

1 Introduction

Unlike other subjects or questions on which I have been working, my thinking about education and growth was spurred by policy demands. First, by the French Conseil d'Analyse Economique which asked me to write a report on the subject back in 2001. And a year later, by the European Commission which asked me to co-author a report (now referred to as the 'Sapir Report') on the causes of the slow growth in Western Europe. A first look at the United States versus the EU in 1999–2000 shows that 37.3 per cent of the United States population aged 25–64 have completed a higher education degree, against only 23.8 per cent of the EU population. This educational attainment comparison is mirrored by that on tertiary education expenditure, with the United States devoting 3 per cent of its GDP to tertiary education versus only 1.4 per cent in the EU. Is this European deficit in tertiary education investment adverse for growth?

When asked to think about growth policy, a natural reflex is to look at the existing literature on education and growth. A first class of models emphasizes (physical or human) capital accumulation as the main source of growth. There, the neo-classical reference is Mankiw-Romer-Weil (1992) [MRW], and the AK reference is the celebrated article by Lucas (1988). In MRW, which is an augmented version of the Solow model with human capital as an additional accumulating factor of production, human capital accumulation slows down the convergence to the steady state by counter-acting the effects of decreasing returns to physical capital accumulation. In Lucas, instead, the assumption that human capital accumulates at a speed proportional to the existing stock of human capital, leads a positive long-run growth rate. Whether on the transition path to the steady state (in MRW) or in steady state (in Lucas), the rate of growth depends upon the rate of accumulation of human capital, not upon the stock of human capital. Moreover, these capital accumulation-based models do not distinguish between primary/secondary and tertiary education: the two are perfect substitutes in these models. Thus, if we believe these models, it is not a problem if the United States spends more than Europe in higher education, as long as total spending and attainment in education as a whole have not increased faster in the United States than in Europe. And indeed they have not done so over the past decade.

Does this mean that education policy is not an issue, or rather that we should not fully believe in these models? That we should not stick to these models has been convincingly argued by Benhabib and Spiegel (1994) who showed, based on cross-country regressions over the 1965–1985 period, that human capital accumulation (where human capital is measured by school enrolment) was not significantly correlated with growth, whereas human capital stocks were. Another source of scepticism is the finding by Ha and Howitt (2005) that the trend growth rate of the number of R&D workers in the United States has gone down over the past fifty years, whereas the trend rate of productivity growth has not. In this chapter we consider an alternative approach to education and growth. Pioneered by Nelson and Phelps (1966), this approach emphasized the complementarity between human capital stocks on the one hand, and the process of innovation and technological catch-up on the other.

2 Nelson–Phelps

More than just questioning the capital accumulation approach to education and growth, Benhabib and Spiegel (1994) resurrected the simple model by Nelson and Phelps (1966). Nelson and Phelps did not have a model of endogenous growth with endogenous R&D and innovation, but they were already thinking of growth as being generated by productivity-improving adaptations, whose arrival rate would depend upon the stock of human capital. More formally, Nelson and Phelps would picture a world economy in which, in any given country, productivity grows according to an equation of the form:

$$\dot{A} = f(h)(\overline{A} - A),$$

where again $\overline{A}$ denotes the frontier technology (itself growing over time at some exogenous rate), and h is the current stock of human capital in the country. A higher stock of human capital would thus foster growth by making it easier for a country to catch up with the frontier technology. Benhabib and Spiegel tested a slightly augmented version of Nelson–Phelps in which human capital not only facilitates the adaptation to more advanced technologies, but also makes it easier to innovate at the frontier, according to a dynamic equation of the form:

$$\dot{A} = f(h)(\overline{A} - A) + g(h)\gamma A,$$

where the second term captures the innovation component of growth.

Using cross-country regressions of the increase in the log of per capita GDP over the period 1965–1985 as a linear function of the sum of logs of human capital stocks over all the years between 1965 and 1985, Benhabib and Spiegel found a significantly positive correlation between the two, which in turn was evidence that the rate of productivity growth is also positively correlated with the stock of human capital. Moreover, they found a larger correlation for countries further below the world technology frontier, which would hint at the catch-up component of growth being the dominant one. Thus, more than the rate of human capital accumulation, it is its stock that matters for growth. Does this help us understand the comparison between Europe and the United States?

Unfortunately, more recent work by Krueger and Lindahl (2001) would temper our optimism. Using panel data over 110 countries between 1960 and 1990, choosing the number of years in education instead of the logarithm of that number to measure human capital,[1] and correcting for measurement errors, Krueger and Lindahl would still find a positive correlation between growth and human capital stocks (although they also found a positive correlation between growth and the rate of accumulation of human capital), however the significance of the correlation between growth and human capital stocks would disappear when restricting the regression to OECD countries.

3 Appropriate education systems

Should we conclude from Krueger and Lindahl that education only matters for catching-up but not for innovating at the frontier and that, consequently, education is not an area which Europe needs to reform in order to resume growing at a rate at least equal to that of the United States? The new hint at that point came from Acemoglu, Aghion and Zilibotti's (2002) idea on appropriate institutions and economic growth, and that hint in turn provided the backbone for the Sapir Report and its application to education led to a report on 'Education and Growth' for the French Conseil d'Analyse Economique.

3.1 Acemoglu–Aghion–Zilibotti

By linking growth to innovation and entrepreneurship, and innovation incentives in turn to characteristics of the economic environment, new growth theories made it possible to analyse the interplay between growth and the design of policies and institutions. For example, the basic model developed in Section 2 suggested that long-run growth would be best enhanced by a combination of good property right protection (to protect the rents of innovators against imitation), a good education system (to increase the efficiency of R&D activities and/or the supply of skilled manufacturing labour), and a stable macroeconomy to reduce interest rates (and thereby increase the net present value of innovative rents). Our discussion of convergence clubs in Section 3 then suggested that the same policies or institutions would also increase a country's ability to join the convergence club.

Now, new growth theories may be criticized by development economists and policy makers, precisely because of the universal nature of the policy recommendations that appear to follow from them: no matter how developed a country or sector currently is, it seems that one should prescribe the same medicine (legal reform to enforce property rights, investment climate favourable to entrepreneurship, education, macrostability, ...) to maximize the growth prospects of that country or sector.

However, in his essay on *Economic Backwardness in Historical Perspective*, Gerschenkron (1962) argues that relatively backward economies could more rapidly catch up with more advanced countries by introducing 'appropriate institutions' that are growth-enhancing at an early stage of development but may cease to be so at a later stage. Thus, countries such as Japan or Korea managed to achieve very high growth rates between 1945 up until the 1990s with institutional arrangements involving long-term relationships between firms and banks, the predominance of large conglomerates, and strong government intervention through export promotion and subsidized loans to the enterprise sector, all of which depart from the more market-based and laissez-faire institutional model pioneered and promoted by the United States.

That growth-enhancing institutions or policies might change with a country's or sector's distance to the technological frontier, should not come as a total surprise to readers at this point: in the previous section, we saw that competition could have opposite effects on innovation incentives depending on whether firms were initially closer to or farther below the fringe in the corresponding industry (it would enhance innovations in neck-and-neck industries, and discourage it in industries where innovating firms are far below the frontier). The same type of conclusion turns out to hold true when one looks at the interplay between countries' distance to the world technology frontier and 'openness'. Using a cross-country panel of more than 100 countries over the 1960–2000 period, Acemoglu-Aghion-Zilibotti (2002), henceforth AAZ, regress the average growth rate over a five-year period on a country's distance to the United States frontier (measured by the ratio of GDP per capita in that country to per capita GDP in the United States) at the beginning of the period. Then, splitting the sample of countries into two groups, corresponding respectively to a high and a low openness group according to Frankel-Romer's openness indicator, AAZ show that average growth decreases more rapidly as a country approaches the world frontier when openness is low. Thus, while a low degree of openness does not appear to be detrimental to growth in countries far below the world frontier, it becomes increasingly detrimental to growth as the country approaches the frontier. AAZ repeat the same exercise using entry costs to new firms instead of openness, and they obtain a similar conclusion, namely that high entry costs are most damaging to growth when a country is close to the world frontier, unlike in countries far below the frontier.

More formally, consider the following multi-country growth model. In each country, a unique final good which also serves as numeraire, is produced competitively using a continuum of intermediate inputs according to:

$$y_t = \int_0^1 (A_t(i))^{1-\alpha} x_t(i)^\alpha di, \tag{1}$$

where $A_t\,(i)$ is the productivity in sector i at time t, $x_t\,(i)$ is the flow of intermediate good i used in final good production again at time t, and $\alpha \in [0,1]$.

As before, *ex post* each intermediate good producer faces a competitive fringe of imitators that forces her to charge a limit price $p_t\,(i) = \chi > 1$. Consequently, equilibrium monopoly profits (gross of the fixed cost) are simply given by:

$$\pi_t\,(i) = \delta A_t\,(i)$$

where $\delta \equiv (\chi - 1)\,\chi^{-1/(1-\alpha)}$.

We still let

$$A_t \equiv \int_0^1 A_t\,(i)\; di$$

denote the average productivity in the country at date t, $\overline{A}_t$ the productivity at the world frontier which we assume to grow at the constant rate g from one period to the next, and $a_t = A_t / \overline{A}_t$ the (inverse) measure of the country's distance to the technological frontier at date t.

Productivity growth occurs as follows. Suppose that intermediate firms have two ways to generate productivity growth: (a) they can imitate existing world frontier technologies; (b) they can innovate upon the previous local technology. More specifically, we assume:

$$A_t\,(i) = \eta \overline{A}_{t-1} + \gamma A_{t-1}, \tag{2}$$

where $\eta \overline{A}_{t-1}$ and γA_{t-1} refer respectively to the imitation and innovation components of productivity growth. Imitations use the existing frontier technology at the end of period $(t-1)$, thus they multiply $\overline{A}_{t-1}$, whereas innovations build on the knowledge stock of the country, and therefore they multiply A_{t-1}.

Now dividing both sides of (2) by $\overline{A}_t$, using the fact that

$$\overline{A}_t = (1+g)\,\overline{A}_{t-1},$$

and integrating over all intermediate sectors i, we immediately obtain the following linear relationship between the country's distance to frontier a_t at date t and the distance to frontier a_{t-1} at date $t-1$:

$$a_t = \frac{1}{1+g}(\eta + \gamma a_{t-1}). \tag{3}$$

This equation clearly shows that the relative importance of innovation for productivity growth increases as: (i) the country moves closer to the world technological frontier, i.e. as a_{t-1} moves closer to 1, whereas imitation is more important when the country is far below the frontier, i.e. when a_{t-1} is close to zero; (ii) a new technological revolution (e.g. the ICT revolution) occurs that increases the importance of innovation, i.e. increases γ.

This immediately generates a theory of 'appropriate institutions' and growth: suppose that imitation and innovation activities do not require the same institutions. Typically, imitation activities (i.e. η in the above equation (3)) will be enhanced by long-term investments within (large) existing firms, which in turn may benefit from long-term bank finance and/or subsidized credit as in Japan or Korea since 1945. On the other hand, innovation activities (i.e. γ) require initiative, risk-taking, and also the selection of good projects and talents and the weeding out of projects that turn out not to be profitable. This in turn calls for more market-based and flexible institutions, in particular for a higher reliance on market finance and speculative monitoring, higher competition and trade liberalization to weed out the bad projects, more flexible labour markets for firms to select the most talented or best matched employees, non-integrated firms to increase initiative and entrepreneurship downstream, etc. It then follows from equation (3) that the growth-maximizing institutions will evolve as a country moves towards the world technological frontier. Far below the frontier, a country will grow faster if it adopts what AAZ refer to as *investment-based* institutions or policies, whereas closer to the frontier growth will be maximized if the country switches to *innovation-based* institutions or policies. In the remaining part of the chapter we simply apply this distinction to education systems.

3.2 Distance to frontier and the composition of education spending

Using the AAZ insight whereby productivity growth can be generated either by implementing (or imitating) the frontier technology or by innovating on past technologies, where both types of activities require different institutions or policies, we will depart from Benhabib and Spiegel by decomposing total human capital stock into primary/secondary and tertiary education, and by arguing that different types of education spending lie behind imitation and innovation activities. In particular, higher education investment should have a bigger effect on a country's ability to make leading-edge innovations, whereas primary and secondary education are more likely to make a difference in terms of the country's ability to implement existing (frontier) technologies. Thus, it is not so much the total *amount* of education, but more importantly the *organization* of education, that impacts on growth differently across countries at different stages of development.

Now, what are the potential implications of this approach for education policy, and is there something to learn from the comparison between Europe and the United States given the disappointing news of Krueger and Lindahl from cross-OECD country regressions? The remaining part of the section is based on work by Vandenbussche, Aghion and Meghir (2004) [VAM], and current work by Aghion, Boustan, Hoxby and Vandenbussche (2005) [ABHV]. The starting point of these two papers is that, in contrast to the Nelson–Phelps or Benhabib–Spiegel models, human capital does not affect innovation and imitation uniformly: more specifically, primary/secondary education tends to produce imitators, whereas tertiary (especially graduate) education is more likely to produce innovators. This realistic assumption, in turn, leads to the prediction that, as a country moves closer to the technological frontier, tertiary education should become increasingly important for growth compared to primary/secondary education (all measured in stocks).

3.2.1 *Solving the Krueger–Lindahl puzzle*

First, note that this simple combination of AAZ with the Nelson–Phelps model of education and growth, provides a solution to the Krueger–Lindahl puzzle. Namely, that total human capital stock

$$U + S$$

is not a sufficient statistic to predict growth in OECD countries. For example, take two countries *A* and *B* at the same distance from the world frontier, with the same total human capital, but

$$S_A > S_B.$$

Country *A* will grow faster if the two countries are sufficiently close to the frontier whereas country *B* will grow faster if both countries are far from it and yet the two countries have the same total amount of human capital.

3.2.2 *A simple model of appropriate education systems*

Now, going into slightly greater detail on formalization, VAM and ABHV focus on the following class of productivity growth functions:

$$A_{it} - A_{it-1} = u_{m,i,t}^{\sigma} s_{m,i,t}^{1-\sigma} \overline{A}_{t-1} + \gamma u_{n,i,t}^{\phi} s_{n,i,t}^{1-\phi} A_{t-1} = g(u,s), \tag{4}$$

where $\overline{A}_{t-1}$ is the frontier productivity last period, A_{t-1} is the average productivity in the country last period, u_m (resp. u_n) is the number of workers with primary/secondary education (unskilled workers) used in imitation (resp. innovation), s_m (resp. s_n) (resp.) is the number of workers with higher education (skilled workers) in imitation, and

$$u = (u_m, u_n); s = (s_m, s_n),$$

and

$$\sigma > \phi$$

so that the elasticity of productivity growth with respect to skilled (resp. unskilled) workers is larger in innovation (resp. in imitation).

Letting $a_t = A_t/\bar{A}_t$ denote the country's proximity to the technological frontier at date, and letting the frontier grow at constant rate $\bar{g}$, the intermediate producer will choose u and s to maximize profits. Dividing through by $\bar{A}_{t-1}$ and dropping time subscripts, the producer's problem simply becomes:

$$\max_{u_m, u_n, s_m, s_n} \{\delta[u_m^{\sigma} s_m^{1-\sigma} + \gamma u_n^{\phi} s_n^{1-\phi} a]\} - w_u(u_m + u_n) - w_s(s_m + s_n),$$

where we eliminate the firm's subscript i since all intermediate firms face the same maximization problem. Moreover, in equilibrium we necessarily have:

$$u_m + u_n = U; s_m + s_n = S,$$

where U and S are the total supplies of workers with primary/secondary education and tertiary education respectively.

What we have here is formally equivalent to a small open economy model with two factors and two products, where the two products are imitation and innovation, whose prices, δ and $\delta\gamma a$ are exogenously given. As in standard trade theory, these given output prices uniquely determine the equilibrium factor prices w_u and w_s. The 'revenue' in firms' objective function is proportional to the growth rate (plus unity). Solving for the equilibrium allocations of skilled and unskilled labour between imitation and innovation as a function of U, S and the proximity to the technological frontier, one can look at how the equilibrium growth rate

$$g^* (U, S, a) = g(u^*(U, S, a), s^*(U, S, a))$$

varies with either of those three variables.

In particular, looking at the cross derivative of g^* with respect to S and a, we find:

$$\frac{\partial^2 g^*}{\partial a \partial S} > 0;$$

in other words, a marginal increase in the fraction of workers with higher education enhances productivity growth all the more the closer the country is to the world technology frontier.

The intuition for this result relies on the Rybczynski theorem in international trade, which in turn implies that a marginal increase in the supply S of highly educated workers leads to an even greater number of skilled workers being employed in innovation. Since the change does not affect equilibrium factor prices, therefore it leaves the factor proportions unchanged in each activity, meaning that innovation also attracts an increased number of unskilled workers. More precisely, since $\sigma > \phi$ so that innovation is the skill-intensive activity, innovation will increase but imitation will decrease. The effect on firms' 'revenue', and hence the effect on the economy's growth rate, is positive. For countries closer to the frontier, where the 'price' of innovation $\delta\gamma a$ is larger, the effect is larger than for countries further from the frontier.

3.3 Cross-country and cross-US-states evidence

3.3.1 Cross-country evidence

VAM confront this prediction with cross-country panel evidence on higher education, distance to frontier, and productivity growth. ABHV test the theory on cross-US-state data. Each approach has its pros and cons. Cross-US-state analysis uses a much richer data set and also very good instruments for higher and lower education spending. However, a serious analysis of the growth impact of education spending across US states, must take into account an additional element not considered in previous models, namely the effects on the migration of skilled labour across states at different levels of technological development. On the other hand, cross-country analysis can safely ignore the migration; however the data are sparse and the instruments for educational spending are weak (they mainly consist of lagged spending). In the remaining part of the section we consider the two pieces of empirical analysis in turn.

VAM consider a panel data set of 22 OECD countries over the period 1960–2000, which they subdivide into five-year subperiods. Output and investment data are drawn from Penn World Tables 6.1 (2002) and human capital data from Barro-Lee (2000). The Barro-Lee data indicate the fraction of a country's population that has reached a certain level of schooling at intervals of five years, so they use the fraction that has received some higher education together with their measure of TFP (constructed assuming a constant labour share of 0.65 across country) to perform the following regression:

$$g_{j,t} = \alpha_0 + \alpha_1\, dist_{j,t-1} + \alpha_2 \Lambda_{j,t} + \alpha_3 (dist_{j,t-1} * \Lambda_{j,t}) + v_j + u_{j,t},$$

where $g_{j,t}$ is country j's growth rate over a five-year period, $dist_{j,t-1}$ is country j's closeness to the technological frontier at $t-1$ (i.e. 5 years before), $\Lambda_{j,t}$ is the fraction of the working age population with some higher education and v_j is a country's fixed effect. The closeness and human capital variables are instrumented with their values at $t-2$ and the equation is estimated in differences to eliminate the fixed effect. Before controlling for country fixed effects,

VAM obtain a statistically significant coefficient of –1.87 for the human capital variable, and a statistically significant coefficient of 2.37 for the interaction variable, indicating that indeed higher education matters more as a country gets closer to the frontier. Controlling for country fixed effects removes the significance of the coefficients; however this significance is restored once countries are regrouped into subregions and country fixed effects are replaced by group fixed effects. This, in turn suggests that cross-country data on only 22 countries are too sparse for significant regression results to survive when we control for country fixed effects.

To see how this result translates in terms of the effect of an additional year of schooling of higher education, they perform the following regression in logs:

$$g_{j,t} = \alpha_0' + \alpha_1' \, dist_{j,t-1}' + \alpha_2' N_{j,t} + \alpha_3' (dist_{j,t-1} * N_{j,t}) + v_j' + u_{j,t}',$$

where this time $dist_{j,t-1}'$ is the log of the closeness to the technological frontier and $N_{j,t}$ is the average number of years of higher education of the population. The econometric technique employed is the same as before. Before controlling for country fixed effects, VAM find the coefficient of the number of years to be 0.105 and of little significance, but the coefficient of the interaction variable to be equal to 0.368 and significant. This result again demonstrates that it is more important to expand years of higher education close to the technological frontier.

3.3.2 *Cross-US-states evidence*

ABHV test the same theory on cross-US-state data instead of cross-country data. As mentioned above, one potential problem when moving from cross-country to cross-region data, is that educational policy should affect migration flow across regions more than it affects migration flows across countries. Thus a suitable model of education and growth across regions within a same country, ought to include an additional equation describing how migration flow varies for example with the wage differential between a particular state and the state currently at the technological frontier. Introducing the possibility of migration reinforces the positive interaction between closeness to the frontier and higher education. Namely, in addition to the Rybczynski effect described above, investing in higher education in a state that is far from the technological frontier, would contribute all the less to growth in that state that the newly skilled workers would migrate to a more frontier state where productivity and therefore wages are higher.

Any regression with growth on the left-hand-side and education on the right-hand-side, raises an obvious endogeneity problem, best emphasized by Bils and Klenow (2000). Here, as in the above cross-country panel regressions, the endogeneity problem can be stated as follows: if states or countries choose their composition of education spending according to the model, then we should see the composition of educational investments being highly correlated with technology and productivity, and therefore the regressions would say nothing about causality.

However, the great advantage of moving from cross-country to cross-state analysis, is that we have access to a natural source of exogenous mistakes in education investment, namely political economy considerations which may lead the Congress or other federal instances to misallocate the funding to higher education across states. For example, because it has a representative on a Congressional commission for higher education, a far-from-the-frontier state may end up mistakenly receiving excessive funding for research-related education. Conversely, because of local political economy considerations, a close-to-the-frontier state may end up mistakenly focusing its investment in primary education, neglecting higher education.

In other words, political economy considerations and the politicians' ability and incentive to deliver 'porks' to their constituencies, provide a natural source of instruments that predict states' tendencies to make exogenous mistakes when investing in education.

The actual instruments used in ABHV are:

1. for research-university education: whether a state has a Congressman on the appropriations committee which allocates funds for research universities but not other types of schools;
2. for 'low-brow' post-secondary education (community colleges, training schools): whether the chairman of the state's education committee represents voters whose children attend one- or two-year post-secondary institutions;
3. for primary and secondary education: whether the overall political balance on the state's supreme court interacts with the state school finance system.

Then, using annual panel data over the period 1970–2000, ABHV perform a two-stage procedure whereby: (i) in first-stage regressions, the various kinds of educational spending are regressed over their respective instruments; (ii) the growth rate in each state and year is regressed over the instruments for the various kinds of educational spending, the state's proximity to the frontier, and the interaction between the two, controlling for state and year fixed effects.

We refer readers to ABHV (2005) for the detailed regression results, which yield the following conclusions. First, in contrast to our previous cross-country analysis, here the correlations remain significant even after controlling for state fixed effects without having to regroup the country dummies. Second, the above instruments are very strong, with F-statistics of more than 10 for the joint significance of the two dummies for Senator and House

Representative on the corresponding appropriation committees as determinants of research education spending. For example, every additional Representative on the House Appropriation Committee increases the expenditure on research-type education by $597 per cohort member, which is considerable. Now, turning to the second-stage regressions, ABHV find that an additional $1000 per person in research education spending raises the state's per-employee growth rate by 0.27 per cent if the state is at the frontier (with a close to 1), whereas it raises it by only 0.09 per cent if the state is far from the frontier (with a close to 0.3). More generally, the closer a state gets to the technological frontier, the more growth-enhancing it becomes to invest in higher education and the less growth-enhancing it becomes to emphasize lower education.

4 Conclusion

What have we learned from our discussion? First, that capital accumulation-based models have little to say about education policy, particularly with regard to the increasing growth gap between Europe and the United States. Second, that Schumpeterian models that emphasize the interplay between human capital stocks and the innovation process, have more potential for delivering policy recommendations, yet when looking at educational spending as a whole there is not much that can be said from looking at cross-OECD comparisons. However, once we distinguish between imitation and frontier innovation and map these two sources of productivity growth to different segments of the education system, then we can come up with relevant policy recommendations for regions such as Europe that have moved closer to the frontier and yet are maintaining very low levels of higher education spending compared to the United States. The above regressions indeed suggest that putting the emphasis on primary/secondary education was fine as long as Europe was technologically far from the United States and therefore relying more on imitation as a main source of growth, but that now that the growth potential of imitation is wearing out, it becomes more urgent to invest more in higher education in order to foster innovation. In fact, the cross-country (cross-OECD) analysis in VAM shows the additional result that if we include a dummy for 1985 (equal to zero before 1985 and to one after) in the regressions, and interact that dummy with all the right-hand-side terms in the regression, one finds that after 1985, the interaction between higher education investment and the proximity to the technological frontier becomes insignificant: this, in turn, indicates that on top of the above consideration, something happened during the 1980s (globalization and/or the IT revolution?) that would make it more growth-enhancing for *all* OECD countries to shift their emphasis to higher education.

Note

1. This change was in turn motivated by the so-called Mincerian approach to human capital, whereby the value of one more year in schooling is measured by the wage increase that is forgone by the individual who chooses to study during that year instead of working. This amounts to measuring the value of a human capital stock by the log of the current wage rate earned by an individual. And that log was shown by Mincer to be positively correlated to the number of years spent at school by the individual, after estimating an equation of the form:

$$\ln w = a_0 + a_1 n.$$

The Mincerian approach can itself be criticized, however, for: (i) assuming perfectly competitive labour markets; (ii) ignoring the role of schools as selection devices; (iii) ignoring interpersonal and intertemporal knowledge externalities.

References

Acemoglu, Daron, Philippe Aghion and Fabrizio Zilibotti (2002) "Distance to Frontier, Selection, and Economic Growth", NBER Working Paper no 9066.

Aghion, Philippe, Leah Boustan, Caroline Hoxby and Jerome Vandenbussche (2005) 'Exploiting States' Mistakes to Evaluate the Impact of Higher Education on Growth', mimeo, Harvard University.

Aghion, Philippe and Peter Howitt (1992) 'A Model of Growth through Creative Destruction', *Econometrica*, vol. 60, pp. 323–51.

Aghion, Philippe and Peter Howitt (1998) *Endogenous Growth Theory* (MIT Press).

Barro, Robert and Jong-Wha Lee (2000) 'International Data on Educational Attainment: Updates and Implications', Working Paper No 42, Center for International Development at Harvard University.

Benhabib, Jess and Mark Spiegel (1994) 'The Role of Human Capital in Economic Development: Evidence from Aggregate Cross-Country Data', *Journal of Monetary Economics*, vol. 34, pp. 143–73.

Bils, Mark and Peter Klenow (2000) 'Does Schooling Cause Growth?' *American Economic Review*, vol. 90, pp. 1160–83.

Gerschenkron, Alexander (1962) *Economic Backwardness in Historical Perspective* (Cambridge, Mass.: Harvard University Press).

Ha, Joonkyung and Peter Howitt (2005) 'Accounting for Trends in Productivity and R&D: a Schumpeterian Critique of Semi-Endogenous Growth Theory', mimeo Brown University.

Krebs, Tom (2003) 'Human Capital Risk and Economic Growth', *Quarterly Journal of Economics*, vol. 118, pp. 709–44.

Krueger, Alan and Mikael Lindahl (2001) 'Education for Growth: Why and For Whom?', *Journal of Economic Literature*, vol. 39, pp. 1101–36.

Lucas, Robert (1988) 'On the Mechanics of Economic Development', *Journal of Monetary Economics*, vol. 22, pp. 3–42.

Mankiw, Gregory, David Romer and David Weil (1992) 'A Contribution to the Empirics of Economic Growth', *Quarterly Journal of Economics*, vol. 25, pp. 275–310.

Nelson, Richard and Edmund Phelps (1966) 'Investment in Humans, Technological Diffusion, and Economic Growth', *American Economic Review*, vol. 61, pp. 69–75.

Romer, Paul (1986) 'Increasing Returns and Long-Run Growth', *Journal of Political Economy*, vol. 94, pp. 1002–37.
Romer, Paul (1990) 'Endogenous Technical Change', *Journal of Political Economy*, vol. 98, pp. 71–102.
Sapir, Andre et al. (2003) *An Agenda for a Growing Europe* (Oxford: Oxford University Press).
Vandenbussche, Jerome, Philippe Aghion and Costas Meghir (2004) 'Growth, Distance to Frontier and the Composition of Human Capital', mimeo, Harvard-UCL.

6

Analysing Institutional Change: Integrating Endogenous and Exogenous Views

Masahiko Aoki
Stanford University, USA

Consensus seems to have emerged among economists, as well as among other social scientists, that 'institutions matter' for understanding differences in economic performance among different economies over time and space. But, if institutions are nothing more than codified laws, fiats, organizations and other such deliberate human devices, why cannot badly performing economies design (emulate) 'good' institutions and implement them? This question would naturally lead to more fundamental questions: how do institutions change? Or, why do they not change in the ways people would like? An answer depends on the still more fundamental, ontological question of what institutions are. These are thorny questions to economists, who have developed a solid frame of analysis based on the equilibrium principle. Indeed, there does not yet seem to be a clear consensus of what institutions are. Are they exogenous constraints for economic equilibrium or endogenous equilibrium outcomes? If the difference is nothing more than semantic, there would be not much sense in wrangling about the ontological question of defining institutions. However, if it has a bearing on understanding how institutions can or cannot be changed, say, by fiat, then it certainly deserves attention.

This chapter tries to integrate and reconcile the seemingly opposing endogenous and exogenous views of institutions in the literature by the construction of a game-theoretic-like conceptual and analytical framework for understanding the nature of institutional change. Within this framework, institutions are conceptualized as being generated as endogenous outcomes of strategic interplays of various boundedly rational social actors, and in turn, becoming exogenous constraints for further institutional evolution over time and across diverse domains of social interactions. Hopefully, this game-theoretic-like apparatus will be useful not only as a conceptual clarification of institutions, but also for analysing the nature of dynamic interdependencies/ linkages of human behaviour and associated institutions across various domains (economic, social, organizational and political) and over time. An understanding of what institutions are thus becomes inseparable from that of how they can change.

1 The game form and alternative views of institutions

In order to construct a conceptual and analytical framework for understanding institutional dynamics, let us begin with specifying the notion of a 'game form' as its building block. We conceive of it as composed of a pair of the domain and consequence functions. The *domain* is further composed of the set of the activated sets of action choices of all the actors who are mutually relevant in certain kinds of social interactions as will be specified later. With each profile of possible action choices by all the actors, the *consequence function* specifies the particular (objective) consequences of concern to some or all the actors.[1] Formally, we may say that the consequence function maps the domain into a range of consequences (rather than subjective utilities pay-offs). More concretely, the set of actors may include not only natural persons but also organizations (such as the government, corporations and the judiciary). The activated set of action choices of a particular actor may be conditioned by his/her mental state and acquired skills in the case of natural persons, and by the accumulated collective know-how and scope of collective attention in case of an organization. Formally, an actor's set of potential action choices can be of an infinite dimension, but only finite dimensions of it can be seen as activated. The consequence function can be conditioned by available technologies, formally specified rules (such as laws and fiats) and other relevant environmental factors (specified below). Thus, the game form can be considered fixed at one point in time, but should be viewed as historically conditioned. As was pointed out some time ago by Field (1981), it is not possible to construct a history-free game form.

Suppose, given the game form, each actor tries to choose an action (or more generally a plan of actions, each contingent on an evolving state of the domain) that (s)he considers the most desirable according to his/her own preferences given his/her expectations about others' choices (plans) and their joint consequences. Thus the actors of the domain can be conceived of as the players of the game with the rules of the game specified by the consequence function. From here, we use the words actors and players interchangeably. Viewing social interactions among relevant actors as a game should not be seen as idiosyncratic to mathematical game-theorists who have developed elaborate analytical frameworks. Such a view can be traced as far back as the writings of Adam Smith (1759), as well as the writings of prominent scholars of trans-disciplinary orientations, such as Hayek (1973) and Braudel (1958).[2]

The reason why we introduce the utility-independent game form prior to the explicit reference to the game is that it can be useful for pinpointing the differences in alternative notions of institutions and the implied nature of institutional change in the literature. That is, we may distinguish:

- *Institutions as particular players of the game*: For example, Nelson identifies institutions as prominent organizations such as 'industry associations, technical societies, universities, courts, government agencies, legislatures, etc.' (Nelson, 1995, p. 57). Then institutional change may be identified with a domain change in the composition of the actors brought about with the emergence or deliberate invention of new types of organizations (e.g. Silicon Valley firms, revolutionary governments).
- *Institutions as the rules of the game*: This view is held among the so-called new institutional economists as represented by North (1990, 1999) and Williamson (2000). They identify institutions by the formal rules of the game such as constitutions, statutory laws, and contracts, as well as informal rules such as social norms. Such rules can be identified with prior specification of the parameters of the consequence function and/or prior constraints on the sets of 'permissible' action choices. One notable problem with this view is how these rules are enforced. They may be enforced by particular organizations such as the court or social sanctions. However, then the question may be raised as to how the enforcer(s) can be motivated to enforce the specified rules, which leads to the infinite regression of who enforces the enforcer(s), who enforces the latter, *ad infinitum*. Another question is who formulates the formal rules and how is this done? They consider that these rules reflect the beliefs of actors (particularly those who are influential) and can be 'changed by fiat' (see for example North, 1999, chapter 5). In other words, they visualize a kind of hierarchical ordering in which the polity (and the society in the case of social norms) formulates rules for the economic domain. But then how are the rules of the polity (and social interactions) formulated? Are they formulated endogenously in the polity (and through social interactions)? Is there not feedback from the domain of economic transactions to the polity?[3]
- *Institutions as an endogenous equilibrium outcome of the game*: A solution to the problem of infinite regression as noted above can be provided by endogenizing the enforceability question. That is, certain rules of the game may be considered sustainable (self-enforcing) and thus become institutionalized only if all the players, including the enforcer of the rules, regard deviation from it as unbeneficial. In other words, an institution is a Nash equilibrium. This idea has been entertained by various authors, using diverse specifications of the game and associated concepts of equilibrium (see for example, Schotter (1981), Young (1998), Greif (1997), Aoki (2001), Dixit (2004)). In the equilibrium approach, how is the notion of institutional change entertained? By the gradual change of an equilibrium in response to changes in the parameters of the game form? Or, can there be any qualitative, endogenous shift in equilibrium à la Schumpeter?

2 The dual nature of institutions

The differences among the above views, as they stand, may appear sharp. However, let us try to explore a way to reconcile them. We do this step-by-step by considering the interactions and interdependencies of games across domains and over time. As a first step, we introduce the stationary concept of an institution, subtly modifying the equilibrium view. We first provide a formal version expressed in game-theoretic-like language and then an informal one in everyday language.

> *An institution is a summary representation of a Nash equilibrium path out of the many possible, held as the players' shared beliefs about ways in which the game is being repeatedly played.*
>
> *An institution is a salient, self-sustaining feature of human interactions, held as the collective knowledge of almost all the actors about the ways in which they are to act/not to act (contingent on the evolving state).*

A few caveats are immediately due. First of all, the formal definition is free from any specific refinement of the equilibrium concept (such as a sub-game perfect equilibrium, an evolutionarily stable equilibrium, and so on) beyond a Nash so that it is applicable to a variety of games. The Nash concept is nothing but an analytical representation of self-enforceability, or self-sustainability, of a strategic profile, from which a unilateral deviation would not benefit any player. Also, this definition presupposes the multiplicity of equilibrium paths, or equivalently a variety in the patterns of human interactions and thus a variety of institutions. If only one equilibrium path existed, it would be nothing but a mechanical transformation of a natural factor beyond the analytical foci of the social sciences.[4]

In order that all the players' action choices become mutually consistent and sustainable (thus in equilibrium), each player does not need to know the details of the other players' intentions and choices. In addition to fine, idiosyncratic information – 'the knowledge of particular circumstances of time and space' (Hayek, 1945) – relevant to their own choices, it may be sufficient for the players to share knowledge or beliefs summarizing the possible consequences of certain types of their own actions via others' reactions. They may normally take the rule-form: 'If I do such and such, then such and such a consequence will occur (via others' actions).' It is an expectation regarding ways in which the game is being played in the domain. In order for such an expectation or belief to be shared, sustained and relevant, it needs to be consistent with the repeated choices of players. For example, the players can be deterred from importing legally prohibited goods, if they believe that 'if they smuggle, they are likely to be caught by the enforcement officer and penalized according to the law'. However, if it is widely believed that many actors are able to import the goods by bribing the law enforcer and thus escape punishment, such beliefs cannot be sustained. The unenforceable law is hardly qualified to be an institution, but the expectation regarding the corrupt law enforcer does qualify.

The institution as defined possesses some subtle dual characteristics. First, there is an endogenous–exogenous duality. Once established, the institution may appear as an exogenous external constraint for each individual actor in his choice of actions which are beyond his control. In the above example, there may be two equilibria and accordingly two institutions: an institution of the rule of law and an institution of bribery. If the rule-of-law institution prevails, then compliance with the law would appear imperative for an individual actor to avoid a penalty. An attempt to smuggle the legally prohibited goods by bribing the enforcement officer would appear futile (except as a random event). Alternatively, in the bribery institution, an attempt by an honest enforcement officer to enforce the law may be frustrated. However, if each institution is to be sustained, corresponding beliefs need to be continually reconfirmed and reproduced by relevant strategic equilibrium plays by the players.[5] Thus the difference between the rules-of-the-game view and the endogenous-outcome-of-the-game view of institutions may be thought of as only arising on different facets of the same entity.

Second, there is an objective–subjective duality. The institution exists as an objective reality because its validity can be tested by an actual choice. For example, the objectivity of the belief that smuggling will be punished can be tested and experienced by actually violating the law. On the other hand, unless it constitutes the internal beliefs of the players, any rule may be irrelevant to their action choices and thus may not be institutionalized. For example, even when the objective existence of a statutory law on the books is unquestionable, if nobody believes it can be implemented and thus relevant, it will not prevail as an institution. This dual characterization indicates the difficulty of changing an institution just by enacting a law. A law may certainly change actors' expectations, but whether they will yield a sustainable outcome consistent with the original intention of the legislature cannot be taken for granted. In a sense, an institution may be thought of as a collective mind-set.[6]

The third duality is a constraining/enabling one. An institution constrains each player's action choices through beliefs implied by it. Indeed, North once defined institutions simply as 'humanly devised constraints that shape human interaction' (1990, p. 3). However, an institution also enables the boundedly rational, information-constrained actors to arrive at mutually consistent choices in an information-efficient manner. This is somewhat analogous to the situation in which the equilibrium market prices summarize information regarding the preferences and technologies facing market participants in the most information-efficient way (they represent the marginal rates of substitution and transformation) for sustaining equilibrium.[7] Each market participant only needs to know prices, of which dimension is equivalent to the number of goods minus one (one good being the *numeraire*). A difference exists, however, in that what is implied in an institution is not a summary representation of exogenous data (in the neoclassical setting) of the game such as technology and preferences, but a summary representation of the players' intentions regarding how to play at equilibrium. Each player may collect information and form expectations regarding other players' choices and intentions in a manner idiosyncratic to his own choices. Therefore there may be wide differences and variety in how finely their information sets are partitioned. However, each player cannot, and need not, know the choices of all other players in their entirety. It may be sufficient for them to share some rough idea regarding how the game is repeatedly played in certain respects, although some others may utilize more detailed (finer) information in the same respect. Then an institution may be perceived as the extent of beliefs/knowledge of the players shared by all of them and consistent with the on-going equilibrium play.[8] In that sense it is a summary representation of equilibrium but not equilibrium as such. But being guided by such information boundedly rational players can economize on information processing and still arrive at mutually consistent choices, although there is no guarantee whatsoever that its outcome is the most efficient one as in a Walrasian equilibrium.

Figure 6.1 may be of some help to represent the dualistic natures of an institution.

3 Prototypes of the domain and associated institutions

So far we have imagined the generic game played in an abstract domain where the parameters are represented by the game form. We have conceptualized an institution, arising as a summary representation of the equilibrium outcome of the game. However, actual institutional dynamics appear to

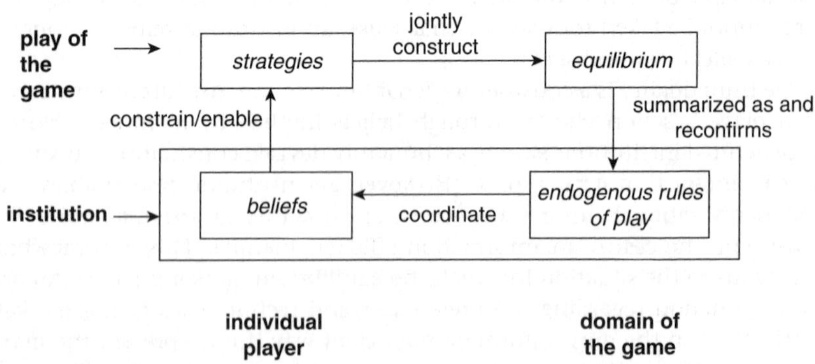

Figure 6.1 An institution as shared beliefs cum summary representation

involve interactions of economic, political, social and organizational factors.[9] As a first step toward the analytical treatment of such an interactive process, this section attempts to specify prototypes of domains that may be useful for capturing minimally essential elements of those interactive factors. The following section seeks to capture the generic nature of the interactions among those factors in the contexts of the games across those domains.

Let us consider the following six prototypes of the domain distinguished by types of players and types of interactive choices. We note for each of them a unique problem that must be solved in order to sustain interactions (exchanges) and the types of institutions that may arise in response to such problems.

- *The economic exchange domain.* This is the domain in which transactions of private goods take place. The most primitive type is the domain composed of only two actors who can potentially repeat the transactions over time. As Hicks once noted, even the simplest exchange of this type is essentially a 'contract': making the agreement to exchange, delivery one way, and delivery the other. 'Trading is trading in promises' (Hicks, 1969). How can this bilateral promise be assured and fulfilled? This is essentially the problem of contract enforcement. A simple institution that can arise in response to this problem is the reputation mechanism, called trust: belief that the default on a contract will be penalized by the other party by refusing to exchange in the future. However, if a large number of domains of this simple kind are bundled together into a complex network with a medium of money, an effective reputation mechanism may not be feasible any more, because the information necessary for identifying and penalizing past cheaters may become increasingly difficult to disseminate. This difficulty can anticipate a solution that can only be facilitated by linking the game in this domain to one in another domain.
- *Domains of the commons.* This is the domain in which common goods are consumed, as well as replenished through collective efforts. The problem unique to this type of domain is the 'tragedy of commons' due to the overconsumption of the goods and/or the shirking of efforts to sustain them. If it is technologically feasible to exclude particular players from the domain, then self-closed institutions such as the establishment of customary property rights, collective norms of consumption and efforts of maintenance and the like, may cope with the problem.[10] But, if not, then these solutions may become problematical.
- *The organizational exchange domain.* The organization may be a player of the game in an economic-exchange domain.[11] At the same time the organization itself may be regarded as constituting a domain of the game involving multiple actors. A prototype of this domain can be conceptualized as one in which the actors are divided into two classes: the helmsman (superordinate, manager) and the at-least-two operatives (subordinates, workers).[12]

The former formulates the collective objective, decomposes the collective task for achieving it into modular tasks and assigns each of them to a particular operative together with the provision of incentives/penalties. The operatives respond with cooperation/non-cooperation in assigned tasks. However, aspects of interactions within this prototype domain may not necessarily be exhausted as a mere bundling of such economic-like exchanges of incentives and acceptance of commands (cooperation). In order for an organization to formulate and pursue the collective objective, complex information exchanges will take place between the helmsman and the operatives as well as across the operatives. Indeed, an organization can be regarded as an information system linking the actors. Through interactions among the actors, a certain pattern of information exchange can be institutionalized.[13] But we will see that this pattern may well be conditioned by the ways in which the organization interacts with other domains (or more simply the ways in which the organization interacts with other actors as a player in other domains).[14]

The three prototype domains introduced above have traditionally been the objects of study in economics, business economics and organization theory, while political and social factors have been taken as the given environments in those analyses. However, recently there has been a growing awareness among social scientists that there are actually important interactions between economic domains, on one hand, and social and political factors, on the other. In order to capture these interactions and the possible institutional linkages between them, we first conceptualize the following two prototype domains.[15]

- *The political exchange domain.* This domain in its prototype may be conceived of as being composed of two types of actors: the government and multiple private actors. This asymmetric structure is somewhat similar to that of the prototype organizational-exchange domain. They are different, however, in that in the organizational domain the members have the option to participate or not, but in the political exchange domain the exit option is not open to the actors. The government protects/transgresses the rights of private actors (property rights, the right to live and so on) in exchange for certain returns (taxes, prestige, etc.). The private actors respond by supporting/resisting/submitting to the government's choice with/without mutual coordination among themselves. Even in this simple game structure a variety of different equilibria can arise, depending on the ways in which coalitions between the government and particular private actors, as well as those among the private actors, are formed. These equilibria can be identified as institutions of the state.[16]
- *The social exchange domain.* This domain may be conceptualized as the one in which social symbols (languages, rituals, gestures, gifts, etc.) that

directly affect the payoffs of players, such as esteem, emotional rejection, sympathy, benign neglect, and so on, are unilaterally delivered and/or exchanged with 'unspecified obligations to reciprocate', sometimes accompanied by gift-giving (Blau, 1964). Institutions that arise in this type of domain are identified with social customs and norms enforced by the threat of social ostracism from the domain, gradational rankings (stratification) of prestige/social status among the actors, etc.[17] Norms are taken as exogenous rules for the 'economic exchange' game in the North–Williamson framework, but their production and reproduction may be susceptible to game-theoretic analysis, to which we return shortly.

We have identified five prototypes of institutions. However, an equilibrium of the game, and consequently an institution, may not arise in a single domain independently of other domains. Rather, institutions are likely to arise across the domains linking games within them and/or institutions in different domains may be interdependent and reinforcing through the interdependence of strategic choices across them in a quasi-parametric manner, leading to a complex overall structure of institutional arrangements.

4 The coherent structure of institutional arrangements across domains

In this section we discuss institutional linkages across the domains using a game-theoretic apparatus. One of the important advantages of the game-theoretic approach to institutions indeed lies in the possibility that the intuitively appealing and plausible notion of institutional interdependencies, coherence and robustness is made analytically tractable rather than presented as an *ad hoc* presumption. From the game-theoretic perspective, there can be two types of institutional linkages: linked games and strategic complementarities. Let us take them up in turn.

Linked games: Games are 'linked', if one or more players coordinates his own choices of strategies across more than one domain so as to gain more pay-offs than the sum that could be gained from playing separately in each of these domains. The reason for this possibility is that by doing so these players can benefit from externalities such that possible gains in one domain can be transferred to another to sustain some strategic profile that would not be profitable in isolation. For example, suppose that there is a commons domain where actors who misuse the commons (abuse, shirking of maintenance efforts, and the like) cannot be excluded from using them for technological reasons so that the reputation mechanism cannot be implemented. However, if the members of the commons domain all belong to a same social exchange domain where large social surpluses can be created by cooperation in rituals, festivities, and assistance in times of private hardships and the like, then misbehaviour in the commons domain can be punished by ostracism in the social exchange domain. (See Aoki (2001) chapter 2, for such a model.) This is an instance where the reputation mechanism may become self-enforcing by linking games even if players are short-sighted and/or cannot be excluded in one particular domain. Specifically, the tragedy of commons can be controlled when the commons domain is embedded in a tight social exchange domain. Essentially the same mechanisms are found in a variety of situations such as: the natural environment that is protected by the community of citizens who share the same values; and free contributions to open-source software development made by individual engineers who aim to enhance their professional reputations, etc.

This type of linkage mechanism corresponds to the sociological notion of 'social embededness' due to Granovetter. It is particularly worth noting that the author made an explicit reference to the endogeneity of norms as well as their strategic nature from a sociological perspective. He argued that 'agents in markets and organizations in the modern society generate trust and discourage malfeasance by being embedded in concrete personal relations and structures (networks)'. The norms and values are not a one-time influence but an ongoing process, continuously needing to be constructed and reconstructed through interactions. In other words, values and norms may be perceived as exogenously received by individuals, though actually they are endogenously shaped by them 'in part for *their own strategic reasons*' (1985, p. 57. Italics by the present author).

Another type of linked games of institutional relevance can be found in the *bundling* of multiple similar or disparate domains. For example, a single employer can bundle multiple employment contracts with workers. Then an equilibrium may emerge that can elicit higher levels of effort from each worker than would be possible under a single contract, because the threat of terminating a contract with a worker who shirks and replacing him/her with another becomes more credible, provided that the employer can prevent collusion among the workers (Murdock, 1996). The economic exchange domains thus bundled are then transformed into a prototype of an organizational domain as defined above. A somewhat similar example is found in the financing of multiple entrepreneurial projects of similar types by a single financier (venture capitalist). In spite of multiple financing costs, multiple contracts under the threat of termination before completion of the project may be beneficial to the financier because they can broaden future options in the presence of high developmental uncertainty. Further, by promising to share a large prize only with the most successful entrepreneur, this type of bundling may also elicit higher developmental efforts by entrepreneurs because of its tournament-like situation. The possibilities of the option value and externalities created by the tournament are considered two fundamental institutional features of the entrepreneurial competition as observed in Silicon Valley. (See Aoki and Takizawa, 2002, for such a model.)[18]

Examples in the above paragraph are of bundling by a single player internal to each of the bundled domains of similar types (employer, financier). Bundling may also be institutionalized by a third party external to domains. Suppose, for example, that the reputation mechanism cannot sustain honest exchanges (mutual contract compliances) between two anonymous traders because they are not expected to meet again. However, if multiple domains of this sort are bundled with an intermediary who can disseminate information regarding the past contractual compliances of the actors, the two-person reputation mechanism can be effectively replicated, provided that honest information processing and dissemination by the third party can be motivated by his/her own reputation concerns (note that we treat the third party as a strategic player). The Law Merchants (Milgrom, North and Weingast, 1990), credit bureaux, escrow services, on-line certification authorities and auction-sites are examples of such third parties. It is important to note that third parties in bundling are by themselves strategic players and they should be treated as such in an analysis of institutionalization.

Still more complex linked games exist between domains of different types. As suggested, the organizational exchange domain may internally generate particular modes of information-systemic and organizational-architectural characteristics. But those characteristics may not be sustainable by themselves. The members of the organization, the helmsman and the operative alike, may also be active actors in particular economic exchange domains (such as financial, labour and political exchange domains) and coordinate their own internal and external strategies. As a result a complex institutional structure, known as corporate governance, may evolve across those domains.[19]

Institutional complementarities: In linked games each actor or a particular actor coordinates his/her own strategic choices across domains and generates a single institution (equilibrium). Alternatively, we can conceive of the possibility that, even if actors may not consciously coordinate their own choices across domains, they regard an institution in another domain as a parameter and accordingly choose strategies in their own domains, and *vice versa*. In such situations, institutions evolving in each of these domains may become interdependent and mutually reinforcing. This intuition can be game-theoretically warranted. Suppose simply that x′ and x″ are two alternative institutions (equilibrium outcomes) in domain X, while z′ and z″ are two alternative institutions in domain Z. Suppose that the utility difference U(x′) – U(x″) increases for all the players in domain X (they do not need to have the same utility function), when z′ rather than z″ prevails in domain Z. By the same token, suppose that the utility difference V(z′) – V(z″) increases for all the players in domain Z (they may be partially or totally overlapped with those in domain X), when x′ rather than x″ prevails in X. Then the games in X and Z are said to be super-modular, and x′ and z′ (alt. x″ and z″) are said to complement each other. If the super-modular condition holds, then the equilibrium combination can be either (x′, z′) or (x″, z″).[20] Further, even if one of them is less efficient in terms of Pareto-ranking, it may still prevail as an equilibrium (an overall institutional arrangement), once it is achieved.

This is a powerful and useful analytical tool for institutional analysis. First, as just mentioned, it explains why there can be a variety of overall institutional arrangements across economies, even if the economies face the same types of domain characteristics (such as technologies or common markets connecting them), as well as why a sub-optimal overall institutional arrangement can persist. Second, institutional complementarities are not necessarily conditional on consensus among actors in domain X regarding the absolute ranking of x′ versus x″ (i.e. it is not required that $U(x') - U(x'') > 0$). Only a weaker agreement in the direction of change in their 'relative' preferences associated with a parametric change in z matter. Thus the emergence and sustenance of an overall institutional arrangement may become stable and robust even if there is a conflict of interests among the actors about the absolute preference for a component institution in isolation.

For example, suppose that the manager prefers retaining the exclusive rights of managerial prerogatives over work within his/her own firm, but wages are set by a corporatist agreement and enforced by the state, as in Germany, rather than through individual contracts. Then the manager's dislike of workers' participating in work control through co-determination and the works council may be somewhat mitigated, because yielding a partial control of rights to the workers may substitute for the missing pecuniary incentives. Then the works council in the organizational-exchange domain and corporatism in the political-economic exchange domain would become institutionally complementary to each other, while the combination of exclusive managerial prerogatives and individual wage contracts would become another possibility.[21]

5 How institutional change occurs

Even if the nature of the overall institutional arrangements can be understood in equilibrium terms, it does not mean that institutions will not change. It would if there could be a substantial equilibrium shift. However, because we have conceptualized an institution as a summary representation of salient features on an equilibrium path, gradual changes in equilibrium as a passive response to continual changes in the parameters of the game form may not be immediately reflected in the form of an institution. In that sense, institutions can be robust and inertial even if the environment of the game is continually changing to a certain extent. Then, when and how does a qualitative change in equilibrium occur that will necessitate a corresponding change in its summary representation? In this section, we consider the generic nature of an institutional change in a domain. In the next section we consider dynamic interactions of institutional changes across domains in a relatively more concrete fashion.

While the game is repeatedly played, the parameters of the game form may gradually change. These parameters may include the mental states and skill levels of the actors that condition the scope and impact of their choices, as well as technologies that define the ways in which their choices are transformed. However, these changes may rather be regarded as partially endogenous in the sense of being induced through the repeated plays of the game and thus patterned after them. Therefore Greif (2006) aptly calls the parameters of the game form 'quasi-parameters'. And because of this quasi-parametric nature, these changes may in turn reinforce the sustenance of an institution, i.e. the salient patterns of plays. But as the patterns of plays repeat and expand, the accumulated consequences can start to generate some inconsistencies *vis-à-vis* the environment of the domain, as are evidenced by the depletion of natural environments and stocks of natural resources increase in friction with the order of surrounding domains (including foreign markets) and the like. In this situation, mutant strategies that have been suboptimal but randomly generated may start to exhibit increasing viability. Also, searches for, and experiments with, new types of strategies consistent with the emergent environments may be earnestly initiated. In other words, actors may seek to expand their activated sets of choices. When such deviations from the existing patterns of playing occur beyond a certain threshold, and the actors' beliefs in the sustainability of existing patterns of playing become problematic, the existing institution may be said to face an *institutional crisis*. Competition between searches for new types of playing on one hand and efforts to preserve the existing pattern of playing on the other may become keener. This competition may eventually result either in convergence to a new equilibrium, the persistent dominance of the existing pattern of playing, or utmost chaos. Concrete cases of these possibilities need to be examined, but we can make comments on two generic points here.

When new types of strategic choices are searched for and experimented with *vis-à-vis* old patterns of strategic choices, what kinds of forces will be operating in this process? Especially, even if there are many possible alternative equilibria, how is one particular equilibrium selected? First, selection may be influenced by the entrepreneurial players pursuing a new type of bundling with predictive beliefs in the viability and/or desirability of a prospective equilibrium, as well as by a charismatic leader/political organization that makes a particular direction of change a 'focal point' through its normative beliefs in the nature of the future equilibrium. Second, the dominating political organization may try to implement its political beliefs through the enactment of statutory laws.[22] What influence does a statutory law have on the formation of new institutions in other domains? Further, does the political initiative only go one-way? In other words, is there no feedback mechanism from other domains to the political-exchange domain? Since the enactment of statutory law may be conceived of as a consequence of strategic interplays in the political domain, the above questions may be reformulated in a more generic form: How do domains interact in the process of institutional change? We argue below that the very same mechanisms that lead to the coherence of the overall institutional arrangements can operate as factors that facilitate or deter institutional change in the longer term.

6 The mechanisms of institutional change

We suggest that there may be two types of generic mechanisms operating in the process of institutional change across domains: (1) linking the same or different domains in a novel way; and/or (2) the creation of a momentum for making hitherto unobserved or sub-optimal choices viable and subsequently establishing and even creating, a new type of domain through complementary interactions across domains. These two types of mechanisms can operate conjointly in a complex manner in the actual process of institutional change, but we begin by treating them separately.

Schumpeterian disbundling and new bundling. We hinted that one aspect of the formation of the firm can be understood as the bundling of multiple employment contracts. The historical emergence of the factory system can be considered in that light as an institutional innovation by the entrepreneurs to provide effective discipline over the workers rather than as merely an adaptive response to technological change. By the same token, the reverse trend from the integrated organizational architecture of the modern corporate firm as envisioned by Chandler (1977) to the spin-offs of hitherto internalized activities to outsourcing, as well as the formation of a supply chain by independent firms, can be thought of as institutional innovations through the reconfiguration of bundling. Also equilibrium shifts from internalized bundling to third-party mediated bundling are often found in the process of institutional change. The emergence of modular entrepreneurial firms in Silicon Valley, whose competition is mediated by venture capital financing, is one example.[23] For another, business groups including trading companies, often emerge in developing economies as ways of enforcing contracts when the rule of law by the state has not been firmly established. However, as professional competence in designing, agreeing upon, and enforcing contracts becomes more available, the relative economic value of the trading company in mediating intra-group transactions may gradually decline. However, even when the institutional value of the grouping gradually erodes, a group may strive for survival in pursuit of the monopoly rents that result from exclusive bundling. An institutional change from corporate grouping to more open contractual relationships governed by a third party (such as the court) is likely to involve a Schumpeterian entrepreneurial challenge, countered by political, economic and social resistance by the old group. Rebundling and disbundling cannot be realized simply with a legislator's pen-stroke.

Overlapping social embeddedness. Let us imagine that the choice set of the actors potentially includes all physically possible action choices (possibly of infinite dimensions), but that the player activates only his/her small subset of finite dimensions as a 'repertoire' of actual choices at any point of time.[24] In general, the player may change this repertoire over time by adding new choice possibilities and deleting those that are obsolete in response to available technological changes and the development of skills, as well as changes in his/her own physical and mental states shaped by training, experience, perception of the external world, etc. However, the speed of this change may vary depending on the type of domain. The choice possibilities open to actors, and accordingly to equilibrium strategy profiles, may change relatively slowly in the social-exchange domain, while those in the organizational exchange domain may change relatively faster, because the organizational architecture may be susceptible to design competition among entrepreneurs subject to constraints imposed by complementary institutions (such as labour and capital markets). Thus it is possible that the same type of choice profile in the social-exchange domain can link itself with different choice profiles in other domains. In other words, the same type of social norms may embed different institutions in other domains over time in an overlapping manner.[25]

For example, consider the opening of exchange opportunities with outside merchants facing a rural community in the pre-capitalist period where the social norm of cooperation in the management of the commons, such as the irrigation system, had prevailed. Until the resurgence of institutional economics in the late twentieth century, various social science disciplines, including economics, sociology and anthropology, have tended to draw a sharp line between community relationships in the pre-capitalist economy and market relationships in the capitalist economy. But the presence of social norms as an institutional device to promote and sustain cooperation in the rural community can facilitate, or deter, its transition to a market economy, contingent on the historical conditions prevailing there. In some cases, the presence of social norms may serve as a transitory mechanism of contract enforcement in the underdevelopment of the rule of law governing the economic exchange domain. It can do so by facilitating collective punishment on breaches of contracts by merchants from the outside, while restraining their own breaches through peer monitoring in order to preserve their collective reputation to outside markets. Cases of these possibilities drawn from experiences in East Asia are documented and their theoretical implications were examined in Aoki and Hayami (2001).

Dynamic institutional complementarities: The concept of static institutional complementarities has a natural dynamic version formulated in the Momentum Theorem by Milgrom, Qian and Roberts (1991). Liberally rephrased, it holds that, even if the initial level of human competence in domain X conducive to the support of potential institution x′ is low, the presence of complementary institutions in other domains may amplify the impact of a policy intended to induce x′, and that once momentum is initiated, x′ may gradually evolve as a viable institution. Conversely, even if laws are introduced to induce institution x′, the absence of complementary institutions and supporting competence in this and other domains may make its realization difficult.

One example is the role played by the institutional infrastructure of contract implementation in Hong Kong in the transition of the Chinese economy to a market economy. It is now well-recognized that China's remarkable growth since reform was initiated in the late 1970s and was largely driven by foreign direct investments and commodity exports. By 1977, however, the Chinese economy was virtually closed to the world market economy, while the domestic economy was largely governed by a command system. How could such an economy attract massive foreign investments in spite of regulations over the remittance of investment returns to home countries? How could it be expected to entertain export contracts in the absence of an effective rule of law governing domestic market exchanges? In fact, large portions of capital inflow and commodity exports were mediated through Hong Kong (Shinohara, 2002), where the legal infrastructure of contract implementation and enforcement was relatively well-developed and the associated competence of individuals in law, accounting, consulting, transportation logistics and foreign languages was already in place or was relatively easily acquired from abroad. Once the Chinese economy became involved in exchange relationships with outside markets, it was able to gradually develop its own competence through complementary reinforcement by the infrastructure in Hong Kong.

7 Conclusion: history and the dual nature of institutions again

We started with the concept of the domain of the game delineated by the game form and then conceptualized institutions as an equilibrium outcome of the strategic interplays of the players in the domain. Then we proceeded to prototype economic, social, political and organizational exchanges in the form of specific domain characteristics and examined possible mechanisms of strategic interdependencies across them to form a coherent, overall institutional arrangement. Finally, we discussed how such interdependencies operate dynamically to condition the direction of institutional change when the equilibrium supporting the overall institutional arrangement is perturbed to a substantial degree.

More specifically, we specified the dynamic mechanisms of Schumpeterian rebundling, overlapping social embeddedness and dynamic institutional complementarities. They are conceptually distinct, but are likely to operate simultaneously and in an interactive manner. While Schumpeterian rebundling can bring more innovative elements into the process of institutional change by destroying old bundling, the overlapping social embeddedness and dynamic institutional complementarities can impact on it with past legacies. However, even innovation-minded Schumpeterian rebundling has to take place in the milieu of complementary institutions/competence inherited from the past while embedded in persistent social norms. On the other hand, overlapping social embeddedness and dynamic complementarities may not necessarily deter institutional innovation. On the contrary, the former may facilitate the transition into a new institutional arrangement, by reproducing the same pattern of social exchanges *vis-à-vis* new emergent domains. The latter may create a momentum for the emergence of a new institution, once complementary links between the old and new domains are initiated.

Thus, institutions in the past and in the future are mutually interlinked in a complex manner. Institutions generated endogenously in one period of time become external constraints and/or enabling facilitators for further institutional dynamics in their own domain as well as beyond. Thus, in a dynamic context the distinction between the endogenous and exogenous views of institutions tends to become blurred; a semantic quarrel over them is fruitless. There are continual and uninterrupted spiral movements for the newly born to be eventually turned into the established, on which basis future innovations will be moulded *ad infinitum*. Both views can be regarded as capturing different aspects of the same entity in incessant motion.

Notes

1. The terminology 'game form' is due to Hurwicz (1996) and distinct from the classical notion of the game defined as 3-tuple of the set of players, the sets of action choices facing them and the profile of pay-off functions over them. In contrast to the pay-off function, which might contain the subjective element of utility, the game form thus defined is meant to capture only objective parameters of the game. By doing so, we can distinguish the different notions of institutions in the literature by focusing on different facets of the game form.
2. Adam Smith refers to 'the great chessboard of human society (in which) every single piece has a principle of motion of its own, altogether different from that which the legislature might chuse to impress upon it' (1759, p. 234). See also the appendix of Hayek (1973). Braudel, the foremost scholar of the French Annales School of History, made an extremely interesting suggestion on the possibility of 'qualitative social mathematics' as tools for comparative and historical analysis, as

well as for crossing lines of different social science disciplines. He was inspired by 'the games of Von Neumann and Morgenstern' (Braudel 1958/1980, particularly pp. 38–52).

3. I discussed these two problems of the view of institutions as rules-of-the-game in greater detail in Aoki (2001), ch.1. Also see Grief (1997, 2006).
4. The multiplicity was emphasized by Sugden (1986) as a precondition of the equilibrium conceptualization of conventions.
5. This exogenous–endogenous duality was the focal point of the phenomenological approach to the sociology of knowledge by Berger and Luckmann (1966).
6. North writes, 'Belief systems are the internal representation and institutions the external manifestation of that representation' (1999, p. 9). However, while North seems to have mainly cultural beliefs and the like on his mind, we refer to beliefs as 'expectations' about ways the game is played at this point of the discussion.
7. See Hayek (1945), Koopmans (1957) and Hurwicz (1960).
8. Technically speaking, the institution thus defined is equivalent to an equilibrium-containing cell (information set) of the finest partition on the set of strategic choices, which is coarser than the partition of any player (see Fagin et al., 1996, pp. 36–40).
9. More generally, one may conceive of types of domains that intersect with other domains and generate cultural values and beliefs, although the ways in which such domains can be analysed in terms of the game have hardly been explored; (see however Kaneko and Matsui, 1999). For an interesting non-game-theoretic exploration, see Ikegami (2005). For the relationships between cultural values and institutions, see Greif (2006), North (1999), Nelson and Sampat (2003).
10. See Aoki (2001), chapter 2.
11. North (1990, 1999) emphatically argues that the organization is a player of the game, but not an institution as are the rules of the game.
12. The terminology 'helmsman' is due to Arrow and Hurwicz (1960). In economics, a prototype organization is often analysed in terms of a two-person contact. But we consider that it is essential to regard the organization as at least a 3-person game.
13. Such a pattern may be thought of as corresponding to the 'routines' in the evolutionary framework of Nelson and Winter (1982). Also see Nelson and Sampat (2003).
14. See 11 above.
15. This framework follows that of Weingast (1993) who considered the democratic state as an equilibrium. We consider the possible multiple equilibria even for this simple prototype.
16. The English words 'stable', 'state' and 'institution' are all said to have been derived from the same Latin word 'status' (standing condition). Thus it seems semantically warranted to conceptualize the 'state' as a political institution to be a stable equilibrium in the political exchange domain. See Aoki (2001, chapter 6) for a variety of prototype states as equilibria.
17. Coleman (1990), Aoki (2001 chs 2.2 and 8).
18. An example of bundling of disparate domains by a single player internal to all of them can be found in 'linked contracts' in the developing economy. See Bardhan (1977).
19. For this, see Aoki (2001), chs 11–14.
20. Topkis (1978), Milgrom and Roberts (1990) and Aoki (2001), ch. 8.
21. See Aoki (2001) ch. 11.2 for a detailed discussion and proof.

22. This last mechanism is the one emphasized by North (1999).
23. This phenomena is discussed in Aoki (2005).
24. The term is due to Dosi and Marengo (1994).
25. Implications of interactions between slow-changing institutions and fast-changing institutions in general are discussed in a recent paper by Roland (2005).

References

Aoki, M. (ed.) (2001) *Toward a Comparative Institutional Analysis* (Cambridge, Mass.: MIT Press).

Aoki, M. (2005) 'Schumpeterian Innovation of Institutions', an invited lecture delivered at the World Congress of the Schumpeter Society, Milan.

Aoki, M. and Y. Hayami (eds) (2001) *Communities and Markets in Economic Development* (Oxford: Oxford University Press).

Aoki, M. and H. Takizawa (2002) 'Information, Incentives, and Option Value: the Silicon-Valley Model', *Journal of Comparative Economics'*, vol. 30, pp. 759–86.

Arrow, K.J. and L. Hurwicz (1960) 'Decentralization and Computation in Resource Allocation', in R.W. Pfouts (ed.), *Essays in Economics and Econometrics* (Chapel Hill: University of North Carolina Press), pp. 34–104.

Bardhan, P. (1977) 'Variations in Forms of Tenancy in a Peasant Economy', *Journal of Development Economics*, vol. 4, pp. 105–18.

Berger, P. and T. Luckmann (1966) *The Social Construction of Reality: a Treatise in the Sociology of Knowledge* (New York: Doubleday Anchor).

Blau, P. (1964/1998) *Exchange and Power in Social Life*, with new introduction (Brunswick, N.J.: Transaction Publishers).

Braudel, F. (1958/1980) 'History and the Social Sciences: The *Longue Duree*', in S. Matthews (trans.), *On History* (Chicago: Chicago University Press), pp. 24–55.

Chandler, A. Jr. (1977) *The Visible Hands: the Managerial Revolution in American Business* (Cambridge, Mass.: Harvard University Press).

Coleman, J. (1990) *Foundations of Social Theory* (Cambridge, Mass.: Harvard University Press).

Dixit, A. (2004) *Lawlessness and Economics* (Princeton, N.J.: Princeton University Press).

Dosi, G. and L. Marengo (1994) 'Some Elements of an Evolutionary Theory of Organizational Competence', in R.W. England (ed.), *Evolutionary Concepts in Contemporary Economics* (Ann Arbor: University of Michigan Press), pp. 157–78.

Fagin, R., J.Y. Halpern, Y. Moses and M.Y. Vardi (1996) *Reasoning about Knowledge* (Cambridge, Mass.: MIT Press).

Field, A.J. (1981) 'The Problem with Neoclassical Institutional Economics: a Critique with Special Reference to the North-Thomas Model of pre-1500 Europe', *Explorations in Economic History*, vol. 18, pp. 174–98.

Granovetter, M. (1985) 'Economic Action and Social Structure: the Problem of Embeddedness', *American Journal of Sociology*, vol. 91, pp. 480–510.

Greif, A. (1993) 'Contract Enforceability and Economic Institutions in Early Trade: the Maghribi Traders' Coalition', *American Economic Review*, vol. 83, pp. 525–48.

Greif, A. (1997) 'Micro Theory and Recent Developments in the Study of Economic Institutions through Economic History', in D. Kreps and K. Wallis (eds), *Advances in Economics and Econometrics: Theory and Applications*, vol. 2 (Cambridge: Cambridge University Press), pp. 79–113.

Greif, A. (2006) *Institutions and the Path to the Modern Economy* (New York: Cambridge University Press).

Hayek, F.A. (1945) 'The Use of Knowledge in Society', *American Economic Review*, vol. 35, pp. 519–30.
Hayek, F.A. (1973) *Law, Legislation, and Liberty*: Rules and Order, vol. 1 (Chicago: University of Chicago Press).
Hicks, J. (1969) *A Theory of Economic History* (Oxford: Oxford University Press).
Hurwicz, L. (1960) 'On the Dimensional Requirements for Non-wasteful Resource Allocation Systems', in K.J. Arrow, S. Karlin, and P. Suppes (eds), *Mathematical Methods in the Social Sciences 1959* (Stanford: Stanford University Press).
Hurwicz, L. (1996) 'Institutions as Families of Game Forms', *Japanese Economic Review*, vol. 47, pp. 13–132.
Ikegami, E. (2005) *Bonds of Civility: Aesthetic Networks and the Political Origins of Japanese Culture* (Cambridge: Cambridge University Press).
Kaneko, M., and A. Matsui (1999) 'Inductive Game Theory: Discrimination and Prejudices', *Journal of Public Economic Theory*, vol. 1, pp. 101–37.
Koopmans, T. (1957) *Three Essays on the State of Economic Sciences* (New York: McGraw-Hill).
Milgrom, P., D. North and B. Weingast (1990) 'The Role of Institutions in the Revival of Trade: the Law Merchant, Private Judges, and the Champagne Fairs', *Economics and Politics*, vol. 2, pp. 1–23.
Milgrom, P., Y. Qian and J. Roberts (1991) 'Complementarities, Momentum, and the Evolution of Modern Manufacturing', *American Economic Review*, vol. 81, pp. 84–8.
Milgrom, P. and J. Roberts (1990) 'Rationalizability, Learning, and Equilibrium in Games with Strategic Complementarities', *Econometrica*, vol. 59, pp. 1255–77.
Murdock, K. (1996) 'The Role of Institutions in Enforcing Implicit Contracts: Analysis of Corporate and Government Policy', Ph.D. dissertation submitted to Stanford University.
Nelson, R. (1995) 'Recent Evolutionary Theorizing about Economic Change', *Journal of Economic Literature*, vol. 33, pp. 48–90.
Nelson, R. and B.N. Sampat (2003) 'Making Sense of Institutions as a Factor Shaping Economic Performance', in G.M. Hodson (ed.), *Recent Developments in Institutional Economics* (Cheltenham: Elgar), pp. 25–48.
Nelson, R. and S. Winter (1982) *An Evolutionary Theory of Economic Change* (Cambridge, MA: Harvard University Press).
North, D. (1990) *Institutions, Institutional Change and Economic Performance* (Cambridge: Cambridge University Press).
North, D. (1999) *Understanding the Process of Economic Change* (London: Institute of Economic Affairs and Princeton, N.J.: Princeton University Press).
Roland, G. (2005) 'Fast-Moving and Slow-Moving Institutions', ch. 7 in this volume.
Schotter, A. (1981) *The Economic Theory of Social Institutions* (Cambridge: Cambridge University Press).
Schumpeter, J. (1912/1934) *The Theory of Economic Development* (Cambridge, MA: Harvard University Press); English translation by R. Opie of *Theorie der Wirtschaftlichen Entwicklung*, 1912.
Shinohara, M. (2002) Chugoku Keizai no Kyodaika to Honkon – Sono Dainamizumu no Kaimei (The Mega-growth of the Chinese Economy and Hong Kong – an Elucidation of its Dynamics), in Japanese (Tokyo: Keiso Shobo).
Smith, A. (1759/1976) *The Theory of Moral Sentiments* (Oxford: Oxford University Press).
Sugden, R. (1986) *The Economics of Rights, Cooperation and Welfare* (Oxford: Basil Blackwell).

Topkis, D. (1978) 'Minimizing a Submodular Function on a Lattice', *Operations Research*, vol. 26, pp. 305–21.
Weingast, B. (1993) 'Constitutions as Governance Structures: the Political Foundations of Secure Markets', *Journal of Institutional and Theoretical Economics*, vol. 149, pp. 286–311.
Williamson, O.E. (2000) 'The New Institutional Economics: Taking Stock, Looking Ahead', *Journal of Economic Literature*, vol. 38, pp. 595–613.
World Bank (2002) *World Development Report 2002: Building Institutions for Markets* (New York: Oxford University Press).
Young, H.P. (1998) *Individual Strategy and Social Structure: an Evolutionary Theory of Institutions* (Princeton, NJ: Princeton University Press).

7

Fast-Moving and Slow-Moving Institutions*

Gérard Roland
University of California, Berkeley, USA

1 Introduction

Understanding the conditions for successful economic growth and development is becoming an increasingly central question in economics. It is the same question that Adam Smith was asking in 1776 when he founded the discipline. For many decades, the central question in economics concerned the comparison of markets and hierarchies in the allocation of resources, and was the focus of the entire general equilibrium programme, but its importance in economics receded with the collapse of central planning. More recently, the very diverse performances of various developing countries and countries in the process of transition from socialism to capitalism have revived the 'Adam Smith question'. For example, why has the growth performance of Russia been so dismal in its first decade of transition, whereas China has been growing at over 8 per cent per year throughout its two decades of transition? Why has the Argentine economy, one of the richest in the world in the early twentieth century, more or less collapsed? Why have the 'Asian tigers' experienced a successful economic take-off, whereas the economies of most African countries have been decimated by misery, war, and disease?

The Adam Smith question is not only central in the economics of development; it is also central in economic history and transition economics. Why the early success of Britain? Why the failure of Spain to take off when Britain was industrializing? How can one explain the success of some of the latecomers to industrialization (Gerschenkron, 1962) and the 'modernization failures' in Egypt and large parts of the former Ottoman empire? Whereas these questions can only be answered by digging into the past, the transition

* I am grateful to Erik Berglöf, Grigore Pop-Eleches, Thad Dunning, and especially Ruth Collier for very helpful comments. I also thank seminar participants at the World Bank. An earlier version was published in *Studies in Comparative International Development*, vol. 38(4) 2004, pp. 109–31.

experience of the 1990s was both a testing ground for the traditional body of economic theory and an invaluable source of new information about conditions for successful capitalist development. It has been a humbling experience for the so-called Washington Consensus and has unveiled many weak spots in the certainties of the economics profession (see Roland, 2002). It has also raised new questions and puzzles, the most important one being the Chinese 'economic miracle' following a strategy quite removed from the one recommended by the Washington Consensus.

The revival of the Adam Smith question has been associated with increased support for the institutionalist school in economics (North, 1990; Williamson, 1975, 1985; and others). Paraphrasing Nixon, we can say 'We are all institutionalists now.' However, there are by now probably as many interpretations of the new institutionalist bible as there are different Protestant churches. What do we mean by institutions? What are the relevant institutions for successful development? Are they complements? Substitutes? Is there one 'first-best' set of institutions, or is the optimality of institutional systems country-specific? To what extent can 'optimal institutions' be imported? How does institutional change occur? How can a country improve its institutions? All of these questions are important, and few have yet received a convincing answer.

In this chapter, I try to make some progress in providing a conceptual framework that would allow us to tackle these questions. It is not my purpose to survey the literature on institutions within the field of economics, but I will discuss some of the contributions along the way. First, I discuss the approaches to institutions in the discipline of economics. Next, I propose a classification of institutions to provide a basis for understanding the interactions among institutions and institutional change. I distinguish between sets of institutions based on whether they change *slowly* and *continuously* or *rapidly* and *irregularly*. I term the former 'slow-moving' and the latter 'fast-moving' institutions. What is often called 'culture', including values, beliefs, and social norms, can be classified as a slow-moving institution. The evolution of culture is closely related to the evolution of technology and scientific knowledge, which obviously plays an important role in understanding growth. Like culture, technology evolves slowly and continuously, although the pace may vary.

Fast-moving institutions do not necessarily change often but can change more quickly – sometimes nearly overnight. Political institutions can be classified as fast-moving institutions. In this chapter, I take an initial look at the interaction between slow-moving and fast-moving institutions and argue that the analysis of the interaction between the two types can shed light on institutional change (why it occurs, how, and when). I suggest some preliminary hypotheses, such as the difficulty of transplanting institutions into different cultural contexts. Finally, I offer some policy implications.

2 Posing the institutional question in economics

One of the main problems in institutional economics is that there exist myriad institutions in an economic system. Economists have taken different approaches to understanding institutions as they attempt to understand which institutions are relevant for growth and development.

2.1 What do I mean by institutions?

In order to identify the relevant institutions, one must first ask exactly what is meant by 'institutions'. North (1990, p. 3) defines institutions as constraints on behaviour imposed by 'the rules of the game' in society: 'Institutions include any form of constraint that human beings devise to shape human interaction.' This definition includes formal and informal institutions. It is a very broad definition in that it includes in particular social norms and all other constraints imposed by a society's system of beliefs and values. In that regard, from North's perspective it does not make sense to distinguish between 'institutions' on the one hand and 'culture' on the other as fundamentally different causal mechanisms to explain growth and development; both are institutional causes, simply different ones. North, however, explicitly excludes organizations as institutions; for example, he considers banks to be organizations, not institutions. Yet the banking system itself is shaped by the institutional system (laws and regulations related to the financial system).

Economists have modelled institutions in two alternative ways: either as exogenously given constraints on behaviour (following North) or as endogenously appearing self-enforcing rules that are the equilibrium of a repeated game (Aoki, 2001; Greif, 1993, 1994). Institutions have no meaning if the constraints they impose are not enforced. In the exogenous models, enforcement relies (often implicitly) on the role of a third party. Such models therefore have the disadvantage of raising the questions of where these third parties derive their enforcement power and what their incentives are to enforce the rules. By contrast, Aoki's (2001) elegant approach to institutions as endogenous, self-enforcing rules does not simply assume away the difficult question of enforcement. However, this approach is mostly tractable when one looks at relatively simple institutions such as contract enforcement. In many cases, one would need to define the self-enforcing object as a large cluster of institutions. A general equilibrium approach is thus very ambitious but also quite complicated. For purposes of the (partial-equilibrium) analysis of specific institutions, it suffices to take institutions as exogenous and to understand their effects on human behaviour and interaction.

To avoid adding semantic confusion, I take as a starting point North's definition of institutions. The next (and probably more important) question is how to classify different institutions. Some sort of classification is important because, in order to understand an economic system, one must have a conceptual framework to understand the interactions between the various institutions at work within that system.

2.2 Approaches to classifying institutions

2.2.1 The functional approach

A first method of classification, often adopted by economists, is provided by a functional approach, which defines institutions by the needs of efficient contracting and investing: we need property rights to write contracts, bankruptcy laws and courts to enforce the contracts, financial market institutions to secure investment, governments to provide public goods and infrastructure, and so forth. Under the functional approach, a specific institution corresponds to each need. This is a straightforward and natural way to think about institutions.

The functional approach, however, is not without its problems. First of all, it is not straightforward to derive specific existing institutions from the needs they are called upon to fulfil. There are many different bankruptcy laws in the world. How does the functional approach account for this diversity? At best, it can provide – with some help from theory – a prescription for the optimal bankruptcy law contingent on differences in economic circumstances. For example, in an economy where agents are very risk-averse and display little taste for entrepreneurship, a bankruptcy law should not be too punitive towards failed entrepreneurs, whereas bankruptcy laws should be tougher towards debtors in an economy where agents are both very entrepreneurial and prone to cheating to make a quick buck. However, this approach does not explain adequately the choice between different institutional arrangements that fulfil the same function, or why some countries end up with inefficient institutions. A second problem is that it is difficult to say something about systems of institutions other than as an average of individual institutions satisfying particular needs. The functional approach does not tell us how institutions interact.

2.2.2 A macrosystemic approach

A second method for classifying institutions is provided by a macrosystemic approach. Subscribers to this approach start from a descriptive list of different institutions, going from general (political, legal, social) to specific categories; political institutions include, for example, regime type, electoral practice, rules affecting legislative bargaining, and the degree of federalism. This approach helps us to understand the effects of particular institutions and to perform a comparative institutional analysis, one of the main goals of the research agenda of institutional economics. Indeed, institutional description allows us to define an extensive-form game that is not arbitrarily given but that follows the description of the institution. For example, to understand the divergent effects of presidential versus parliamentary democracies, one defines extensive-form games based on the existing constitutional features of the different political systems (e.g. Persson, Roland and Tabellini, 2000). Analysis of the equilibria of those games suggests which institutional details may be relevant and which may not be: the irrelevant details are the ones that, when varied or changed, do not affect the equilibrium of the game. This is a pretty foolproof method, using tools of game theory to determine which institutional details are relevant and which are not.[1]

Not only can the macrosystemic approach provide a natural method for understanding the effects of specific institutions, it also allows us to conceptualize and analyse systems of institutions. For example, recent research has emphasized the different sets of institutions in common law versus civil law countries (La Porta et al., 1998a, 1998b, 1999, 2000); portfolio- versus bank-oriented systems of finance (e.g. Mayer, 1987; Berglöf, 1990); and parliamentary versus presidential systems (Persson et al., 2000); as well as in countries with different electoral rules (e.g. Lizzeri and Persico, 2001; Persson and Tabellini, 1999; Milesi-Ferretti et al., 2002; Persson et al., 2003), federal versus centralized government (Weingast, 1995; Cai and Treisman, 2001); and democracy versus dictatorship (Acemoglu and Robinson, 2005).

Systems of institutions are characterized by complementarities and substitutability of different institutions. This observation raises questions about the interactions among specific institutions within any institutional system. What, for example, are the interactions between antitrust institutions that foster market competition and managerial incentive structures? Between incentive structures and property rights, social norms and legal arrangements, or corporate governance and labour-market institutions? What is the relationship between labour-market institutions and social-insurance systems? How are economic institutions related to electoral rules and other aspects of the political system? Asking these questions about interactions between institutions seems to make the task of understanding institutions even more daunting. One must understand not only myriad real-world institutions but also the interactions among them. The combinations appear astronomically complex.

In practice, however, this is not the case. Kornai (1995), for example, noted a strong congruence among economic institutions for allocation of resources and forms of ownership. Institutional systems are generally not a modular construction where one module can be replaced easily by another. If this were so, 'institutional shopping' would be nearly as easy as supermarket shopping. Institutions generally form a system in the sense that each institution in the system is complemented by others, achieving a certain systemic consistency. Replacing one institution by another can in some cases dangerously disrupt this systemic consistency. Piecemeal institutional change in some directions is made impossible when there are strong complementarities among institutions.

These strong institutional complementarities have figured prominently in debates about the optimal institutional reform strategy from socialism to capitalism in the former communist countries.[2] Post-socialist transition is, however, not the only example. Institutional congruence may help to explain why institutional transformation in Japan appears to be so difficult. The Japanese economy has been ailing for more than ten years, and no fundamental institutional reform has taken place. Reform-minded politicians seem to face insurmountable obstacles.

The existence of complementarities among institutions suggests that analysts should examine systems of institutions and that countries can be classified accordingly. A distinction made by Evans (1989) and picked up by Acemoglu and Robinson (2002) and many others (e.g. Shleifer and Vishny, 1994) is that between 'predatory' and 'developmental' institutions. Predatory institutions allow the minority in power (usually, although not necessarily, under a dictatorship) to use its power to prey upon economic agents, thereby reducing the latter's incentive to invest and produce. Developmental institutions, by contrast, encourage development and growth by providing a 'helping hand' to private agents, providing public goods such as education, infrastructure and incentives to invest. This distinction between predatory and developmental institutions is certainly the most important classification economists can think of, given the interest in the Adam Smith question.

However important this distinction, it is based on outcomes, and does not specifically identify the relevant institutions. What are the predatory institutions? What are the developmental institutions? In other words, what are the main institutional mechanisms that lead to stark differences in growth outcomes? Much empirical research does a poor job of dealing with these questions because the indicators used are mostly surveys among businesspeople and economic agents asking about the security of property rights. Not only are these measures subjective and imprecise, but it is difficult to tell how well they separate perceptions of bad institutions (the cause) and bad economic performance (the effect). Identifying the precise mechanisms leading to predatory and developmental institutions is important from a policy perspective. Are predatory institutions essentially the product of multiple regulations put in place by corrupt bureaucrats to extract bribes? Are they the result of an inadequate separation of power within the government and the bureaucracy? Or are they related to differences in the culture, education and quality of bureaucrats? Clearly, different answers to these questions lead to quite different policy conclusions, reinforcing the need for a better understanding of institutional systems worldwide.

A major empirical challenge is to disentangle the relative importance of different institutions: the quality of the legal system and of law enforcement; the quality and integrity of the bureaucracy; the nature of the political regime, electoral rules and the degree of federalism; social capital; and social norms and values. Ideally, we would be able to measure the separate effects of different institutions or the joint effect of a subset of institutions, but this task is not easy. First of all, as mentioned above, many institutions are strongly correlated. This does not pose too big a problem, however, because factor analysis allows us to deal with a large number of correlated independent variables. One can even argue that factor analysis is a good strategy for empirical research on institutions, because identification of clusters of institutional variables will be very helpful for further conceptualization of institutional systems. A bigger obstacle than correlation is the identification problem; institutions are usually not exogenous but may themselves be the product of other institutional constellations. Are legal arrangements causing social norms, or is it the other way around? Considerable craftsmanship and innovation in datasets will be required to find adequate estimation strategies to tackle those questions.

2.3 Change and persistence of institutions

2.3.1 The functionalist pitfall

We have seen that a functionalist approach poses important problems in the classification of institutions. Functionalism also provides the biggest pitfall in trying to understand institutional change. The functionalist view is that institutions change by necessity in response to a change in their environment that diminishes the efficiency of existing institutions; it does not explain the mechanisms by which change takes place or fails to take place. It is rather like the social scientific equivalent of the Lamarckian view that organisms evolve in order to adapt to changes in their environment (as opposed to the Darwinian view that genetic mutations are random and that, when the environment changes, the mechanism of natural selection promotes the survival of the fittest). While functionalism has been criticized at length and has been deeply discredited in the political and social sciences (e.g. Elster, 1982), it has remained quite alive in economics, where it has a long tradition from Marx to Gerschenkron. In modern economics, functionalist explanations are justified by the assumption (mostly associated with the Chicago school) that economic agents can efficiently bargain to create adequate institutions. Institutions can be seen as the result of some kind of Coasian bargain within society (see Acemoglu, 2003, for a contrary view). Therefore, institutions should in general be both efficient and adapted to the existing social and economic environment.

2.3.2 The persistence of inefficient institutions

Decades ago, however, Olson (1965) refuted the view that institutions are the result of an efficient Coasian bargain, by emphasizing the collective action problems of large groups. The Olsonian view stands in stark contrast to the Chicago view: inefficient institutions may survive for a long time because groups with stakes in institutional change fail to get organized and solve their collective action problem. However, collective action problems are not necessarily the only reason for the persistence of inefficient institutions.

Acemoglu and Robinson (2000, 2001, 2005) have emphasized the commitment problem that governments in general face, since there is usually not a third party to enforce agreements between various groups in society. Whatever group holds power will use that power in its own best interest. Thus, ruling elites who have a vested interest in maintaining their power in societies with inefficient institutions may not agree to give up that power because the winners of institutional change may not be able to commit to compensation schemes for the losers. Inefficient institutions may therefore persist because of the combined effect of social conflict and lack of commitment. For example, the Russian tsarist regime and the Austro-Hungarian Empire were much more resistant to change than Germany. In the former cases, aristocratic interests remained purely in land and had no commercial or industrial interests. The industrial bourgeoisie was seen as a threat to the power of the existing elite (Acemoglu and Robinson, 2002). In Germany, by contrast, the Napoleonic wars had deeply shaken the powers of the landed aristocracy, and the Prussian elite experienced an inter-penetration between industry and land.

So how does change come about? In the Acemoglu–Robinson models, from time to time exogenous and stochastic events give power to certain groups in society. Workers may be disorganized most of the time, but in a crisis are able to unite and have the strength to overthrow the existing regime. This model makes sense: it is important to recognize that the ability of social groups to organize depends partly on existing institutions. Dictatorships tend systematically to repress the collective action of those not in power, whereas democracy provides an institutional framework for the large majority of the poor to solve their collective action problem *via* political competition and elections. This is partly why universal suffrage was such a big battle at the turn of the twentieth century. For the poor, it represented an institutional change that could maintain the momentum of exceptional moments, such as general strikes, in which the collective action problem could be solved momentarily. For the rich, however, the franchise was a way to commit to redistributive transfers toward the poor while avoiding a revolution (Acemoglu and Robinson, 2000).

A key insight from this discussion is that institutions impact the ability of different groups in society to solve their collective action problems. Therefore, institutional change is itself the object of political and social conflicts.

3 A framework for understanding institutional change

In order to have a meaningful understanding of institutions as systems, we need to understand interactions between different institutions; we must also have a way to understand institutional change. To make some progress along these lines, I propose a classification that is based on the capacity of institutions to change rapidly or slowly, and whether or not that change is continuous.

3.1 Fast-moving and slow-moving institutions

I start with a fundamental distinction between slow-moving and fast-moving institutions. The former generally change slowly, incrementally and continuously, whereas the latter are more given to rapid, discontinuous change in large steps. Political institutions, for example, have the potential for centralized decisional changes in large steps. In this sense, they can be fast-moving institutions, which change nearly overnight when there are revolutionary moments. In contrast, social norms are more often an example of slow-moving institutions. While some social norms and values can change very rapidly in historical terms (e.g. a society's tolerance for cigarettes), in general, social norms and values change slowly. Even individual social norms, such as attitudes towards the death penalty or acceptance of corruption, tend to change rather slowly, possibly because many norms are rooted in religions whose basic precepts have changed remarkably little for centuries and even millennia; the major world religions have shaped and still shape the basic values and preferences of individuals, what they consider important in life, and how they expect other people to behave toward them. One can always find examples to the contrary, but values and social norms, seen as a whole, tend to change slowly.

It is not my purpose here to analyse why social norms or values change slowly, but simply to state the fact. An important element, however, is whether or not institutions can change by authoritative decision. Legal systems tend to be faster-moving institutions than social norms but slower-moving than political institutions. A given law can be changed overnight, but legal systems are rarely changed as rapidly as political institutions, such as electoral rules. On the other hand, the effectiveness of the legal system and the enforcement of laws depend on their acceptance and legitimacy in society and on the expectations of many actors. Thus the legal system is very similar to social norms, except that the system of rewards and punishments is legally codified and can be changed more rapidly than social norms, which can never change by *fiat*.

I also add a word about which institutions tend to change continuously and which discontinuously. Compared to social norms, political institutions may change more discontinuously; they may change little for prolonged periods of time, then change very abruptly. Social norms, on the other hand, tend to change continuously, albeit slowly.[3] Legal arrangements are again somewhat in between. While the size of the increments of change and the extent to which change unfolds continuously or discontinuously are not identical concepts, there is an obvious, close relationship between these two aspects of slow- and fast-moving institutions; if steps of change are large but are taken rarely, for example, change occurs discontinuously.

What is the relationship between fast- and slow-moving institutions? Slow-moving institutions are by definition good candidates to influence fast-moving institutions, since the former may change a little at a time when the latter is changing dramatically. On the other hand, for this perspective to make any sense, slow-moving institutions must also change continuously, so as to produce inconsistencies with fast-moving institutions and thereby create pressures for change. An appropriate analogy is an earthquake: pressures along fault lines build up continuously but slowly, then suddenly provoke an earthquake that abruptly changes the topography of a given area. Slow-moving institutions are the equivalent of these tectonic pressures; fast-moving institutions are the equivalent of the topography.

Marx's theory of institutional change has some parallels to the one posed here. What he called 'productive forces' are analogous to slow-moving institutions, in that they change slowly and continuously yet create pressures for change in what Marx termed the 'superstructure' (what I term 'fast-moving institutions'). However, technology was the main component of Marx's productive forces, and technology is not an institution. Thus, the Marxian scheme classified all institutions as part of the superstructure, including (following the philosopher Ludwig Feuerbach) ideas and culture. However, seen as the broader set of both social norms and values, culture is typically a slow-moving institution, one that influences fast-moving institutions. The present model thus differs from that of Marx, and is, in a sense, closer to Max Weber's emphasis on the importance of culture in explaining institutional and economic change. The approach described in this chapter is, in that sense, neo-Weberian.

3.2 Technology, culture and growth

Technology is a fundamental explanatory factor for economists seeking to understand growth. Technology is the accumulated stock of knowledge embodied in human society. Where does technology stand in our analytical scheme? Technology relates to a broader set of beliefs about the operation of the physical world and about the nature of interactions between humans and their physical environment. Culture, by contrast, comprises social norms, which refer to ideas about interactions among human beings, and the broader set of underlying values.

However, culture and technology have many things in common. Both tend to evolve continuously and slowly, although technology may be more prone to irregular bursts of change clustered around particular moments in time. Both involve research and experimentation, trial and error and learning. Education is the acquisition of both technology and culture. Moreover, the evolution of technology and culture is difficult to predict because they obey the laws of the evolution of knowledge: both are subject to unpredicted innovations that emerge in association with random, mutation-like recombinations of subsets of the existing stock of knowledge. These commonalities between culture and technology also mean that they evolve in parallel. Sets of beliefs related to technology influence sets of beliefs related to interactions among humans.

Culture, understood in terms of social norms and underlying values, must therefore be analysed in conjunction with technology and with the growth of knowledge. Just as we are familiar with analysing technological innovation and its role in economic growth, we should also look at cultural innovations and analyse their broad social and economic effects. Examples in history abound. Different societies have throughout history exhibited different attitudes toward manual labour and work in general, toward thrift and usury (and even toward the use of interest rates), toward respect of private property and of creativity, and towards the participation of women in different economic activities. Obviously, these cultural differences have had a profound impact on economic development and growth.

It is in a way strange that most economists have shied away from incorporating cultural differences and cultural innovations in economic analysis.[4] The process of economic growth tends currently to be seen by economists as a combination of technology and institutions. I propose to view institutional change as the interaction between slow-moving institutions, culture in particular, and fast-moving institutions such as political and legal institutions. It is this interaction that drives institutional change, and it is the interaction between institutional change and technology that drives economic growth.

3.3 Interests and institutional change

An important question arises: if Olsonian interests play an important role in processes of institutional change, how should we understand the causal role of slow-moving institutions? Are they redundant as an explanatory factor? Change is driven by social forces that favour it and opposed by social forces that would lose from it. The balance of power between those two groups determines the dynamics of change. Yet, how the relative strengths of forces of change and of conservatism map onto conflict and change also depends on the existing institutions, on how they help or hinder groups in solving their collective action problem, and on how representative and participatory the political institutions are.

While it would, therefore, be wrong to exclude the role of interests from discussions of institutional change, interests are not sufficient either to explain why institutional change takes place or to elucidate the direction of change. The institutional changes that took place in Western Europe in the eighteenth and nineteenth centuries would be difficult to imagine without the intellectual turmoil created by the Renaissance and the ideas of the Enlightenment, which were spread by communication technology such as the printing press. Ideas of equality and human rights led to enormous changes in forms of government, and to the long transition from absolutism to democracy. This contrasts sharply with China, where Confucianism and related ideas were miles away from the Renaissance and Enlightenment ideas. China has experienced time and again large rebellions of peasants (larger than in ancient Rome or feudal Europe), some of which even managed to overthrow the empire. However, given the ideological background of these revolts, most only led to a change of emperor or of dynasty, because the purpose of the rebellion was to replace the emperor with a 'more just' one.

The interests of oppressed groups always play an important role in institutional change. However, the ability of oppressed groups to organize often relies on commitment to particular world-views. On the one hand, oppressed groups are often mobilized by elites who are driven by certain ideologies or world-views. The October Revolution in Russian is probably a good example: organized elites with a certain world-view managed to seize power in a situation of semi-anarchy after a military defeat. On the other hand, solving collective action problems of oppressed groups also depends on rank-and-file militants who care so much about the ideas they fight for that they are ready to pay enormous costs (often, their lives). To these people, the free-riding incentive that may normally bedevil collective action does not apply. Thus there is an important role for culture, world-views and ideological commitment in explaining institutional change. Thinking that only interests drive institutional change implies the dangerous assumption that economic prosperity will make Islamic fundamentalism quietly disappear.

4 Some hypotheses using this framework

To shed light on the Adam Smith question with which I began, it is necessary to understand how the interaction of slow- and fast-moving institutions creates pressures for institutional configurations that may be growth-enhancing or growth-inhibiting. This interaction is not one-sided: slow-moving institutions exercise causal pressures on fast-moving institutions, and, by the same token, the latter have a life their own and can influence the path of slow-moving institutions. Moreover, different slow- and fast-moving institutions may have different effects on economic growth in their own right, while the form of existing fast-moving institutions may promote or, alternatively, may inhibit further institutional change, with positive or negative implications for economic growth.

These issues are quite complicated and demand a major research effort in many directions. Nonetheless, in this section I use the framework developed above to suggest some working hypotheses about the institutional conditions for successful economic growth and development.

4.1 The failure of institutional transplantation

A first hypothesis is that transplanting institutions is likely to be unsuccessful. Support for this hypothesis is provided by the fact that transplantation of European institutions did not work well outside the settler colonies. Colonial settlers transplanted European institutions, fast-moving by definition, into a setting to which they brought their stock of knowledge, their technology, and their culture. The countries that grew from these settler colonies are now counted among the rich, advanced economies of the world. Contrast this economic outcome with post-colonial India, where British institutions were transplanted into a different cultural context, including a deeply rooted caste system. An even stronger contrast is Africa, where conscious attempts to introduce the Western-style institutions of the democratic, modern European nation-states pathetically failed to produce economic growth. Transplantation often does not work well precisely because institutions are characterized by the complex interaction between slow-moving and fast-moving institutions, and the former change slowly and are largely autonomous. Trying to impose Western fast-moving institutions adequate to the West's own slow-moving institutions in countries with a very different history and culture is not likely to meet the same economic success.

The interaction between slow-moving and fast-moving institutions thus provides an explanation for why the transplantation of 'best-practice' institutions (or 'institutional monocropping'[5]) does not work. It provides content to the idea that different countries have different 'local conditions', which arise from each country's slow-moving institutions. It also provides a rationale for why reforms in a given country must build on these local conditions. In other words, countries with different cultural and historical paths must find within their existing slow-moving institutions the roots for changes in their fast-moving institutions.

4.2 The advantage of accumulated knowledge

Another hypothesis stems from a 'Jared Diamond' (1998) vision of the world, which proposes to explain the unequal development of civilization by the differences in the initial conditions facing early humans. Focusing on domesticable plants and animals and the (latitudinal or longitudinal) shapes of the continents, Diamond argues that the best conditions for developing civilizations were met in Eurasia, and within Eurasia, mostly in the Middle East and the Mediterranean. Favourable initial conditions led to population growth, which led in turn to higher production of surplus via division of labour. The latter led in turn to a higher production of knowledge, both scientific and cultural.

Let us take as a starting point this stock of knowledge dating to antiquity in the Mediterranean. This higher stock of knowledge does not refer only to scientific knowledge; the study of mathematics in Ancient Greece was more developed than anywhere else in the world, but the region's cultural diversity was also quite impressive, as evidenced by the number of competing religions in the Mediterranean at that time. Institutional innovation was also thriving: the variety of political systems in the region was much greater than elsewhere. Most of the forms of government known throughout history were invented in the Mediterranean and in the Old World (Finer, 2001); even today, 'old Europe' is experimenting with supranational forms of democracy at the level of the European Union.

The evolution of knowledge and culture may be linked to political institutions; the vigorous development of technologies suggests the parallel development of ideas concerning political innovations. Indeed, it is reasonable to think that innovation should apply not only to technology but also to the political and social spheres (although, since social and political innovations are much more costly to experiment with than are technological innovations, they may occur less frequently). Since knowledge and culture accumulate slowly, geographic areas with environmental conditions that promoted the interaction of diverse cultures, and hence, large stocks of accumulated knowledge, may have had greater potential for fast-moving institutional change. It may, therefore, be no coincidence that Europe, historically diverse and geographically favourable to interaction between cultures, was the location of most of the political innovations throughout history. How can we explain Western Europe's economic dominance over much of the rest of the world in the last several centuries? One hypothesis is that the initial conditions proposed by Diamond favoured a cross-cultural exchange of ideas, and that this exchange permitted an accumulation of knowledge that gave Europe an institutional 'head start'.[6]

4.3 Accumulated stocks of knowledge

Europe, of course, did not experience an uninterrupted accumulation of knowledge, a fact which suggests that countries with accumulated knowledge may witness historical setbacks for prolonged periods due to war or internal institutional failures. However, to the extent that stocks of knowledge and cultural capital remain preserved, these countries may be positioned for a more solid growth path once they are on a favourable track as far as their fast-moving institutions are concerned. Flanders, for example, experienced a cultural flowering during the Middle Ages and early Renaissance, when it was one of the richest areas in the world, and even recovered (albeit centuries later) from the massive losses inflicted by the Spanish Inquisition.

Consider also the case of China: the twentieth century was certainly one of the worst in all of Chinese history, but until the seventeenth or eighteenth century, China had the most advanced economy in the world. While Europe, despite its earlier superiority in terms of the development of knowledge, was mired for centuries in bloody wars, China developed its economy through centuries of relative peace and remarkable institutional stability equalled only by ancient Egypt. Since then, China has undergone more than two centuries of relative decline. However, considering the success of Chinese transition, with an average growth rate of over 8 per cent per year, it is difficult not to think that there is not some kind of 'reversion to the mean' and that the accumulated knowledge and culture from the country's past have helped in this process. Sachs et al. (1994) present almost the opposite perspective, attributing China's recent high growth rates to the country's 'backwardness' in the immediately preceding period. Seen in a long-run historical perspective, however, China has been anything but backward. For example, Chinese agriculture, which was the initial engine of growth early in the transition, has always been among the most productive in the world. I therefore suggest that one of the clues to the success of China's transition is not its 'backwardness' at the onset of the transition but the inherited high level of knowledge and culture relative to its economic performance.

Based on its existing stock of cultural knowledge (which differs strongly from that in the West), China, like other Asian countries, has developed unique fast-moving institutions in achieving its recent growth trajectory. Thus, China is experimenting with its own institutions for the market economy instead of importing Western institutions. Whether Asian capitalist institutions are more efficient is not the right question to ask here. A more appropriate question relates to the one posed earlier about institutional transplantation: what would have happened if Western-style institutions had been directly imported into a cultural context that exhibits deep differences from those of the West?

4.4 Dictatorship and growth

Whereas we have seen above that the transplantation and development of fast-moving institutions are affected in important ways by slow-moving institutions, one-way causality is not necessarily implied. Fast-moving institutions may impede the development or deployment of stocks of knowledge. In the context of the modern 'knowledge economy', the most important impediment to growth for countries beyond a certain level of economic development may be repressed circulation of ideas. Countries governed by totalitarian dictatorships may fall behind in economic development.

This hypothesis is compatible with the finding of Przeworski et al. (2000) that dictatorship may be at odds with modern economic development. It may also help to explain the economic trajectory of the Soviet Union, in which, after several decades of successful industrialization under a repressive centralized regime, economic growth slowed significantly during the 1970s and 1980s; the new 'computer age' was incompatible with the Communist regime's attempts to control the use of typewriters, photocopiers, and other tools for widespread communication. Similarly, if the Chinese Communist regime continues to limit access to the Internet, this will undoubtedly have negative economic consequences. Of course, not all dictatorships repress the exchange of knowledge. For example, pro-business dictatorships do not generally attempt to exercise totalitarian control over the circulation of ideas. Nevertheless, it is still clear that dictators try to prevent the free circulation of any ideas that may hurt them politically. Since intellectual freedom is a precondition for innovation and technological and cultural creativity, institutions that encourage the circulation of ideas may be increasingly necessary for growth in a global, information-based economy.

4.5 Concentration of power affects institutional change

The form of fast-moving political institutions may greatly affect the manner in which institutional change occurs, with important consequences for economic development and growth. In particular, this subsection focuses on the implications of the relative (de)centralization of political power for the dynamics of institutional change.

Although much work remains to be done, recent research suggests that decentralization through federalist democracies encourages experimentation. American federalism is often considered a 'laboratory of the states', where some states initiate and experiment with innovative institutions. Other states may imitate the successful results (see the framework of Qian, Roland, and Xu, 2003 on flexibility and organizational forms). At the other extreme, as discussed above, totalitarian regimes are likely to prevent not only technological and cultural but also political innovations, resulting in pronounced institutional uniformity and rigidity. Even in centralized democratic states, such as France and Japan, major changes in government programmes, such as education and banking reforms, require initiation by the responsible ministries and coordination by the central government.

The degree of centralization and power concentration has important implications not only for institutional experimentation but also for the nature and speed of political change. Political institutions that concentrate power in the hands of a few tend toward patterns of infrequent and abrupt change because, relative to institutions in which power is more dispersed, institutions with concentrated power leave more room for discretionary behaviour and abuse of power by those holding office. As a corollary, the high economic stakes of political power in centralized regimes tend to translate into a more pronounced temptation to resort to coercive methods to retain power.

Many historical examples illustrate this phenomenon. One is the well-known comparison between the evolution of the British Crown and that of absolute monarchy in France. The English monarchy was historically relatively weak, and in consequence the king had to share powers with feudal lords. Frequent attempts to strengthen the power of the king were mostly defeated. Although the episode of the Glorious Revolution of 1688 and the subsequent separation of powers between the monarch and the House of Lords – one of history's most important political innovations – has been documented at length (e.g. North and Weingast, 1989), previous episodes, such as the drafting of the Magna Carta in 1215, reveal a constant check on the king by the feudal lords in medieval England. Importantly, the English political system is also probably the prime example of an evolutionary political system that has adjusted in a flexible way throughout the last centuries.

Consider, by contrast, the consequences of centralized power in France: ironically, the French king began much weaker relative to noble lords than the English monarch, and remained so for centuries. It was only much later, in a Europe divided by religious wars, that the power of the French monarchy began to strengthen, until it achieved its absolutist status under Louis XIV. It took the French Revolution, centuries later, to trigger abrupt political change. Unlike the flexible and evolutionary political system that arose due to the separation of powers in medieval England, then, the centralization of power in France under an absolutist monarch made political change particularly discontinuous.

Another example comes from the comparison of the Ottoman Empire and feudal Europe. Machiavelli noted in *The Prince* that it was much easier to conquer feudal France than the Ottoman Empire, but it was much more difficult to occupy the former than the latter. In France, prior to the concentration of power by an absolutist monarch, feudal lords were relatively independent and did not rely much on the king. Therefore, they were not very loyal to the latter and would change allegiance whenever it best suited their interests. They could therefore be easily bribed by a would-be conqueror into betraying the French king. By the same token, however, feudal lords could also betray any occupying power. By contrast, the governors of the Ottoman Empire had no property of their own and depended for their resources on the emperor, who threatened to have them executed if they lost territory to an enemy. Therefore, they would fight to the death against any occupant. On the other hand, once successfully invaded, Ottoman territory was easily occupied because the Ottoman institutions collapsed like a house of cards. More centralization in the Ottoman Empire therefore meant that change through successful invasions was less frequent and more abrupt when it came, whereas greater dispersion of power in pre-absolutist France allowed for more frequent foreign influence and institutional change.

However, pre-existing institutional patterns (such as centralized systems of governance) do not automatically translate into preordained trajectories of institutional change. The comparison between the transitions in China and the Soviet Union is instructive in this regard. In the former, a commitment to safeguarding some of the crucial political and economic interests of potential losers, the Communist Party old guard, allowed reformers to maintain the support of conservatives and brought with it an incremental process of change. In the latter, by contrast, the lack of such a commitment provoked a backlash by potential losers and, with it, discontinuous change.

Let us consider this comparison between China and the Soviet Union in more detail. In principle, one would think that institutional change in the transition from socialism must proceed in one leap, because power was concentrated in the hands of a relatively small group, the *nomenklatura*. However, it is wrong to claim that the *nomenklatura* was consistently against transition to the market economy. Indeed, many members of the *nomenklatura* were among the first to become successful entrepreneurs and directors of privatized enterprises. Socialist economies were distinct in the sense that few identifiable social groups could be directly labelled *ex-post* as 'losers' or 'winners' from transition; instead, the constellation of winners and losers crossed all levels of society (Roland, 1989). Thus, even though power was concentrated in the hands of the *nomenklatura*, reform packages could potentially be designed that lowered the stakes and facilitated a more continuous kind of political change.

In China, although the old guard within the Communist Party had much to lose from institutional change, Deng Xiaoping, the father of Chinese economic reforms, proceeded in two ways.[7] First, he launched a gradualist strategy, hoping that the first economic reforms would be successful. He thus started out with the reforms that would have the highest likelihood of being popular (see Roland, 2000 for analysis). In fact, decollectivization turned out to be a huge success, which strongly reinforced the position of Deng within the Communist Party. However, despite the success of the changes, the Party's old guard became increasingly nervous because they were afraid that this process of institutional change would eventually lead to their demise. Deng therefore constantly tried to show that he was committed to not excluding them from power. For example, at times of protest such as the Wall of Democracy in 1980 or the Tiananmen Square events, Deng never hesitated to purge reformist Party leaders who were in favour of greater dialogue with student protestors. In this way, he managed to show his commitment to not purging the old guard. Later on, this commitment was institutionalized by introducing an age limit for party cadres and introducing a favourable retirement package for the older conservative communist leaders, which now works to ensure a smooth rotation of the leadership and creates an element of stability.

It is interesting to contrast this pattern of reform with the experience of the Soviet Union. When Gorbachev came to power, the Central Committee of the Soviet Communist Party was entirely composed of Brezhnevites, partisans of stagnation (Brezhnev's period was called *zastoinyi period* or 'stagnation period'). Gorbachev nevertheless managed to manoeuvre very adeptly within the first two years he was in power to replace the Central Committee and introduce like-minded politicians who wanted change – that is, those elements of the *nomenklatura* who were interested in reforms (see Roland, 1991; Hough, 1988). His *glasnost'* and *perestroika* programmes were challenged not only by conservatives but also by Yeltsin, who favoured more radical reforms that were totally unacceptable to the conservative wing of the Communist Party. Unlike Deng in China, Gorbachev was not willing to repress radical reformers in order to show his commitment to the old guard. Furthermore, unlike Deng, Gorbachev had not been able to strengthen his position sufficiently with successful economic reforms, The most positive thing he did on the economic front was to introduce cooperatives, the early form of small private enterprise, but their effect was relatively meagre. On the negative side of the ledger, Gorbachev also made economic mistakes such as granting more autonomy to enterprises, which had an inflationary effect that, given the absence of free pricing, only led to increased shortages.

Thus, whereas Deng had been able to lower the stakes of holding on to power and commit not to purge hard-line elements, thereby pacifying elements of the old guard, Gorbachev soon turned conservative elements against him. His unwillingness to repress reformers was felt quickly in the satellite states, which seized the opportunity to overthrow their own Communist regimes in 1989. For example, Gorbachev intervened personally during the East German events to prevent Honecker and the hard-line communists from firing on demonstrators in Leipzig. When the Soviet republics began preparing to break away, and especially when East Germany joined Germany and NATO, conservatives saw events getting out of control. They thus staged the coup that ousted Gorbachev, led to a complete implosion of the communist regime, and ultimately propelled Yeltsin to power. Thus, in neither the Chinese nor the Soviet cases did the pre-transition concentration of power in the hands of the *nomenklatura* inevitably lead to abrupt, discontinuous institutional change. Instead, the particular strategies chosen by reformist leaders such as Deng and Gorbachev influenced the extent to which power seemed 'indivisible' to hard-line elements. Further research should trace the conditions under which the implications of concentrated power for the discontinuity of change may be mitigated, as in the Chinese case, and thus lead to gradualist trajectories of reform.

5 Some policy implications

The interaction between slow-moving and fast-moving institutions implies that different cultural paths (slow-moving institutions) may affect the appropriate choices of fast-moving institutions. Given our limited knowledge of these interactions, caution is required. Yesterday's conventional wisdom has often been overturned. Sixty years ago, most intellectuals were convinced that central planning was more efficient than markets. Hardly anybody believes that today. Similarly, only ten years ago, Asian economies were praised for the marvellous effect of Confucian values (family, hard work, and savings). Yet, when the Asian economies were hit by the 1997 crisis, 'crony capitalism' became the only term used to name those economies. This discussion carries a number of possible policy implications.

5.1 The dangers of transplanting 'best-practice' institutions

First, one should take a sceptical attitude towards transplantation of institutions, because the different dynamics of slow-moving institutions may make some fast-moving institutions inadequate in some countries. The above framework provides a rationale for such scepticism. The appropriate question for analysts of development may not be what constitutes a globally optimal set of institutions, but rather whether fast-moving institutions are appropriate to the slow-moving institutions with which they interact. Thus reforms of fast-moving institutions in a given country must in part build on existing slow-moving institutions that have arisen in countries with different cultural and historical pasts. Ignoring these pasts in designing institutional reforms is likely to be a recipe for failure. The interaction of slow- and fast-moving institutions therefore provides an important caution to any development specialist seeking to export 'best-practice' institutions.

5.2 The importance of gradualism and experimentation

Secondly, our current relative ignorance about the interaction between fast-moving institutions and the slow-moving institutions of different countries provides a strong rationale for certain kinds of experimentation and gradualism and, conversely, a strong reason for opposing the imposition of irreversible institutional change in a given country. Dewatripont and Roland (1995) and Roland (2000) have shown that in the presence of aggregate uncertainty about large-scale institutional change, as well as high costs of institutional reversal, the optimal approach to institutional reform is gradualism. Indeed, gradualism provides an option of early reversal if the prospects look bad after the introduction of the first reforms, an option that actually makes it *easier* to gain political support and build constituencies for institutional change.

As I stress above, this gradualist approach has been followed in the Chinese success story of transition from socialism to capitalism. The transition process started with decollectivization in agriculture, which itself was preceded by experiments of decollectivization in different provinces. The experimental approach was later used again and again, whether with the special economic zones or with privatization (see Naughton, 1995; Qian, 2002). The territorial organization of the Chinese government, following the pattern of the M-form organization (Chandler, 1962; Williamson, 1975), in contrast to the functional organization of the Soviet government, following more the U-form organization, has provided a more flexible framework for setting up reform experiments (see Qian and Xu, 1993; Qian, Roland, and Xu, 2003). The dual-track approach to reform has also provided a smart way to reform gradually while respecting the complementarity of reforms. Thus with dual-track price liberalization, the planned production obligations and planned delivery rights of enterprises under the plan were frozen at a pre-existing level, and enterprises had continuing obligations and rights under the plan track. On the other hand, enterprises were given freedom to set prices, contract, and retain profits from transactions on the new market track. The dual-track system therefore allowed for the introduction of liberalization across all markets – which avoids the distortions that arise from liberalization only in some markets – while avoiding the disruption of output collapse by maintaining a frozen plan track (Roland and Verdier, 2003). Moreover, price liberalization at the margin has the same efficiency properties as full liberalization (Lau et al., 1997) and the dual track has the attractive property of being Pareto-improving – that is, hurting no one while improving the welfare of others (Lau et al., 2000). Notice also that the dual track approach reduces reversal costs, which makes adopting it even more attractive.

Rodrik (2000) documents the positive experience of reform in Mauritius in the light of a dual-track strategy. Mauritius established an export processing zone operating under complete free-trade and free-market principles in 1970, while keeping the domestic sector highly protected until the 1980s. Moreover, the country kept the two sectors as segmented as possible to prevent negative spillovers (of wages, in particular) from the export processing zone to the domestic sector. The development of the former had a positive impact on the domestic economy that could pave the way for later liberalization. Interestingly, this was done in a very participatory political context where most interests of the population had to be involved in the decision-making process in a way similar to those mentioned by Evans (2003) when discussing the effect of participatory institutions.[8]

5.3 The importance of policy dialogue

A third implication of this discussion is, therefore, that policy dialogue may be needed more than trying to impose 'one-size-fits-all' solutions for different countries. Policy dialogue has been viewed with suspicion in the past, on the grounds that a doctor does not dialogue with his patient about making a health diagnosis. This suspicion was based on the doubly erroneous view that technocrats in international financial institutions possess superior knowledge about economic development and that local elites either have mostly 'wrong' views about solutions for their countries or lack the incentives to do something about it. As the preceding discussion has suggested, however, while slow-moving institutions may hamper the proper functioning of implanted fast-moving institutions, local knowledge about a country's slow-moving institutions is not part of the problem but part of the solution. Therefore, only dialogue can help formulate adequate development policies. This does not mean that there are no local elites with vested interests in maintaining inefficient institutions. Yet those are not the local elites with whom a fruitful dialogue can be established; rather, one should enter into a dialogue with elites who have an interest in development. Such elites are not necessarily represented in governments but are very active in civil society. Policy dialogue therefore entails not just a dialogue with governments but also with different components of civil society at large.

A few further comments are in order before closing. First, one hypothesis outlined above concerned the importance of the separation of powers in promoting experimentation (federalism) as well as in engendering continuous, flexible institutional evolution. A caveat is important here: although different forms of separation of powers diffuse the powers of government, there is a danger that this may go too far. Involvement of many different groups in decision-making may lead to an excess number of veto players, which may be stifling and prevent institutional innovation (Olson, 1982). In such cases, the danger of anarchy looms. Government resources can come to be treated as a common pool into which different groups can dip their hands. The common-pool problem is a feature of many modern democracies and tends to lead to budgetary disasters, Argentina being a particularly salient example. There is thus a fine line between healthy separation of powers within governments and forms of anarchy within governments (see Persson, Roland and Tabellini, 1997, on the difference between separation of powers and the common pool problem). This shows the necessity of comparative political analysis to achieve a better understanding of how the different democratic systems function.

Second, anarchy is the big challenge at a global level today. Globalization of markets has created the need for provision of international public goods (e.g. environmental preservation, peace, disease prevention, free movement of goods and services, global financial stability). However, we lack adequate institutions at the world level to tackle these problems. Here, we are still closer to anarchy and generalized free-riding than to a democratic international order. These issues have become increasingly acute in the last few years. Nonetheless, constituencies may be forming to demand such an institutional change, as globalization of the economy, of science and knowledge, and of cultural interactions leads to increased demands for such changes.

6 Conclusion

Let us return to the bigger questions, and in particular to the Adam Smith question. Why did England industrialize more quickly than continental Europe? Why has development failure in the last few decades been so massive in so many areas of the world, with the exception of Asia? Why is China so successful in its transition? Explaining these phenomena *via* differences in institutions across countries begs the question of *how* the different institutions have evolved in different countries, which depends to a certain extent on how pre-existing institutions have empowered different groups in society so that they could solve their collective action problem. This in turn begs the question of how these pre-existing institutions came about. It seems that the reasoning must stop either at specific exogenous events at some points in history or that we must go down the entire path of human history. This is not quite infinite regression, but in history, one cannot go further than that.

But even if we look to history to explain institutions, how can we be sure that the subsequent chain of events obeys a predictable pattern? Are some institutional changes or their absence necessarily the consequence of pre-existing institutions, or is there an infinity of possibilities, in which case it would be futile to try to establish strong causal links? How can one distinguish between predictable patterns of institutional change and purely random historical events?

These are obviously hard questions. Above, I have proposed a framework for thinking about institutional change. In order to have a meaningful understanding of institutions as *systems*, we need to understand interactions between different institutions. The proposed classification of institutions is intended as a step in understanding institutional change. These suggestions are still very tentative. Much empirical work is needed to better understand the interactions between different institutions. We also need better to ground empirically our knowledge of the determinants of institutional change. This will require a major effort not only for those who study development and transition but perhaps most of all for economic historians, because history provides a very rich ground for studying institutional change.

Nonetheless, the framework I have outlined above may be one helpful way to start thinking about institutional change. Economists have been reluctant to discuss the relationship of social norms and cultural values to economic growth. Instead, recent cutting-edge work in economics has proposed economic growth as a product of the combination of ideas and institutions. Yet ideas are closely related to culture, understood both as values (world-view) and as social norms. And as I have suggested in this chapter, institutions may themselves be viewed as the interaction of fast-moving (political) and slow-moving (cultural) institutions. In order better to understand the determinants of economic growth, then, economists should seek a better understanding of the role of values and norms in shaping both ideas and institutions.

Notes

1. Of course, this is an empirical question as well, given that no formal model can capture all the potentially relevant factors.
2. This has led some, such as Jeffrey Sachs and others (1994), to argue that the 'big bang' approach to transition, whereby all institutions are changed simultaneously and as fast as possible, is the only one possible. The existence of complementarities, however, does not rule out certain forms of gradualism. Indeed, as I have emphasized in my work on transition (see e.g. Roland, 2000), a gradualist strategy may even be superior, as the Chinese experience has demonstrated. Institutional complementarities point to the art of reform sequencing as one of the most difficult in the transition process. Transition is akin to changing the engines of a plane while the plane is still flying.
3. This does not mean that the speed of change of slow-moving institutions is constant over time. There can be periods of relatively faster change. For example, after Christianity became the official religion of the Roman Empire and after the establishment of the caliphate following the death of Mohammed, one can imagine that the spread of Catholicism and Islam was faster. It would, however, be wrong to think that millions of people thereafter drastically changed their world view and

values as a result of forms of forced conversion. This would be a severe overestimation of state capacity in those days. It is only in the twentieth century (and maybe in the late nineteenth century) that governments have acquired the capacity of totalitarianism.

4. A major exception is Weitzman and Xu (1993), who argue that the very strong development of township and village enterprises in China, despite the absence of well-defined property rights, can be traced back to cultural differences between Western and Chinese values.
5. See Peter Evans (2003).
6. This should not, however, lead us to conclude that there is necessarily a deterministic relationship between initial material conditions and future economic development; many other factors play a key role.
7. What follows is very schematic. Reality was more complex, but I want to get to the gist of the story.
8. The relevance of the Chinese experience is often dismissed because of the dictatorial character of its regime. However, it is interesting to note that, despite the political regime, it is not the case that painful reforms have been brutally imposed on the population. On the contrary, both the sequencing and the design of reforms have been tailored so as to benefit a majority without hurting a minority. The choice of dual-track price liberalization was therefore precisely designed to be Pareto-improving. It is not clear that the Chinese reform process would have been politically infeasible if China had not been a democracy or whether no democratic system could have sustained such a process. If anything, the absence of democracy has made it more difficult to enforce private property rights and the rule of law and to encourage the development of a *sui generis* private sector. Recent research (Che and Qian, 1998) suggests that the development of township and village enterprises was a spontaneous response to the specific Chinese institutional situation with absence of the rule of law and the absence of sufficient safeguards against predatory government behaviour.

References

Acemoglu, D. (2003) 'Why Not a Political Coase Theorem? Social Conflict, Commitment and Politics', *Journal of Comparative Economics*, vol. 31, pp. 620–52.

Acemoglu, D., Johnson, S. and Robinson, J. (2001) 'The Colonial Origins of Comparative Development: an Empirical Investigation', *American Economic Review*, vol. 91, pp. 1369–401.

Acemoglu, D. and J. Robinson (2000) 'Why Did the West Extend the Franchise? Democracy, Inequality, and Growth in Historical Perspective', *Quarterly Journal of Economics*, vol. 115, pp. 1167–99.

Acemoglu, D. and Robinson (2001) 'A Theory of Political Transitions', *American Economic Review*, vol. 91, pp. 938–63.

Acemoglu, D. and J. Robinson (2002) *Economic Backwardness in Political Perspective* (London: Centre for Economic Policy Research).

Acemoglu, D. and J. Robinson (2005) *Economic Origins of Dictatorship and Democracy* (Cambridge: Cambridge University Press).

Aoki, M. (2001) *Toward a Comparative Institutional Analysis* (Cambridge, Mass.: MIT Press).

Berglöf, E. (1990) 'Capital Structure as a Mechanism of Control: a Comparison of Financial Systems', in Masahiko Aoki, Bo Gustavsson and Oliver Williamson (eds), *The Firm as a Nexus of Treaties* (London: European Sage).

Cai, H. and D. Treisman (2001) 'State Corroding Federalism: Interjurisdictional Competition and the Weakening of Central Authority', *Journal of Public Economics*, vol. 88, pp. 443–93.

Chandler, A. (1962) *Strategy and Structure: Chapters in the History of the American Industrial Enterprise* (Cambridge, Mass.: MIT Press).

Che, J. and Y. Qian (1998) 'Insecure Property Rights and Government Ownership of Firms', *Quarterly Journal of Economics*, vol. 113(2), pp. 467–96.

Dewatripont, M. and G. Roland (1995) 'The Design of Reform Packages under Uncertainty', *American Economic Review*, vol. 85, pp. 1207–23.

Diamond, J. (1998) *Guns, Germs and Steel* (New York: Norton).

Elster, J. (1982) 'Marxism, Functionalism and Game Theory: the Case for Methodological Individualism', *Theory and Society*, vol. 11(4), pp. 453–82.

Evans, P. (1989) 'Predatory, Developmental and Other Apparatuses: a Comparative Political Economy Perspective on the Third World State', *Sociological Forum*, vol. 4(4), pp. 561–87.

Evans, P. (2003) 'Development as Institutional Change: the Pitfalls of Monocropping and Potentials of Deliberation', mimeo, University of California, Berkeley.

Finer, S.E. (2001) *The History of Government from the Earliest Times* (Oxford: Oxford University Press).

Gerschenkron, A. (1962) *Economic Backwardness in Historical Perspective* (New York: Praeger).

Greif, A. (1993) 'Contract Enforceability and Economic Institutions in Early Trade: the Maghribi Traders' Coalition', *American Economic Review*, vol. 83(3), pp. 525–48.

Greif, A. (1994) 'Cultural Beliefs and the Organization of Society: a Historical and Theoretical Reflection on Collectivist and Individualist Societies', *Journal of Political Economy*, vol. 102(5), pp. 912–50.

Hough, J. (1988) *Opening up the Soviet Economy* (Washington, DC: Brookings Institution).

Kornai, J. (1980) *The Economics of Shortage* (Amsterdam: North-Holland).

Kornai, J. (1995) *Highways and Byways* (Cambridge, Mass.; MIT Press).

La Porta, R., F. Lopez-de-Silanes, A. Shleifer and R. Vishny (1998a) 'Law and Finance', *Journal of Political Economy*, vol. 106, pp. 1113–55.

La Porta, R., F. Lopez-de-Silanes, A. Shleifer, and R. Vishny (1998b) 'Legal Determinants of External Finance', *Journal of Finance*, vol. 52, pp. 1131–50.

La Porta, R., F. Lopez-de-Silanes, A. Shleifer, and R. Vishny (1999) 'Corporate Ownership around the World', *Journal of Finance*, vol. 54, pp. 471–517.

La Porta, R., F. Lopez-de-Silanes, A. Shleifer, and R. Vishny (2000) 'Agency Problems and Dividend Policies around the World', *Journal of Finance*, vol. 55, pp. 1–33.

Lau, L., Y. Qian and G. Roland (1997) 'Pareto-improving Economic Reforms through Dual-Track Liberalization', *Economics Letters*, vol. 55(2), pp. 285–92.

Lau, L., Y. Qian and G. Roland (2000) 'Reform without Losers: an Interpretation of China's Dual-Track Approach to Transition', *Journal of Political Economy*, vol. 108(1), pp. 120–43.

Lizzeri, A. and N. Persico (2001) 'The Provision of Public Goods under Alternative Electoral Incentives', *American Economic Review*, vol. 91(1), pp. 225–45.

Mayer, C. (1987) 'Financial Systems and Corporate Investment', *Oxford Review of Economic Policy*, vol. 3(4), pp. i–xvi.

Milesi-Ferretti, G-M., R. Perotti and M. Rostagno (2002) 'Electoral Systems Public Spending', *Quarterly Journal of Economics*, vol. 117, pp. 609–57.

Naughton, B. (1995) *Growing Out of the Plan* (Cambridge: Cambridge University Press).

North, D. (1990) *Institutions, Institutional Change and Economic Performance* (Cambridge: Cambridge University Press).

North, D. and B. Weingast (1989) 'Constitutions and Commitment: Evolutions of Institutions Governing Public Choice', *Journal of Economic History*, vol. 49, pp. 803–32.
Olson, M. (1965) *The Logic of Collective Action: Public Goods and the Theory of Groups* (Cambridge, Mass.: Harvard University Press).
Olson, M. (1982) *The Rise and Decline of Nations: Economic Growth, Stagflation and Social Rigidities* (New Haven, Conn.: Yale University Press).
Persson, T., G. Roland and G. Tabellini (1997) 'Separation of Powers and Political Accountability', *Quarterly Journal of Economics*, vol. 112, pp. 310–27.
Persson, T., G. Roland and G. Tabellini (2000) 'Comparative Politics and Public Finance', *Journal of Political Economy*, vol. 108(6), pp. 1121–61.
Persson, T., G. Roland and G. Tabellini (2003) 'Electoral Rules Shape Party Structure and Government Spending in Parliamentary Democracies', UCLA Department of Economics Working Paper.
Persson, T. and G. Tabellini (1999) 'The Size and Scope of Government: Comparative Politics with Rational Politicians', Marshall Lecture, *European Economic Review*, vol. 42, pp. 699–736.
Przeworski, A., M. Alvarez, J. Cheibub and F. Limongi (2000) *Democracy and Development: Political Institutions and Well-Being in the World, 1950–1990* (Cambridge: Cambridge University Press).
Qian, Y. (2002) *How Reform Worked in China* (London: Centre for Economic Policy Research).
Qian, Y., G. Roland and C. Xu (2003) *Coordinating Tasks in M-form and U-form Organizations* (London: Suntory Centre, London School of Economics).
Qian, Y., and C. Xu (1993) 'Why China's Economic Reforms Differ: the M-Form Hierarchy and Entry/Expansion of the Non-State Sector' *Economics of Transition*, vol. 1(2), pp. 135–70.
Roland, G. (1989) *Economie politique du système soviétique* (Paris: Editions de l'Harmattan).
Roland, G. (1991) 'The Political Economy of Transition in the Soviet Union', *European Economy*, vol. 49, 1993, pp. 197–216.
Roland, G. (2000) *Transition and Economics: Politics, Markets and Firms* (Cambridge, Mass.: MIT Press).
Roland, G. (2002) 'Ten Years After ... Transition and Economics', *IMF Staff Papers*, vol. 48, Special Issue, 2002, pp. 29–52.
Roland, G. and T. Verdier (2003) 'Law Enforcement and Transition', *European Economic Review*, vol. 47(4), pp. 669–85.
Sachs, J., W. Woo, S. Saucher and G. Hughes (1994) 'Structural Factors in the Economic Reforms of China, Eastern Europe, and the Former Soviet Union', *Economic Policy*, vol. 9, no. 18, pp. 101–45.
Shleifer, A. and R. Vishny (1994) 'Politicians and Firms', *Quarterly Journal of Economics*, vol. 109, pp. 995–1025.
Weingast, B. (1995) 'The Economic Role of Political Institutions: Market-Preserving Federalism and Economic Growth', *Journal of Economics, Law and Organization*, vol. 11, pp. 1–31.
Weitzman, M. and C. Xu (1993) 'Chinese Township and Village Enterprises as Vaguely Defined Cooperatives', *Journal of Comparative Economics*, vol. 3, pp. 276–308.
Williamson, O. (1975) *Markets and Hierarchies* (New York: Free Press).
Williamson, O. (1985) *The Economic Institutions of Capitalism* (New York: Free Press).

8

The Endowment Effect and the Origin of Private Property

*Herbert Gintis**
Santa Fe Institute, USA

and

Central European University, Hungary

1 Introduction

Experimental studies have shown that subjects exhibit a systematic endowment effect. Since there is no plausible cultural norm fostering the endowment effect, the behaviour likely involves a genetic predisposition, and hence may well be the product of some evolutionary adaptation. If this is correct, the bulk of human evolution occurred before the appearance of institutions protecting property rights, so bargaining over the exchange of property rights cannot explain the endowment effect. This chapter shows that the endowment effect can be modelled as respect for private property *without* legal institutions ensuring third-party contract enforcement. In this sense, pre-institutional 'natural' private property has been observed in many species, in the form of the recognition of territorial possession. We develop a model loosely based on the Hawk, Dove, Bourgeois game and the War of Attrition to explain the natural evolution of private property.

We show that if agents in a group exhibit the endowment effect for an indivisible resource, then property rights in that resource can be established on the basis of incumbency, assuming incumbents and those who contest for incumbency are of equal perceived fighting ability.[1] The enforcement of these rights will then be carried out by the agents themselves, so no third-party enforcement is needed. This is because the endowment effect leads the incumbent to be willing to expend more resources to protect his

*I would like to thank Eldridge Adams, Carl Bergstrom, Chris Boehm, Samuel Bowles, Peter Hammerstein, Marc Hauser, Mike Mesterton-Gibbons and John Maynard Smith for helpful comments, and the John D. and Catherine T. MacArthur Foundation for financial support.

incumbency than an intruder will be willing to expend to expropriate the incumbent. For simplicity, we consider only the case where the marginal benefit of more than one unit of the resource is zero (e.g. a homestead, a spider's web, or a bird's nest).

The model assumes the agents know the present value π_g of incumbency, as well as the present value π_b of non-incumbency, measured in units of biological fitness. We assume utility and fitness coincide, except for one situation, described below – this situation explicitly involves *loss aversion,* where the disutility of loss exceeds the fitness cost of loss. When an incumbent faces an intruder, the intruder determines the expected value of attempting to seize the resource, and the incumbent determines the expected value of contesting versus ceding incumbency when challenged. These conditions will not be the same, and in plausible cases there is a range of values of π_g/π_b for which the intruder decides not to fight, and the incumbent decides to fight if challenged. We call this a (natural) *private property equilibrium.* In a private property equilibrium, since the potential contestants are of equal power, it must be the case that individuals are *loss averse,* the incumbent being willing to expend more resources to hold the resource than the intruder is to seize it.

Of course, π_g and π_b will generally be endogenous in a fully specified model. Their values will depend on the supply of the resource relative to the number of agents, the intrinsic value of the resource, the ease in finding an unowned unit of the resource, and the like.

Our model of decentralized private property is like the 'Bourgeois' equilibrium in the Hawk, Dove, Bourgeois game, in that agents contest for a unit of an indivisible resource, contests may be very costly, and in equilibrium, incumbency determines who holds the resource without costly contests. Our model, however, fills in critical gaps in the Hawk, Dove, Bourgeois game. The central ambiguity of the Hawk, Dove, Bourgeois game is that it treats the cost of contesting as exogenously given, and taking on exactly two values, high for Hawk and low for Dove. Clearly, however, these costs are in large part under the control of the agents themselves, and should not be considered exogenous. In our model, the level of resources devoted to a contest is endogenously determined, and the contest itself is modelled explicitly as a modified War of Attrition, the probability of winning being a function of the level of resources committed to combat. One critical feature of the War of Attrition is that the initial commitment of a level of resources to a contest must be *behaviourally ensured by the agent,* so that the agent will continue to contest even when the costs of doing so exceed the fitness benefits. Without this pre-commitment, the incumbent's threat of 'fighting to the death' would not be credible (i.e. the chosen best response of the agent would not be subgame perfect). From a behavioural point of view, this pre-commitment can be summarized as the incumbent have a degree of *loss aversion* leading his utility to differ from his fitness.

Our fuller specification of the behavioural underpinnings of the Hawk, Dove, Bourgeois game allows us to determine the conditions under which a property equilibrium will exist while its corresponding anti-property equilibrium (in which a new arrival rather than the first entrant always assumes incumbency) does not exist. This aspect of our model is of some importance, because the inability of the Hawk, Dove, Bourgeois game to favour private property over anti-private property is a serious and rarely addressed weakness of the model.

2 The endowment effect and territoriality

The endowment effect, according to which a good is more highly prized by an agent who is in possession of the good than one who is not, was first documented by the psychologist Daniel Kahneman and his co-workers (Tversky and Kahneman, 1981). Richard Thaler (1992) describes a typical experimental verification of the phenomenon as follows. Seventy-seven students at Simon Fraser University were randomly assigned to one of three conditions, Seller, Buyer, or Chooser. Sellers were given a mug with the University logo (selling for $6.00 at local stores) and asked whether they would be willing to sell at a series of prices ranging from $0.25 to $9.25. Buyers were asked whether they would be willing to purchase a mug at the same series of prices. Choosers were asked to choose for each price between receiving a mug or that amount of money. The students were informed that a fraction of their choices, randomly chosen by the experimenter, would be carried out, thus giving the students a material incentive to reveal their true preferences. The average Buyer price was $2.87, while the average Seller price was $7.12. Choosers behaved like Buyers, being on average indifferent between the mug and $3.12. The conclusion is that owners of the mug valued the object more than twice as highly as non-owners.

The aspect of the endowment effect that promotes natural private property is known as *loss aversion*: the disutility of giving up something one owns is greater than the utility associated with acquiring it. Indeed, losses are commonly valued at about twice that of gains, so that to induce an individual to accept a lottery that costs $10 when one loses, it must offer a $20 pay-off when one wins. Assuming that an agent's willingness to combat over possession of an object is increasing in the subjective value of the object, owners will be prepared to fight harder to *retain* possession than non-owners are to *gain* possession. Hence there will be a bias in favour of recognizing private property by virtue of incumbency, even where third-party enforcement institutions are absent.

We say an agent *owns* (is incumbent of) something if the agent has exclusive access to it and the benefits that flow from this privileged access. We say ownership (incumbency) is *respected* if it is rarely contested and, when contested, generally results in ownership remaining with the incumbent.

The dominant view in Western thought, from Hobbes, Locke, Rousseau and Marx to the present, is that private property is a human social construction that emerged with the rise of modern civilization. However, evidence from studies of animal behaviour, gathered mostly in the past quarter-century, has shown this view to be incorrect. Various territorial claims are recognized in non-human species, including butterflies (Davies, Wood Butterfly, 1978), spiders (Riechert, 1978), wild horses (Stevens, 1988), finches (Senar, Camerino and Metcalfe, 1989), wasps (Eason, Cobbs and Trinca, 1999), non-human primates (Ellis, 1985) and many others.

In non-human species, that an animal owns a territory is generally established by the fact that the animal has marked the territory (e.g. by constructing a nest, burrow, hive, dam, or web, or by marking its limits with urine or faeces). In humans there are other criteria of ownership, but physical possession and first to occupy remain of great importance. According to John Locke, for example,

> ... every man has a property in his own person ... The labour of his body, and the work of his hands, we may say, are properly his. Whatsoever then he removes out of the state that nature hath provided, and left it in, he hath mixed his labour with, and joined to it something that is his own, and thereby makes it his property.
>
> *Second Treatise on Government, §27 (1690)*

Since private property in human society is generally protected by law and enforced by complex institutions (judiciary and police), it is natural to view private property in animals as a categorically distinct phenomenon. In fact, however, decentralized, self-enforcing types of private property, based on behavioural propensities akin to those found in non-human species (e.g. the endowment effect), are important for humans, and arguably lay the basis for more institutional forms of property rights. For instance, many developmental studies indicate that toddlers and small children use behavioural rules similar to those of animals in recognizing and defending property rights (Furby, 1980).

How respect for ownership has evolved and how it is maintained in an evolutionary context is a challenging puzzle. Why do loss aversion and the endowment effect exist? Why do humans fail to conform to the smoothly differentiable utility function assumed in most versions of the rational actor model? The question is equally challenging for non-humans, although we are so used to the phenomenon that we rarely give it a second thought.

Consider, for instance, the sparrows that built a nest in a vine in my garden. The location is choice, and the couple spent days preparing the structure. The nest is quite as valuable to another sparrow couple. Why does another couple not try to evict the first? If they are equally strong, and both value the territory equally, each has a 50 per cent chance of winning the territorial battle. Why bother investing if one can simply steal? Of course, if stealing were profitable, then there would be no nest building, and hence no sparrows. But that heightens rather than resolves the puzzle.

One common argument, borrowed from Trivers (1971), is that the original couple has more to lose, since it has put a good deal of effort already in the improvement of the property. This, however, is a logical error that has come to be known as the *Concorde* or the *sunk cost* fallacy: to maximize future returns, an agent ought consider only the future pay-offs of an entity, not how much the agent has expended on the entity in the past.

The Hawk, Dove, Bourgeois game was offered by Maynard Smith and Parker (1976) as a logically sound alternative to the sunk cost argument. In this game Hawks and Doves are phenotypically indistinguishable members of the same species, but they act differently in contesting over ownership rights to a territory. When two Doves contest, they posture for a bit, and then each assumes the territory with equal probability. When a Dove and a Hawk contest, however, the Hawk takes the whole territory. Finally, when two Hawks contest, a terrible battle ensues, and the value of the territory is less than the cost of fighting for the contestants. Maynard Smith showed that, assuming that there is an unambiguous way to determine who first found the territory, there is an evolutionarily stable strategy in which all agents behave like Hawks when they are *first* to find the territory, and like Doves otherwise.

The Hawk, Dove, Bourgeois game is an elegant contribution to explaining the endowment effect, but the cost of contesting for Hawks and the cost of display for Doves cannot plausibly be taken as fixed and exogenously determined. Indeed, it is clear that Doves contest in the same manner as Hawks, except that they devote fewer resources to combat. Similarly, the value of the ownership is taken as exogenous, when in fact it depends on the frequency with which ownership is contested, as well as other factors. Clearly, the costs and benefits of possession depend on the state of the population, the density of high-quality territories, the cost of search, and other variables that might well depend on the distribution of strategies in the population.

First, however, it is instructive to consider the evidence for a close association, as Locke suggested in his theory of property rights, between ownership and incumbency (physical contiguity and control) in children and non-human animals.

3 Property rights in young children

Long before they become acquainted with money, markets, bargaining and trade, children exhibit possessive behaviour and recognize the property rights of others on the basis of incumbency. In one study (Bakeman and Brownlee, 1982) participant observers studied a group of 11 toddlers (12 to 24 months old) and a group of 13 preschoolers (40 to 48 months old) at a day care centre. The observers found that each group was organized into a fairly consistent linear dominance hierarchy. They then catalogued *possession episodes*, defined as a situation in which a *holder* touched or held an object and a *taker* touched the object and attempted to remove it from the holder's possession. Possession episodes averaged 11.7 per hour in the toddler group, and 5.4 per hour in the preschool group.

For each possession episode, the observers noted (a) whether the taker had been playing with the object within the previous sixty seconds (prior possession), (b) whether the holder resisted the take attempt (resistance), and (c) whether the take was successful (success). They found that success was strongly and about equally associated with both dominance and prior possession. They also found that resistance was associated mainly with dominance in the toddlers, and with prior possession in the preschoolers. They suggest that toddlers recognize possession as a basis for asserting control rights, but do not respect the same rights in others. The preschoolers, more than twice the age of the toddlers, use physical proximity both to justify their own claims and to respect the claims of others.

4 Respect for possession in non-human animals

In their famous paper, cited above, Maynard-Smith and Parker asserted 'If two animals are competing for some resource (e.g. a territory), and if there is some discernible asymmetry (e.g. between an "owner" and a later animal), then it is evolutionarily stable for the asymmetry to settle the contest conventionally, without fighting.' Among the many animal behaviourists who put this theory to the test, perhaps none is more elegant and unambiguous than Davies (1978), who studied the speckled wood (*Pararge aegeria*), a butterfly found in the Wytham Woods, near Oxford, England. Territories for this butterfly are shafts of sunlight breaking through the tree canopy. Males occupying these spots enjoyed heightened mating success, and on average only 60 per cent of males occupied the sunlit spots at any one time. A vacant spot was generally occupied within seconds, but an intruder on an already occupied spot was invariably driven away, even if the incumbent had occupied the spot only for a few seconds. When Davies 'tricked' two butterflies into thinking each had occupied the sunny patch first, the contest between the two lasted, on average, ten times as long as the brief flurry that occurs when an incumbent chases off an intruder.

Stevens (1988) found a similar pattern of behaviour for the feral horses occupying the sandy islands of the Rachel Carson Estuarine Sanctuary near Beaufort, North Carolina. In this case, it is fresh water that is scarce. After heavy rains, fresh water accumulates in many small pools in low-lying wooded areas, and bands of horses frequently stop to drink. Stevens found that there were frequent encounters between bands of horses competing for water at these temporary pools. If a band approached a water hole occupied by another band, a conflict ensued. During 76 hours of observation, Stevens observed 233 contests, of which the resident band won 178 (80 per cent). In nearly all cases of usurpation, the intruding band was larger than the resident band. These examples, and many others like them, support the presence of an endowment effect and suggest that incumbents are willing to fight harder to maintain their position than intruders are to usurp the owner.

Examples from non-human primates exhibit behavioural patterns in the respect for property rights much closer to that of humans. In general, the taking of an object held by another individual is a rare event in primate societies. A reasonable test of the respect for property in primates with a strong dominance hierarchy is the likelihood of a dominant individual refraining from taking an attractive object from a lower-ranking individual. In a study of hamadryas baboons (*Papio hamadryas*), for instance, Sigg and Falett (1985) have a subordinate allowed to manipulate a food-can and eat from it for five minutes before a dominant individual who had been watching from an adjacent cage was allowed to enter the subordinate's cage. A 'takeover' was defined as the rival taking possession of the can before thirty minutes had elapsed. They found that (a) males never took the food-can from other males; (b) dominant males took the can from subordinate females 2/3 of the time; and (c) dominant females took the can from subordinate females 1/2 of the time. With females, closer inspection showed that when the difference in rank was one or two, females showed respect for the property of other females, but when the rank difference was three or greater, takeovers tended to occur.

Hans Kummer and Marina Cords (1991) studied the role of proximity in respect for property in long-tailed macaques (*Macaca fascicularis*). As in the Sigg and Falett study, they assigned ownership to a subordinate and recorded the behaviour of a dominant individual. The valuable object in all cases was a plastic tube stuffed with raisins. In one experiment, the tube was fixed to an object in half the trials, and completely mobile in the other half. They found that with the fixed object, the dominant rival took possession in all cases and very quickly (median one minute), whereas in the mobile condition, the dominant took possession in only 10 per cent of cases, and then only after a median delay of 18 minutes. The experiment took place in an enclosed area, so the relative success of the incumbent was not likely due to the ability to flee or hide. In a second experiment, the object was either mobile, or attached to a fixed object by a stout two metre or four metre rope. The results were similar. A third case, in which the non-mobile object was attached to a long dragline that permitted free movement by the owner, produced the following results. Pairs of subjects were studied under two conditions, one where the rope attached to the dragline was 2 metres in length, and a second where the rope was 4 meters in length. In 23 of 40 trials, the subordinate maintained ownership with both rope lengths, and in 6 trials the dominant rival took possession with both rope lengths. In the remaining

11 trials, the rival respected the subordinate's property in the short rope case, but took possession in the long rope case. The experimenters observed that when a dominant attempts to usurp a subordinate when other group members are around, the subordinate will scream, drawing the attention of third parties, who frequently force the dominant individual to desist.

No primate experiment, to my knowledge, has attempted to determine the probability that an incumbent will be contested for ownership by a rival who is, or could easily become, closely proximate to the desired object. This probability is probably very low in most natural settings, so the contests described in the papers cited in this section are probably rather rare in practice. At any rate, in the model of respect for property developed in the next section, we make informational assumptions that render the probability of contestation equal to zero in equilibrium.

5 Conditions for private property equilibrium

Suppose that two agents, prior to fighting over possession, simultaneously precommit to expending a certain level of resources to the contest. As in the War of Attrition, a higher level of resource commitment entails a higher fitness cost, but increases the probability of winning the contest. We assume throughout this chapter that the two contestants, an incumbent and an intruder, are *ex ante* equally capable contestants in that the costs and benefits of battle are symmetric in the resource commitments s_o and s_u of the incumbent and intruder, respectively and $s_o, s_u \in [0, 1]$. To satisfy this requirement, we let $p_u = s_u^n / (s_u^n + s_o^n)$ be the probability that the intruder wins, where $n > 1$. Note that larger n implies that resource commitments are more decisive in determining victory. We assume that combat leads to injury $\beta \in (0, 1]$ to the losing party with probability $p_d = (s_o + s_u)/2$, so $s = \beta p_d$ is the expected cost of combat for both parties.

This chapter uses a territorial analogy throughout, some agents being incumbents and others being migrants in search of either empty territories or occupied territories that they may be able to occupy by displacing its current incumbent. Let π_g be the present value of being a currently uncontested incumbent, and let π_b be the present value of being a migrant searching for a territory. We assume throughout that $\pi_g > \pi_b > 0$. Suppose a migrant comes upon an occupied territory. Should the migrant contest, the condition under which it pays an incumbent to fight back is then given by

$$\begin{aligned}\pi_c \equiv p_d(1 - p_u)\pi_g + p_d p_u(1 - \beta)(1 - c)\pi_b \\ + (1 - p_d)(1 - p_u)\pi_g + (1 - p_d)p_u\pi_b(1 - c) > \pi_b(1 - c).\end{aligned}$$

The first term in π_c is the product of the probabilities that the intruder loses $(1 - p_u)$ and sustains an injury (p_d), times the value π_g of incumbency, which the incumbent then retains. The second term is the product of the probabilities that the incumbent loses (p_u), sustains an injury (p_d), survives the injury ($1 - \beta$), and survives the passage to migrant status ($1 - c$), times the present value π_b of being a migrant. The third and fourth terms are the parallel calculations when no injury is sustained. This inequality simplifies to

$$\frac{\pi_g}{\pi_b(1 - c)} - 1 > \frac{s_u^n}{s_o^n} s. \tag{1}$$

The condition for a migrant refusing to contest for the territory, assuming the incumbent will contest if the migrant does, is

$$\pi_u \equiv p_d(p_u\pi_g + (1 - p_u)(1 - \beta)(1 - c)\pi_b) \tag{2}$$

$$+ (1 - p_d)(p_u\pi_g + (1 - p_u)\pi_b(1 - c)) < \pi_b(1 - c). \tag{3}$$

This inequality reduces to

$$\frac{s_o^n}{s_u^n} s > \frac{\pi_g}{\pi_b(1 - c)} - 1. \tag{4}$$

A private property equilibrium occurs when both inequalities obtain:

$$\frac{s_o^n}{s_u^n} s > \frac{\pi_g}{\pi_b(1 - c)} - 1 > \frac{s_u^n}{s_o^n} s. \tag{5}$$

An incumbent who is challenged will choose S_o to maximize π_c, and then contest if and only if the resulting $\pi_c^* > \pi_b(1 - c)$, since the latter is the value of simply leaving the territory. It is easy to check that $\partial\pi_c/\partial s_o$ has the same sign as

$$\frac{\pi_g}{\pi_b(1 - c)} - \left(\frac{s_o\beta}{2n(1 - p_u)} + 1 - s\right).$$

The derivative of this expression with respect to s_o has the same sign as $(n - 1)\beta\pi_b/(1 - p_u)$, which is positive. Moreover, when $s_o = 0$, $\partial\pi_c/\partial s_o$ has the same sign as

$$\frac{\pi_g}{\pi_b(1 - c)} - 1 + \frac{s_u\beta(1 - c)}{2},$$

which is positive. Therefore, $\partial\pi_c/\partial s_o$ is always strictly positive, so $s_o = 1$ maximizes π_c.

In deciding whether or not to contest, the migrant chooses s_u to maximize π_u, and then contests if this expression exceeds $\pi_b(1-c)$. But $\partial\pi_c/\partial s_o$ has the same sign as

$$\frac{\pi_g}{\pi_b(1 - c)} - \left(s - 1 + \frac{s_u\beta}{2np_u}\right),$$

which is increasing in s_u and is positive when $s_u = 0$, so the optimal $s_u = 1$. The condition for not contesting the incumbent is then

$$\frac{\pi_g}{\pi_b(1 - c)} - 1 < \beta. \tag{6}$$

In this case, the condition (4) for the incumbent contesting is the same as (6) with the inequality sign reversed.

By an *anti-private property* equilibrium we mean a situation where intruders always contest, and incumbents always relinquish their possessions without a fight. We have

> Theorem 1. If $\pi_g > (1 + \beta)\pi_b(1 - c)$ *there is a unique equilibrium in which a migrant always fights for possession and an incumbent always contests. When the reverse inequality holds, there exist both a private property equilibrium and an anti-private property equilibrium.*

Theorem 1 implies that private property is more likely to exist when combatants are capable of inflicting great harm on one another, so β is close to its maximum of unity, or when migration costs are very high, so c is close to unity.

Theorem 1 may apply to a classic problem in the study of hunter-gatherer societies, which are important not only in their own right, but because our ancestors lived uniquely in such societies until about 10,000 years ago, and hence their social practices have doubtless been a major environmental condition to which the human genome has adapted. One strong uniformity across current-day hunter-gatherer societies is that low-value foodstuffs (e.g. fruits and small game) are consumed by the families that produced them, but high-value foodstuffs (e.g. large game and honey) are meticulously shared among all group members. The standard argument is that high-value foodstuffs exhibit a high variance, and sharing is a means of reducing individual variance. But an alternative with much empirical support is the *tolerated theft* theory that holds that high-value foodstuffs are worth fighting for (i.e. the inequality in Theorem 1 is satisfied), and the sharing rule is a means of reducing the mayhem that would inevitably result from the absence of secure property rights in high-value foodstuffs.[2]

The only part of Theorem 1 that remains to be proved is the existence of an anti-private property equilibrium. To see this, note that such an equilibrium exists when $\pi_c < \pi_b(1 - c)$ and $\pi_u > \pi_b(1 - c)$, which, by the same reasoning as above, occurs when

$$\frac{s_u^n}{s_o^n} > \frac{\pi_g}{\pi_b(1 - c)} - 1 > \frac{s_o^n}{s_u^n}s. \tag{7}$$

It is easy to show that if the incumbent contests, then both parties will set $s_u = s_o = 1$, in which case the condition for the incumbent to do better by not contesting is exactly as in the private property equilibrium.

The result that there exists an anti-private property equilibrium exactly when there is a private property equilibrium is quite unrealistic, since few, if any, anti-private property equilibria have been observed. Our model of course shares this anomaly with the Hawk, Dove, Bourgeois model, for which this weakness has never been analytically resolved. In our case, however, when we expand our model to determine π_g and π_g, the anti-private property equilibrium will generally disappear. The problem with the above argument is that we cannot expect π_g and π_b to have the same values in a private and an anti-private property equilibrium.

6 Property and anti-property equilibria

To determine π_g and π_b, we must flesh out the above model of incumbents and migrants. Consider a field with many patches, each of which is indivisible, and hence can have only one owner. In each time period, a fertile patch yields a benefit $b > 0$ to the owner, and dies with probability $p > 0$, forcing its owner (should it have one) to migrate elsewhere in search of a fertile patch. Dead patches regain their fertility after a period of time, leaving the fraction of patches that are fertile constant from period to period. An agent who encounters an empty fertile patch invests an amount $\nu \geq 0$ in preparing the patch for use, and occupies the patch. An agent suffers a fitness cost $c > 0$ each period he is in the state of searching for a fertile patch. An agent who encounters an occupied patch may contest for ownership of the patch, according to the War of Attrition structure analysed in the previous section.

Suppose there are n_p patches and n_a agents. Let r be the probability of finding a fertile patch, and let w be the probability of finding a fertile unoccupied patch. If the rate at which dead patches become fertile is q, which we assume for simplicity does not depend on how long a patch has been dead, then the equilibrium fraction f of patches that are fertile must satisfy $n_p fp = n_p(1 - f)q$, so $f = q/(p + q)$. Assuming that a migrant finds a new patch with probability ρ, we then have $r = f\rho$. If ϕ is the fraction of agents who are incumbents, then writing $\alpha = n_a/n_p$, we have

$$w = r(1 - \alpha\phi). \tag{8}$$

Assuming the system is in equilibrium, the number of incumbents whose patch dies must be equal to the number of migrants who find empty patches, or $n_a\phi(1 - p) = n_a(1 - \phi)w$. Solving this equation gives ϕ, which is given by

$$\alpha r\phi^2 - (1 - p + r(1 + \alpha))\phi + r = 0. \tag{9}$$

It is easy to show that this equation has two positive roots, exactly one lying in the interval (0,1).

In a private property equilibrium, we have

$$\pi_g = b + (1 - p)\pi_g + p\pi_b(1 - c) \tag{10}$$

and

$$\pi_b = w\pi_g(1 - \nu) + (1 - w)\pi_b(1 - c). \tag{11}$$

Note that the cost ν of investing and c of migrating are interpreted as fitness costs, and hence as probabilities of death. Thus, the probability of a migrant becoming an incumbent in the next period is $w(1 - \nu)$, and the probability of remaining a migrant is $(1 - w)$. This explains (11). Solving these two equations simultaneously gives equilibrium values of incumbency and non-incumbency:

$$\pi_g^* = \frac{b(c(1 - w) + w)}{p(c(1 - \nu w) + \nu w)} \tag{12}$$

$$\pi_b^* = \frac{b(1 - \nu)w}{p(c(1 - \nu w) + \nu w)}. \tag{13}$$

Note that $\pi_g, \pi_b > 0$, and

$$\frac{\pi_g^*}{\pi_b^*} - 1 = \frac{c(1 - w) + w\nu}{w(1 - \nu)}. \tag{14}$$

By Theorem 1, the assumption that this is a private property equilibrium is satisfied if and only if this expression is less than β, or

$$\frac{c(1 - w) + wv}{w(1 - v)} < \beta. \tag{15}$$

This inequality shows that, in addition to our previous result that low fighting cost and high migration cost undermine the private property equilibrium, a high probability w that a migrant encounters an incumbent undermines the private property equilibrium, and a high investment v has the same effect.

Suppose, however, that the system is in an anti-private property equilibrium. In this case, letting q_u be the probability that an incumbent is challenged by an intruder, we have

$$\pi_g = b + (1 - p)(1 - q_u)\pi_g + (p(1 - q_u) + q_u)\pi_b(1 - c) \tag{16}$$

and

$$\pi_b = w\pi_g(1 - v) + (r - w)\pi_g + (1 - r)\pi_b(1 - c). \tag{17}$$

Solving these equations simultaneously gives

$$\pi_g^* = \frac{b(c(1 - r) + r)}{((p(1 - q_u) + q_u))(vw + c(1 - vw))} \tag{18}$$

$$\pi_b^* = \frac{b(r - vw)}{(((p(1 - q_u) + q_u))(vw + c(1 - vw)))}. \tag{19}$$

Also, $\pi_g, \pi_b > 0$, and

$$\frac{\pi_g^*}{\pi_b^*} - 1 = \frac{c(1 - r) + vw}{r - vw}. \tag{20}$$

Note that $r - vw = r(1 - v(1 - \alpha\phi)) > 0$. We must check whether a non-incumbent mutant who never invests, and hence passes up empty, fertile patches, would be better off. In this case, the present value of the mutant, π_m, satisfies

$$\pi_m - \pi_b^* = (r - w)\pi_g^* + (1 - r + w)\pi_b^*(1 - c) - \pi_b^*$$

$$= \frac{bw(\nu(r - w) - c(1 - \nu(1 - r + 2))}{(p(1 - q_u) + q_u)(\nu w + c(1 - \nu w))}.$$

It follows that if

$$\nu \leq \frac{c}{(r - w)(1 - c) + c} \tag{21}$$

then the mutant behaviour (not investing) cannot invade, and we indeed have an anti-property equilibrium. Note that (21) has a simple interpretation. The denominator in the fraction is the probability that search ends either in death or finding an empty patch. The right-hand side is therefore the expected cost of searching for an occupied patch. If the cost ν of investing in a empty patch is greater than the expected cost of waiting to usurp an already productive (fertile and invested in) patch, no agent will invest.

However, if (21) is violated then migrants will refuse to invest in an empty fertile patch. Then (9), which implicitly assumed that a migrant would always occupy a vacant fertile patch, is violated. We argue as follows. Assume the system is in the anti-property equilibrium as described above and, noting the failure of (21), migrants begin refusing to occupy vacant fertile patches. Then, as incumbents migrate from newly dead patches, ϕ will fall, and hence w will rise. This will continue until (21) is satisfied as an equality. Thus, we must redefine an anti-property equilibrium as one in which (9) is satisfied when (21) is satisfied, and otherwise (21) is satisfied as an equality and (9) is no longer satisfied. Note that in the latter case the equilibrium value of ϕ will be strictly less than in the private property equilibrium. We then have

Theorem 2. *Suppose (21) is violated when ϕ is determined by (9). Then the anti-private property equilibrium exhibits a lower average pay-off than the private property equilibrium.*

The reason is simply that the equilibrium value of ϕ will be lower in the anti-property equilibrium than in the property equilibrium, so there will be on average more migrants and fewer incumbents in the anti-property equilibrium. But incumbents earn positive returns b per period, while migrants suffer positive costs c per period.

Theorem 2 helps explain why we rarely see anti-property equilibria in the real world. If two groups differ only in that one plays the private property equilibrium and the other plays the anti-private property equilibrium, the former will grow faster than and hence displace the latter, provided that there is some scarcity of resources leading to a limitation on the combined size of the two groups.

This argument does not account for private property equilibria in which there is virtually no investment by the incumbent. This includes the butterfly and feral horse examples, among others. In such cases, the property and anti-property equilibria differ in only one way: the identity of the patch owner changes in the latter more rapidly than in the former. It is quite reasonable to add to the model a small cost δ of ownership change, for instance because the intruder must physically approach the patch and engage in some sort of display before the change in incumbency can be effected. With this assumption, the anti-private property equilibrium again has a lower average pay-off than the private property equilibrium, so will be disadvantaged in a competitive struggle for existence.

The next section shows that if we respecify the ecology of the model appropriately, the unique equilibrium is precisely the anti-private property equilibrium.

7 An anti-private property equilibrium

Consider a situation in which agents die unless they have access to a fertile patch at least once every *n* days. While having access, they reproduce at rate *b* per period. An agent who comes upon a fertile patch that is already owned may value the patch considerably more than the current owner, since the intruder will have, on average, less time to find another fertile patch than the current owner, who has a full *n* days. In this situation, the current owner may have no incentive to put up a sustained battle for the patch, whereas the intruder may. The newcomer may thus acquire the patch without a battle. Thus there is a plausible anti-private property equilibrium.

To assess the plausibility of such a scenario, note that if π_g is the fitness of the owner of a fertile patch, and $\pi_b(k)$ is the fitness of a non-owner who has *k* periods to find and exploit a fertile patch before dying, then we have the recursion equations

$$\pi_b(0) = 0 \tag{22}$$

$$\pi_b(k) = w\pi_g + (1 - w)\pi_b(k - 1) \qquad \text{for } k = 1,\ldots,n, \tag{23}$$

where *r* is the probability that a non-owner becomes owner of a fertile patch, either because it is not owned, or the intruder costlessly evicts the owner. We can solve this, giving

$$\pi_b(k) = \pi_g + (1 - (1 - r)^k) \qquad \text{for } k = 0, 1,\ldots,n. \tag{24}$$

Note that the larger *k* and the larger *r*, the greater the fitness of a intruder. We also have the equation

$$\pi_g = b + (1 - p)\pi_g + p\pi_g(n), \tag{25}$$

where p is the probability the patch dies or the owner is costlessly evicted by an intruder. We can solve this equation, giving

$$\pi_g = \frac{b}{p(1 - r)^n}. \tag{26}$$

Note that the larger b, the smaller p, the larger r, and the larger n, the greater the fitness of an owner.

As in the previous model, assume the intruder devotes resources $s_u \in [0, 1]$ and the incumbent devotes resources $s_o \in [0, 1]$ to combat. With the same notation as above, we assume a fraction f_o of incumbents are contesters, and we derive the conditions for an incumbent and an intruder who has discovered the owner's fertile patch to conform to the anti-private property equilibrium. When these conditions hold, we will have $f_o = 0$.

Let π_c be the fitness value of contesting rather than simply abandoning the patch. Then we have

$$\pi_c = s(1 - p_u)\pi_g + (1 - s)((1 - p_u)\pi_g + p_u\pi_b(n)) - \pi_b(n),$$

which reduces to

$$\pi_c = \frac{\pi_g}{2}\left(\frac{s_u^2 + s_o(2 + s_u)}{s_o + s_u}(1 - r)^n - s_u\right). \tag{27}$$

Moreover, π_c is increasing in s_o, so if the owner contests, he will set $\sigma_o = 1$, in which case the condition for contesting being fitness-enhancing for the owner then becomes

$$\frac{s_u + 2/s_u + 1}{1 + s_u}(1 - r)^n > 1. \tag{28}$$

Now let $\pi_u(k)$ be the fitness of a non-owner who must own a patch before k periods have elapsed, and comes upon an owned, fertile patch. The agent's fitness value of usurping is

$$\begin{aligned}\pi_u(k) = {} & (1 - f)\pi_g + f(sp_u\pi_g + (1 - s)(p_u\pi_g + (1 - p_u)\pi_b(k - 1))) \\ & - \pi_b(k - 1).\end{aligned}$$

The first term in this equation is the probability the owner does not contest, times the intruder's gain if this occurs. The second term is the probability the owner does contest times the gain if the owner does contest, and the final term is the fitness value of not usurping. We can simplify this equation to

$$\pi_u(k) = \pi_g \frac{s_o(1 - f) + s_u}{s_o + s_u}. \tag{29}$$

This expression is always positive, and is increasing in s_u and decreasing in s_o, provided $f_o > 0$. Thus, the intruder will always set $s_u = 1$. Also, as one might expect, if $f_o = 0$, the migrant usurps with probability 1, so $\pi_u(k) = \pi_g$. At any rate, the migrant always contests, whatever the value of f_o. The condition (28) for not contesting, and hence for there to be a globally stable anti-private property equilibrium, becomes

$$2(1 - r)^n < 1, \tag{30}$$

which will be the case if either r or n is sufficiently large. When (30) does not hold, there will be an anti-private property equilibrium.

The anti-private property equilibrium is not often entertained in the literature, although John Maynard Smith (1982) describes the case of the spider *Oecibus civitas*, where intruders virtually always displace owners without a fight. More informally, I observe the model in action every summer's day at my bird feeders and bathers. A bird will arrive, eat or bathe for a while, and if the feeder or bath is crowded, then will be displaced, without protest, by another bird, and so on. It appears that, after having eaten or bathed for a while, it simply is not worth the energy to defend the territory.

8 Conclusion

Humans share with many other species a predisposition to recognize private property. This takes the form of *loss aversion*: an incumbent is prepared to commit more vital resources to defending his property, *ceteris paribus*, than an intruder is willing to commit to taking the property. The major proviso is that if the property is sufficiently valuable, a private property equilibrium will not exist (Theorem 1).

History is written as though private property is a product of modern civilization, a construction that exists only to the extent that it is defined and protected by judicial institutions operating according to legal notions of ownership. However, it is likely that private property in the fruits of one's labour existed for as long as humans lived in small hunter-gatherer clans, unless the equality in Theorem 1 holds, as might plausibly be the case for big game. The true value of modern private property, if the argument in this chapter is value, is fostering the accumulation of property even when $\pi_g > (1 + \beta)\pi_b(1 - c)$. It is in this sense only that Thomas Hobbes may have been correct in asserting that life in an unregulated state of nature is 'solitary, poor, nasty, brutish, and short'. But even so, it must be recognized that modern notions of property are built on human behavioural propensities that we share with many species of non-human animals. Doubtless, an alien species with a genetic organization akin to our ants or termites, would find our notions of individuality and privacy curious at best, and probably incomprehensible.

Notes

1. The assumption of indivisibility is not very restrictive. In some cases it is naturally satisfied, as in a nest, web, dam, or mate who provides for offspring. In others, such as a hunter's kill, a fruit tree, a stretch of beach for an avian scavenger, it is simply the minimum size worth fighting over rather than dividing or sharing.
2. For Theorem 1 to apply, the resource in question must be indivisible. In this case, the 'territory' is the foodstuff that delivers benefits over many meals, and the individuals who partake of it are temporary occupiers of the territory.

References

Bakeman, R. and J. Brownlee (1982) 'Social Rules Governing Object Conflicts in Toddlers and Preschoolers', in K. Rubin and H. Ross (eds), *Peer Relationships and Social Skills in Childhood* (New York: Springer Verlag), pp. 99–112.

Davies, N. (1978) 'Territorial Defence in the Speckled Wood Butterfly (*Pararge aegeria*): the Resident Always Wins', *Animal Behaviour,* vol. 26, pp. 138–47.

Eason, P., G. Cobbs and K. Trinka (1999) 'The Use of Landmarks to Define Territorial Boundaries', *Animal Behaviour,* vol. 58, pp. 85–91.

Ellis, L. (1985) 'On the Rudiments of Possession and Property', *Social Science Information,* vol. 24(1), pp. 113–43.

Furby, L. (1980) 'The Origins and Early Development of Possessive Behavior', *Political Psychology,* vol. 2(1), pp. 30–42.

Kummer, H. and M. Cords (1991) 'Cues of Ownership in Long-tailed Macaques, emphMacaca fascicularis', *Animal Behaviour,* vol. 42, pp. 529–49.

Maynard Smith, J. (1982) *Evolution and the Theory of Games* (Cambridge: Cambridge University Press).

Maynard Smith, J. and G. Parker (1976) 'The Logic of Asymmetric Contests', *Animal Behaviour,* vol. 24, pp. 159–75.

Riechert, S. (1978) 'Games Spiders Play: Behavioural Variability in Territorial Disputes', *Journal of Theoretical Biology,* vol. 84, pp. 93–101.

Senar, J., M. Camerino and N. Metcalfe (1989) 'Agonistic Interactions in Siskin Flocks: Why Are Dominants Sometimes Subordinate?' *Behavioral Ecology and Sociobiology,* vol. 25, pp. 141–5.

Sigg, H. and J. Falett (1985) 'Experiments on Respect of Possession and Property in Hamadryas Baboons', *Animal Behaviour,* vol. 33.

Stevens, E. (1988) 'Contests between Bands of Feral Horses for Access to Fresh Water: the Resident Wins', *Animal Behaviour,* vol. 36, pp. 1851–3.

Thaler, R. (1992) *The Winner's Curse* (Princeton, NJ: Princeton University Press).

Trivers, R. (1971) 'The Evolution of Reciprocal Altruism', *Quarterly Review of Biology,* vol. 46, pp. 35–57.

Tversky, A. and D. Kahneman (1981) 'Loss Aversion in Riskless Choice: a Reference Dependent Model', *Quarterly Journal of Economics,* vol. 106, pp. 1039–61.

9

The Complex Evolution of a Simple Traffic Convention: the Functions and Implications of Habit*

Geoffrey M. Hodgson
The Business School, University of Hertfordshire, UK

and

Thorbjørn Knudsen
Department of Marketing and Management,
University of Southern Denmark, Denmark

1 Introduction

This chapter presents an agent-based simulation of the emergence of a traffic convention – concerning whether to drive on the left or the right of the road. The interaction between agents and structures involves causal influences in two directions, showing how agents constitute institutions and how institutions can have reconstitutive causal effects on individuals.

The evolution of conventions and institutions has become the subject of much analysis, modelling and discussion.[1] We raise here some further analytical and conceptual issues on the basis of a heuristic, agent-based simulation with heterogeneous agents. The general *outcome* of the simulation is relatively uncomplicated because we choose one of the most straightforward of decisions and conventions: whether to drive on the right or on the left of the road. In our model, artificially intelligent 'drivers' in 'cars' are programmed to negotiate a circular road configuration along with a number of other, similar vehicles. We show that the emergence of a convention is possible but by no means guaranteed. Furthermore, some manipulation of the decision processes

* This chapter is a shortened version of Hodgson and Knudsen (2004), excluding some of its data, regression and bibliographic references. The authors wish to thank Brian Arthur, Kenneth Binmore, Nathalie Lazaric, Axel Leijonhufvud, Paul Ormerod, J. Barkley Rosser, Jr., Koye Somefun, Robert Sugden, Margherita Turvani, Viktor Vanberg, Kumaraswamy Velupillai, Ulrich Witt, anonymous referees and others for their comments on earlier drafts.

through which these 'drivers' decide to move to the left or the right provides a basis to consider some of the deeper conceptual issues that are involved in the evolution of conventions, such as the nature of rational decision-making and its possible reliance upon habit.

Each driver is boundedly rational. To negotiate the track and avoid collision, it would seem to be rational for each driver at least to consider *conformity* with the perceived distribution of traffic to the left and right and *avoidance* of cars that are immediately ahead. To these factors, our model adds *habit*.

Any left/right convergence outcome in this model is likely to depend on initial conditions and circumstances. Strong path dependence is likely, but we are more interested in the degree and resilience of any emergent convention than whether it is on the left or the right.

We show that in following or avoiding other traffic in some circumstances, strength of habit and processes of habituation can play a vital role alongside rational deliberation and selection pressure. This outcome not only raises important questions concerning the role of habit in decision-making, but also it challenges the frequent assumption that preference functions should always be taken entirely as exogenously given.

The chapter is structured in seven parts. As well as defining some key terms, the second part considers the theoretical background and points to some important differences of view concerning the manner in which institutions and conventions evolve. The heuristic model is presented in the third part. In the fourth part the basic results of the simulations are reported. The implications of the simulations concerning the concept of habit and regarding the concept of 'downward causation' are discussed in the fifth and sixth parts, respectively. The seventh part concludes the chapter.

2 The evolution of conventions and institutions

We define institutions as durable systems of established and embedded social rules that structure social interactions. A convention is a particular instance of an institutional rule (Sugden, 1986). For example, all countries have traffic rules, but it is a matter of (arbitrary) convention whether the rule is to drive on the right or on the left.

Carl Menger pioneered a basic analysis of how institutions evolve. His chosen example was money. Menger saw the institution of money as emanating in an undesigned manner from the communications and interactions of individual agents. Traders look for a convenient and frequently exchanged commodity to use in their exchanges with others. Once such regularities become prominent, a circular process of institutional self-reinforcement takes place. Emerging to overcome the difficulties of barter, money is chosen because it is convenient, and it is convenient because it is chosen.[2]

In this Mengerian approach, individual preference functions are taken as given. Menger thus inspired a central, unifying project in the 'new institutional economics': to explain the existence of political, legal, or social institutions by reference to a model of given, individual behaviour, tracing out its consequences in terms of human interactions.[3]

However, theoretical analyses or simulation of the evolution of institutions have proved to be remarkably problematic. For example, in the work of Ramon Marimon et al. (1990) an attempt is made to model the emergence of money with artificially intelligent agents. Their results are qualified and partially inconclusive. A single monetary unit does not always readily emerge. Menger's discursive analysis of an emergent convention has proven to be difficult to replicate in a computer simulation. Our simulations also show the difficulties in reaching convergence even with a very simple convention.

The central hypothesis behind the present chapter is that there is often more to the emergence of real world institutions than mere matters of convenience and calculation by individual agents. Additional psychological factors intervene, including emotions, instincts and other dispositions. This basic idea can be found in the writings of the neglected tradition of 'old' institutionalism. For instance, arguing that the evolution of money cannot be understood simply in terms of cost reduction and individual convenience, Wesley Mitchell maintained that money 'stamps its pattern upon wayward human nature, makes us all react in standard ways to the standard stimuli it offers, and affects our very ideals of what is good, beautiful and true' (Mitchell, 1937, p. 371). Accordingly, the evolution of money changed the mentality, preferences and thinking patterns of individuals themselves. This does not necessarily mean that Menger's account is wrong, but that it is sometimes inadequate. At least in some circumstances, it may have to be supplemented by an analysis of how institutions can change individual perceptions and preferences.

The idea of the malleability of individual preferences pervades the 'old' institutional economics, from Thorstein Veblen to John Kenneth Galbraith. However, it has not yet been shown why some preference malleability may be necessary for the emergence and sustainability of institutions. In this chapter we begin to fill this gap by showing how a limited form of preference malleability can improve the possibility and stability of an equilibrium convention.

What is at issue here is the adequacy of the standard account of the emergence of institutions. Just as individuals constitute institutions, individuals may also be partially reconstituted by institutions. Once we raise this possibility, however, we encounter some conceptual problems concerning the specification of such preference endogeneity. It is not our intention to replicate a widely criticized picture of individuals as puppets of institutions, roles or cultural values. To avoid such pitfalls, we have to specify adequately the limits, nature and mechanisms of this reconstitution.

It is here that we come to the concept of habit. The simulation outlined in the next section shows how habit can be significant for institutional evolution, especially in circumstances of limited information. Circumstances help to form the predispositions of individuals by forming and changing their habits. Of course, several attempts have been made to accommodate a notion of habit within relatively sophisticated rational choice models.[4] In these models, any habit is seen as ultimately an outcome of a rational choice. In contrast, in the pragmatist tradition of Charles Sanders Peirce, William James, George Herbert Mead and John Dewey, any rational deliberation is always seen as grounded on habit. The question then is whether rational choice is the foundation of habit, or whether the reverse is true (Becker, 1992; Hodgson, 1998, 2004). The discussion of the simulation, in section 6, addresses this dilemma. It is shown that the concept of habit developed in the cited rational choice models is not the same as the concept in our model and in the tradition of pragmatist thought.

Our intention is not to treat habit as some kind of psychological panacea, but to investigate its significance in the 'experimental' context of a simulation. The model shows that in some circumstances habit can assist convergence to a left/right convention but it also depends upon, and interacts with, other variables and processes. We do not argue that habit is the only factor involved in convergence, but under frequent conditions it is important when allied with other factors. We also find that in some circumstances habit can be disruptive.

3 The simulation model

3.1 The decision problem and the environment of choice

In our model,[5] 40 agents drive around a 100 × 2 grid, arranged in a ring, with two lanes and 100 zones. We use the terms 'agent', 'driver', and 'car' synonymously. The drivers are unique individuals, born to drive either clockwise or counter-clockwise around the ring, referred to as lengthways movement. Half of the agents drive clockwise and the other half counter-clockwise. For each car, the direction of its lengthways movement cannot be changed.

At time $t = 0$, the drivers are randomly assigned a zone and a position on one of the two sides of the ring. The cars then move in turn. During each move, each driver must decide whether to drive on the left or the right side of the ring when making their next lengthways movement. This left/right movement is the driver's only choice variable. Each driver performs an incremental lengthways movement, placing itself in the next zone ahead, on either its left or its right lane.

The left/right decision is partly based on information about the traffic in front of the driver. The driver looks 10 increments ahead and counts in that region the number of cars in each lane and the number of cars going in each direction. Based on this information and given its behavioural and cognitive dispositions (defined below), the driver will decide on which side of the ring to drive in its next move. Each car drives around the ring until it is involved in a collision. A collision occurs when a car moves into a zone occupied by another car that is also in the same lane, irrespective of the direction of movement of the cars. Then both drivers die and new cars and drivers replace them. As a result, the number of cars on the grid is always 40. The replacement routine also ensures that the number of cars moving clockwise and counter-clockwise is always 20.

3.2 Behavioural and cognitive dispositions

Initially our objective was to make the drivers as 'intelligent' as possible, subject to the constraint of a limited number of cognitive and behavioural variables. After numerous runs with additional cognitive parameters, we found that a highly parsimonious model was very effective. Additional decision parameters had little effect in enhancing the survival of individual cars or the convergence characteristics of the model.[6]

When first placed on the ring, each driver receives a unique set $\{S_{Sensitivity_n}, O_{Sensitivity_n}, A_{voidance_n}, H_{abitgene_n}, H_{abituation_{n,t}}\}$ of five cognitive and behavioural dispositions. The first four of these dispositions are randomly assigned and cannot be changed. These variables are randomly chosen according to normal distribution with mean 1 and standard deviation δ (referred to as the mutation variable). Negative numbers are truncated to zero, but there is no upper bound.[7] The only disposition that can be changed during the life of the car is the car's acquired habits ($H_{abituation_{n,t}}$). Furthermore, for all original or newborn drivers, the initial level of the habituation variable is zero ($H_{abituation_{n,0}} = 0$).

Note that the terms 'left' and 'right' are relative to the driver involved. A car driving clockwise on the right will not collide with a car driving counter-clockwise on the right. The same applies to two cars both on the left, likewise moving in opposite directions. The terms 'ahead' and 'behind' are also relative to the car and its movement. A car may collide with another car moving in the same direction, but only if that other car is one zone ahead and does not move first, or if that other car is one zone behind and does move first.

(i) *Same-direction sensitivity.* Each driver looks forward and observes the number of cars going in the same direction as itself up to and including 10 zones ahead, and calculates the proportion of this number driving on the left (or right) hand side of the road. (If no car is going in the same direction as itself, up to and including 10 zones ahead, then the proportion is taken as 0.5.) The variable $S_{Sensitivity_n}$ indicates the degree to which driver n takes account of this ratio in determining its next move. If this variable is high then the car will tend to conform to the pattern of behaviour of the cars ahead of itself and moving in its own direction.

(ii) *Opposite-direction sensitivity*. Each driver *n* looks forward and observes the number of cars going in the opposite direction to itself, up to and including 10 zones ahead, and calculates the proportion of this number driving on *their* left (or right) hand side of the road. (Again, if no car is going in the opposite direction as itself, up to and including 10 zones ahead, then the proportion is taken as 0.5.) The coefficient $O_{Sensitivity_n}$ indicates the degree to which car *n* takes account of this ratio in determining its next move. As well as a rationale to conform to the convention established by others, there is an incentive to avoid this traffic coming in the opposite direction.

(iii) *Avoidance*. This coefficient captures a tendency for each driver *n* to avoid collision with close, oncoming traffic. Each driver looks forward and observes the number of cars going in both directions, *one* zone ahead, and calculates the number on the left and right-hand side of the road, relative to the driver. Because each car moves in turn, another car that is positioned one zone ahead of driver *n* poses a collision danger, regardless of its direction of movement: cars moving in both directions threaten driver *n* with immediate collision. Driver *n*'s avoidance is captured by the coefficient $A_{voidance_n}$, referring to the situation one zone ahead.

(iv) *Habit gene*. A driver's habit gene must be distinguished from its habituation. The habit gene is the instinctive tendency that a driver has to take account of its acquired habituation. The habit gene cannot change but habituation can. The role of the habit gene is explained in the discussion of habituation below. Driver *n*'s habit gene is captured by the coefficient $H_{abitgene_n}$.

Every driver receives a unique personal profile in which the values of the above four behavioural and cognitive variables are randomly assigned. However, the following variable can change through the course of a driver's life.

(v) *Habituation*. Every driver starts with a habituation variable set initially at zero. As time goes on, this variable will be revised according to the car's movements. For instance, if a car has a history of moving on the left-hand side of the road then the habituation variable is likely to be positive, and if a car has generally moved on the right-hand side of the road then the habituation variable is likely to be negative. A more precise account of the habituation process is given below. The habit gene coefficient expresses the degree to which driver *n* takes its habituation into account. Driver *n*'s habituation at time *t* is captured by the coefficient $H_{abituation_{n,t}}$.

3.3 Calculation, habituation, decision and movement

Each car is addressed and moves sequentially. With no simultaneous moves, some associated problems of interpretation of the intentions of others are thus avoided. In each period, all drivers in turn make a (subjective) decision based on the (objective) information about the traffic ahead. Again the purpose was to make the drivers as 'intelligent' as possible, making use of the most important information for their survival, subject to reasonable computational constraints. As each car can only move one zone ahead, there is no reason to take account of traffic to its rear. As noted above, at time t, each driver calculates the following variables:

$S_{L,n}$ = the proportion of all cars, going in the *same* direction as driver n, up to and including 10 zones ahead, that are driving on the left-hand side of the road, where $0 \leq S_{L,n} \leq 1$. If no car is going in the same direction as driver n, up to and including 10 zones ahead, then $S_{L,n} = 0.5$.

$O_{L,n}$ = the proportion of all cars, going in the direction *opposite* to driver n and up to and including 10 zones ahead, that are driving on *their* left hand side of the road, where $0 \leq O_{L,n} \leq 1$. If no car is going in the opposite direction as driver n, up to and including 10 zones ahead, then $O_{L,n} = 0.5$.

$C_{L,n}$ = the number of very close cars, going in any direction, exactly one zone ahead of driver n, that are driving on the left-hand side of the road relative to driver n, where $C_{L,n} = 0$ or 1.

$C_{R,n}$ = the number of very close cars, going in any direction, exactly one zone ahead of driver n, that are driving on the right-hand side of the road relative to driver n, where $C_{R,n} = 0$ or 1.

After having gathered this information and calculated the above ratios, the driver then updates its habit function according to the following formula:

$$Habituation_{n,t} = Habituation_{n,t-1} + LR_{n,t}/(K + Moves_{n,t}),$$

where $LR_{n,t}$ is the situation of car n at time t, whether it is on the left ($LR_{n,t} = 1$) or on the right ($LR_{n,t} = -1$) hand side of the road. K is an arbitrary positive constant and $Moves_{n,t}$ is the total number of moves the driver has undertaken, up to and including the present move at time t. In addition, $Habituation_{n,t}$ is bounded between -1 and 1. Clearly the tendency to change habit decreases with the number of moves; the habit function is cumulative with a decreasing increment. The driver uses the above equation to update its habituation variable.[8]

To make a decision to go left or right, the value of the following expression is calculated:

$$\begin{aligned} LREvaluation_n = {} & w_{Sdirection} \times SSensitivity_n \times (2S_{L,n,t} - 1) \\ & + w_{Odirction} \times OSensitivity_n \times (2O_{L,n,t} - 1) \\ & + w_{Avoidance} \times Avoidance_n \times (C_{R,n,t} - C_{L,n,t}) \\ & + w_{Habit} \times Habitgene_n \times Habituation_{n,t}. \end{aligned}$$

The w_X coefficients ($w_{Sdirection}$, $w_{Odirection}$, $w_{Avoidance}$, and w_{Habit}) are fixed, non-negative weights common to all 40 drivers. The weights determine how much the components of every driver's unique set of cognitive and behavioural dispositions will influence the driver's subjective evaluation and thus its choice to go left or right at time *t*. The coefficient w_{Habit} is referred to as the 'habit weighting'. The term $w_{Habit} \times Habitgene_n \times Habituation_{n,t}$ is referred to as 'the strength of habit' of a car.

Note that each term on the right-hand side of the equation above includes two positive elements plus one element with expected values equally distributed around zero, all multiplied together. Hence each term on the right-hand side has expected values equally distributed around zero. As a result, there is no bias to the right or the left in the model.

The subjective evaluation of each car is given by the variable $LR_{Evaluation_n}$. If $LR_{Evaluation_n}$ is greater than zero then the car intends to move to the left. Otherwise it intends to move to the right. The final element to be taken into consideration is the possibility of error. An error probability variable ε is preset at the beginning of the simulation. A random number generator is used to determine whether each car, with probability ε, makes the move opposite to its subjective evaluation. At this final stage, the left or right inclination of the car in the upcoming move is determined.

The car then moves one increment forward onto the next zone, on the left or right as determined. If there is no other car on the same side of the road and in the same zone, then there is no collision. In each period, all drivers in turn go through these steps.

The drivers in the model are boundedly rational. Taking account of the most important local information, each car responds and manoeuvres in order to survive. The decision algorithm combines decision elements that vary according to the cognitive personality of the driver and the global parameter weights. The population of varied decision algorithms itself evolves due to selection pressure, leading to surviving decision algorithms of some fitness value.

3.4 Replacement of colliding drivers

If there is neither birth nor death, then the pool of fixed characteristics among the population cannot change. At least a small amount of death and replacement is necessary to select the combinations of fixed cognitive and behavioural dispositions that are conducive to survival. However, this means that a replacement routine is necessary for new cars and its form can influence the outcomes in the model. It should be emphasized, however, that the overwhelming majority of deaths generally occur in the early, transition phase of the simulations.

If there is a collision, then – regardless of blame or circumstances – the two drivers die and are replaced by two new cars and drivers. The weights w_X are common to all agents and also used by the newborn drivers. However, the two newborn drivers require a new set of four fixed cognitive and behavioural dispositions $\{S_{Sensitivity_n} O_{Sensitivity_n}, A_{voidance_n}, H_{abitgene_{nt}}\}$. These were chosen randomly in the same manner as the cars in the population at the beginning of the simulation, with the habituation level $\{H_{abituation_{n,t}}\}$ always set initially to zero.

Their cognitive and behavioural characteristics being determined, each new car is allocated to a random position on the track. However, to reduce the frequency of immediate collisions, no new car is allocated to a zone occupied by another car.

3.5 Design adjustments and parametric searches

Experiments were performed with different values of the mutation variable δ. Although a convention emerged with many runs with a higher value, a relatively low value of 0.2 was chosen in order to achieve a lower and more plausible degree of mutation. Different values of K in the function above for $H_{abituation_{n,t}}$ were also tried. Clearly, as K decreases to zero, the left/right choice by the car in its first move will increasingly dominate its strength of habit. The outcomes were relatively insensitive to variations in this coefficient, but habit had a slightly improved positive effect on convergence with values of K in the region of 10. This value ensured that habituation adjusted at a significant but modest rate.

The decision horizon is the number of zones ahead that a driver scans to estimate the traffic pattern. These data affect the driver's 'conformist' calculations concerning same-direction and opposite-direction sensitivity. As summarized in an appendix in the original article, a number of simulations were performed with various decision horizons greater than 10 zones ahead, including the possibility that drivers see all 100 zones of the entire ring. It was found that habit significantly improves convergence for values of the horizon from zero up to and including 25 zones. The maximum habit effect appears with a horizon of 10, which is the value used in the standard runs reported in the main text below.

After all the design adjustments were complete, the values of the first three non-negative weights $\{w_{Sdirection}, w_{Odirection},$ and $w_{Avoidance}\}$ were considered by searching through their multidimensional parametric space, with progressively decreasing increments of search, with w_{Habit} always set at zero. The three positive weights were always normalized according to the rule that their average was unity. The convergence performance, death rates and other aspects of the model were monitored during these searches. At each search point, a sample of at least 100 repeated simulations were made to obtain mean values. Also at each point, error was increased uniformly from zero to 0.02, across the set of 100 or more samples. This search of parameter space identified the point of maximum convergence $\{w_{Sdirection} = 1.4, w_{Odirection} = 0.9,$ and $w_{Avoidance} = 0.7\}$ with $w_{Habit} = 0$.[9]

4 Simulation results for the standard model

4.1 Preliminary remarks

The principal aim of the simulations is to gauge the degree of left/right convergence in multiple runs of the model, exploring different points of parameter space and assessing the impact of different levels of habit and error.

Generally, when an equilibrium outcome emerges, the resulting convention, whether drive-to-the-right or drive-to-the-left, can be highly sensitive to initial conditions. Once the system begins to swing decisively and permanently one way or the other and a convention begins to emerge, then it can become locked into a process that is the cumulative result of tiny initial movements.

However, two factors can disturb this process of convergence to a left/right convention. The first, and more ubiquitous, is error. The effects of error can be particularly disruptive in the early phases of this process. However, even in later phases, errors can trigger deaths that lead to replacements that are ill-adapted for the road conditions, leading to further collisions, and so on. It is possible for such processes of positive feedback to destroy an established convention.

The second disturbing factor emerges under specific conditions only. It is prevalent in a relatively small neighbourhood of parameter space. In some circumstances agile drivers can evolve, typically with a low but positive level of the habit gene. These drivers are sufficiently agile to avoid the traffic ahead, by moving repeatedly from one side of the road to the other if required. A 'cycling' pattern can occur, when cohorts of agile drivers repeatedly move safely and laterally to avoid other oncoming groups. There may be a degree of local convergence in each group, but the conventions in different groups may be different. If there are no further collisions then replacement and mutation through death cannot occur. Consequently, a unanimous convention will not emerge among the population as a whole.

4.2 Some illustrative simulations

Illustrative results from two different runs are displayed in Figure 9.1. The vertical scale measures the average inclination of the cars to the left or right. The horizontal scale measures the number of car moves enacted through time. In Figures 9.1 and 9.2, a value of unity on the vertical scale would correspond to the unanimous use of either the right or the left-hand side of the road by all cars. A value of 0.5 on the vertical scale would indicate that the cars were equally distributed on the right or the left. The expected value at the start of the run is 0.5. With a run of 20,000 car moves, the mean of the 20,000 vertical values is computed.

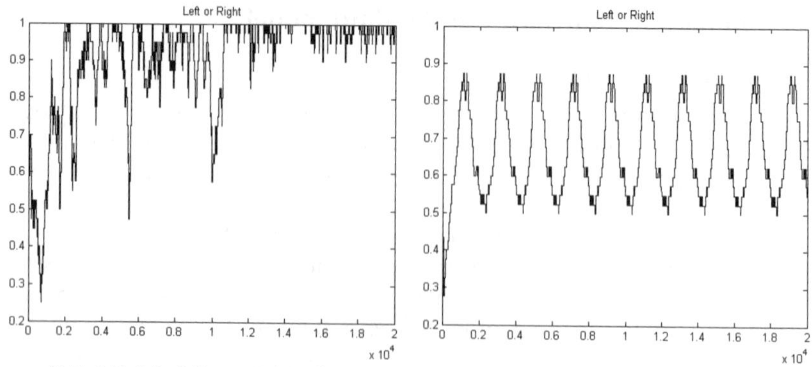

w_X = (0.5, 0.5, 2.0, 0.2), ε = 0.01. C =0.9056 w_X = (0.5, 2.0, 0.5, 0.1), ε = 0. C =0.6641

Figure 9.1 Two illustrative runs

In order to compare results whether the drivers happened to converge on the left or the right, we used the following standardization procedure. If this average is less than 0.5, then it is subtracted from 1, ensuring that the overall convergence outcome (C) is always greater than or equal to 0.5 and less than or equal to 1. With this measure of convergence success, higher values indicate a greater degree of convergence. A figure of 0.95 would indicate that on average, for one entire run, 95 per cent of the cars were on one particular side of the road.

Hence the degree of convergence (C) for m moves with c cars is the total number of moves in which a car is on the left/right, divided by $c \times m$. In this calculation all cars are considered for each individual move of every car through the entire run. The choice of left or right in this definition is made to ensure that $C \geq 0.5$. Hence $0.5 \leq C < 1$.

In the run displayed on the left of Figure 9.1 there is imperfect and incomplete convergence to one side of the track. The small amount of error slightly disturbs the emergent convention and prevents complete convergence. The death rate (not illustrated) is fairly steady and does not greatly subside. In the run displayed on the right of the figure, complete convergence to a left/right convention is prevented by a minority cohort of 18 cars that defy convention and have a disposition to drive on the other side. When they meet oncoming cars they are able to manoeuvre to avoid collision. Partly because the error coefficient is zero in this case, no collisions or deaths occur after the first few moves. Consequently, no further evolution of the model in this run is possible and the 'cycling' pattern becomes permanent.

Many thousands of distinct runs were tried. In some simulations, the habit weighting (w_{Habit}) took the values of 0, 0.5, 1.0, 1.5 and 2.0 in turn. The purpose was to show the effects of increasing weightings to the habit term in the decision function for every car. For each level of w_{Habit}, the error probability

ε took the values of 0.000, 0.005, 0.010, 0.015 and 0.020. This meant that 25 combinations of different levels of w_{Habit} and ε were explored. We tried 200 runs, each with 20,000 car moves, for each of the 25 different combinations of the values for w_{Habit} and ε. This meant a total of 5,000 runs and 100 million car moves.[10]

We found that the degrees of convergence, the death rates, the effects of error, and the impact of habit can vary substantially, depending on the values of the three parameters $\{w_{Sdirection}, w_{Odirection},$ and $w_{Avoidance}\}$. In some regions of parameter space, with a given level of error, increases in the overall strength of habit in the population as a whole (formed by the terms $w_{Habit} \times H_{abitgene} \times H_{abituation}$) can often help to improve the speed of convergence to a left/right convention. In addition, w_{Habit} can sometimes help the system cope with error and subvert 'cycling' behaviour. In other parts of parameter space, the impact of habit on convergence is small or negative.

However, it is important to emphasize that convergence is never achieved by the force of habit alone. Furthermore, convergence can sometimes occur with low or zero levels of habit. Crucially, habit helps convergence only when it is combined with selection pressure on the fixed 'instincts' in the population of cars.

The results of a multiple simulation with different levels of w_{Habit} and ε are reported in Figure 9.2. The three weights in this model are from the point in parameter space where convergence is maximized with zero habit. The vertical axis on Figure 9.2 shows the degree of convergence to a left/right convention. The higher the value the greater the degree of convergence.

$$w_X = (1.4, 0.9, 0.7, w_{Habit})$$

A striking outcome displayed in Figure 9.2 is the sensitivity of convergence to the habit weighting (w_{Habit}) and strength of habit. As w_{Habit} increases, at least from zero to unity, mean convergence levels improve for all levels of error (ε). Habit generally improves convergence.[11]

4.3 Multiple simulations in parameter space

The simulation reported in the previous section is from a point in parameter space where the convergence is maximized with zero habit. The question is raised whether other parts of parameter space exhibit the same positive habit effect, and if so, to what degree.

In Hodgson and Knudsen (2004) we developed techniques for the systematic search through the entire parameter space. Based on the data from hundreds of observations in this parameter space, habit emerged as the most significant factor determining the degree of convergence.

No other variable emerged in general to improve convergence in our simulations. For instance, while the avoidance coefficient can help the drivers to survive, it does not significantly assist convergence.

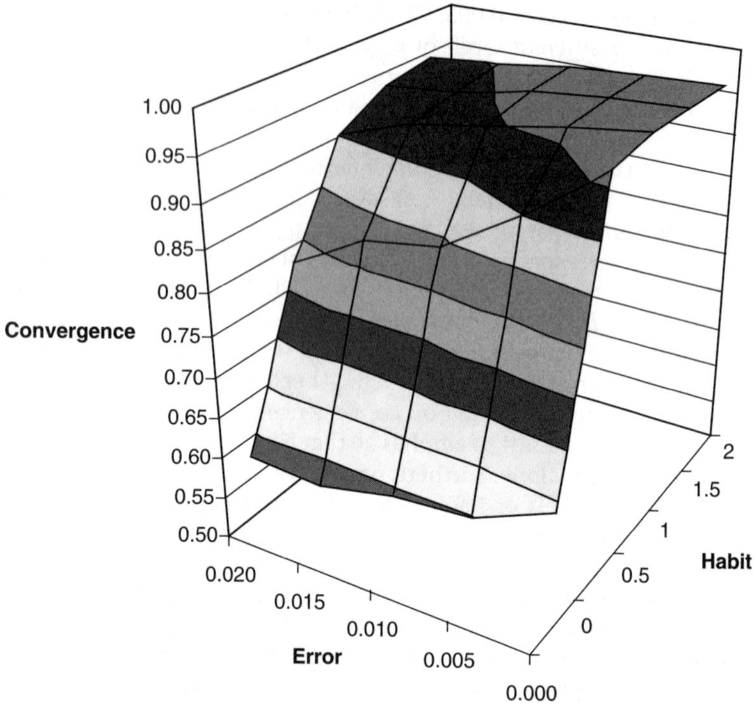

Figure 9.2 Degrees of convergence with 200 runs for each level of habit and error

We conclude that in this boundedly rational situation, where drivers cannot see the whole of the ring, habit emerged as the single most significant factor improving convergence. If drivers can see further ahead (Hodgson and Knudsen, 2004, Appendix 2), habit still has a positive effect. In addition, when the decision horizon is greater than 10, and hence there is more information concerning the traffic ahead, 'conformist' factors related to the $w_{Sdirection}$ and $w_{Odirection}$, coefficients become significant and more important in aiding convergence. The relative importance of habit is inversely related to omniscience.[12]

5 Discussion – the nature of habit

The most important result of the simulations described in section 4 concerns the effect of introducing processes of habituation into the modelling of agent behaviour. In a substantial region of parameter space, strength of habit can increase the systemic rate of convergence towards a left/right convention. In some circumstances it can also enhance systemic resistance to error.

In the above model, each car is programmed by three parameters ($S_{Sensitivity_n}$, $O_{Sensitivity_n}$, $A_{voidance_n}$) governing its sensitivity to traffic patterns ahead and its propensity to make an avoidance manoeuvre. A fourth parameter ($H_{abitgene_{nt}}$) governs the tendency that a driver has to take account of its acquired habituation. The values of these four exogenously given parameters are akin to instincts: they are fixed for the lifetime of each car. By contrast, a fifth parameter ($H_{abituation_{n,t}}$) governing the particular habitual disposition to go left or right is an outcome of the actual behaviour of the car. The value of this parameter is not given and is literally path dependent.

The conception and role of habit in this model contrast greatly with a definition of habit elsewhere. Gary Becker (1992, p. 328) writes: 'I define *habitual* behavior as displaying a positive relation between past and current consumption.' Becker here defines habit not as a behavioural propensity but as sequentially correlated behaviour. A car may manoeuvre to the left to avoid oncoming traffic, but its propensity may still be to drive to the right. If there is an observed succession of left-driving behaviour, this is not necessarily the underlying disposition of the agent. Becker's definition conflates propensity with actuality. However, if past behaviour were taken to mean a potentially infinite sequence of past events, then a propensity acquired through habituation could approximate to mean past behaviour. In this extreme case, propensity with actuality could coincide, but in general, and in contrast to Becker, we distinguish between habit and behaviour by defining habit as a disposition or propensity, rather than correlated behaviour.

Becker (1992, p. 331) is on stronger ground when he writes: 'Habit helps economize on the cost of searching for information, and of applying the information to a new situation.' It is true that habit removes some actions from conscious deliberation and helps the agent to focus on other, more strategic or immediate decisions. However, the model here suggests that there is something more to habit than economizing on decision-making. After all, each car in the model makes only one simple binary decision at each point of time. Habit is doing much more in our model than simply economizing on the time taken to search for and process information.

The model suggests that a crucial role played by habit is to build up and reinforce an enduring disposition in each agent concerning the appropriate side of the road on which to drive, especially in a situation where information concerning the traffic ahead is limited. A sequence of similar and repeated behaviours creates in each agent a habitual predilection, which can stimulate a 'belief' or 'conviction' that a particular behaviour is appropriate.

Again this is reminiscent of the arguments of pragmatists such as Peirce and James, who saw acquired habits as the basis of firmly held beliefs. Habit is more than a means of economizing on decision-making for individuals; it is a means by which social conventions and institutions are formed and preserved.

Our model raises questions concerning the distinction between preference exogeneity and endogeneity. By introducing the concept of meta-preferences, Becker and others have argued that habit-formation is not an example of meta-preference endogeneity. Becker's (1992) argument is that habits and addictions can be placed within a meta-preference function in which data concerning 'different variables and experiences', pertaining to different time periods, enter as arguments. These

> *meta* preferences are stable. ... The message is not that preferences at time *t* for different people depend in the same way on their consumption at time *t*. Rather, it is that common rules determine the way different variables and experiences enter the meta preferences that motivate most people at most times. (p. 340)

It is instructive to consider the scale of the mental operation that is implied here. Note that as the number of time periods increases, the number of arguments in Becker's meta-preference function must increase proportionately. Essentially, Becker argues that utility is a function of the following type:

$$U = f(\boldsymbol{x}_1, \boldsymbol{x}_2 \dots \boldsymbol{x}_i \dots \boldsymbol{x}_t)$$

where U is utility and each $\boldsymbol{x}_i$ is a vector of 'variables and experiences' at time i. In each complete standard run of our model, each surviving agent moves 500 times, meaning that its preference function would have to have 500 arguments for each of the five variables involved. However, ours is an extremely simple model, running overall for only 500 iterations per surviving agent. Assume that a nearer-to-human individual lives for 30,000 days, and makes 10^4 decisions each day, governing 10^4 variables. If so, the Beckerian meta-preference function must have 3×10^{12} arguments. It is likely that the demands of the Beckerian meta-preference function significantly exceed the computational capacities of the human brain. To use the words of Roy Radner (1970, p. 457), the unboundedly rational agent requires 'capabilities of imagination and calculation that exceed reality by many orders of magnitude'.

Habit, in the sense that we are using the term, makes computation manageable by vastly reducing the computational and memory requirements of the agent. Habit works not simply or principally by reducing the 'cost of searching for information' but also by reducing the memory and computational capacity required to make any decision to act. In formal terms,

$$U = f(\boldsymbol{h}, \boldsymbol{m}_{t-s}, \boldsymbol{m}_{t-s+1} \dots \boldsymbol{m}_{t-1}, \boldsymbol{x}_t)$$

where $\boldsymbol{h}$ is the vector of habits and $\boldsymbol{m}_{t-s} \dots \boldsymbol{m}_{t-1}$ constitute the selective memories of past events, where s is less than t. The number of elements in the vector $\boldsymbol{h}$ and in any vector $\boldsymbol{m}_i$ are each less than the number of 'variables and experiences' in $\boldsymbol{x}_t$.

The attribution of a Beckerian preference function to each driver in our model would mean that each driver would have to remember simultaneously, and *for every one of its moves*, at least three computed variables ($S_{L,n,t}$, $O_{L,n,t}$, $C_{R,n,t} - C_{L,n,tt}$) plus all of its past left/right positions. If the maximum number of moves were 500, then each agent would require a mental storage for at least 2000 scalar variables. With a greater number of moves the memory requirement increases in proportion. Instead, in our model, only *two* scalar variables (current habituation, plus the number of past moves) have to be stored in the memory of each car at any point in time, *for any length of run*.

Another aspect of Becker's treatment of individual preferences is also questionable. Becker (1992, p. 340) continues, in the same passage as above,

> forward-looking rational actors maximize the utility from their meta preferences, not from current preferences alone, because they recognize that choices today affect their utilities in the future.

In contrast, it could be argued that many actions of agents in the real world, in this respect like the actions of drivers in our model, are not forward-looking in the sense that they consider the full consequences of present actions in the future. Habit is a disposition, sometimes even reinforced by ethical conviction; it does not typically involve a detailed or extensive consideration of future outcomes. No agent in the model considers whether the future emergent convention will be to the left or to the right. It just acts, in part to survive the traffic maelstrom and in part according to its acquired propensity or 'belief' that one type of behaviour is more appropriate. Of course, things are much more complicated in the real world. People do make decisions based on forward-looking considerations. However, the suggestion here is that forward-looking decisions cannot account for all of behaviour, including behaviour that is habit-driven. Habit is a past-driven propensity, and not necessarily the outcome of a forward-looking calculation.

For these reasons it is preferable to regard habit formation as an endogenous change of preferences rather than an outcome of decisions governed by a meta-preference function that deals with a number of variables over a series of time periods.

6 Discussion – downward causation

Another use of our model is that it provides a heuristic framework to consider the nuanced interpretations and meanings of the idea of 'downward causation' – a concept largely unfamiliar to economists but quite well known in the philosophy of psychology and the philosophy of biology (Campbell, 1974; Sperry, 1991).

The concept of downward causation depends upon the ontological notion that any complex system has 'higher level' systemic properties as well as 'lower level' components. At the systemic level there may exist 'emergent properties' that are, by definition, additional properties that depend upon, but are not explicable or predictable from, an analysis of the components at the lower level. The concept of emergent properties has recently become prominent in discussions of the complex simulations, pioneered in Santa Fe and elsewhere (Lane, 1993).[13]

Downward causation refers to possible effects of higher-level properties on lower-level components. It has weak and strong forms. In our model, this weaker form of downward causation is clearly present. As a left/right driving convention begins to be formed, more and more cars drive in conformity with that emerging convention. If a convention begins to emerge, then those that survive tend to be those that conform. Evolutionary selection acts on the population of agents, causing a shift in the characteristics of the population as a whole. This is an outcome of 'natural selection' and amounts to weak downward causation.

In the population as a whole, this evolutionary selection works on both the four fixed parameters and the single variable expressing habit. The set of values in the population as a whole changes by means of the death of the unsuccessful and the birth of the new agents. However, for any individual agent, evolutionary selection does not cause a change in the values of the four fixed parameters.

The stronger notion of 'reconstitutive downward causation' involves changing individuals as well as populations as a result of causal powers associated with higher levels (Hodgson, 2004). However, Sperry (1991) and other authors insist that explanations based on downward causation should be carefully focused on real causal mechanisms. This is the problem: while it is tempting to explain the behaviour of units in terms of collectives or wholes, the precise causal mechanism is difficult to determine.

If there is some mechanism whereby an actual or emerging convention can affect or 'reconstitute' the characteristics of the individual units, then this would amount to reconstitutive downward causation. System-wide outcomes (at a 'higher' level) would affect the characteristics of individual units (at a 'lower' level).

In our model, this stronger form of downward causation is also present and is associated with a discernible causal mechanism because as the left/right convention begins to emerge, more and more surviving cars develop the habit to drive on the left or the right, according to that convention. Strength of habit is based on two of the five variables that form the 'preference function' of each agent. For each individual, one of these preference elements ($H_{abituation_{n,t}}$) can change. In this way, emerging and enduring systemic properties reconstitute 'downwards' the preferences of the agent. Part of the achievement here is to show that both forms of downward causation can be represented in an agent-based model. In particular, we can identify a specific causal mechanism of reconstitutive downward causation.

Another crucial point to recognize is the specific mechanism by which reconstitutive downward causation operates. It is on *habits* rather than merely on behaviour, intentions or other preferences. Clearly, the definitional distinction between habit (as a propensity or disposition) and behaviour (or action) is essential to make sense of this statement.

The existence of a viable mechanism of reconstitutive downward causation contrasts with other, untenable 'top down' or 'methodologically collectivist' explanations in the social sciences where there are unspecified 'structural', 'cultural', or 'economic' forces controlling individuals. Crucially, the mechanism of reconstitutive downward causation that is outlined here affects the dispositions, thoughts, and actions of human actors. It is highly inadequate to regard preferences or purposes as changing simply as a result of unspecified cultural or social forces. What does happen is that the framing, shifting and constraining capacities of social institutions give rise to new perceptions and dispositions within individuals. Upon new habits of thought and behaviour, new preferences and intentions emerge.

Hence the concept of reconstitutive downward causation does not rely on new or mysterious types of cause or causality. We exclude any version of methodological collectivism or holism where an attempt is made to explain individual dispositions or behaviour entirely in terms of institutions or other system-level characteristics. Instead, we are obliged to explain particular human behaviour in terms of causal processes operating at the individual level, such as individual aspirations, dispositions or constraints.

It is a central tenet of the pragmatist philosophical and psychological perspective to regard habit and instinct as foundational to the human personality. Reason, deliberation and calculation emerge only after specific habits have been laid down; their operation depends upon such habits. In turn, the development of habits depends upon prior instincts. Instincts, by definition, are inherited. Accordingly, *reconstitutive* downward causation upon instincts is not possible. However, as noted above, the weaker form of downward causation does operate on whole populations and on its pool of habits and instincts.

The ongoing acquisition and modification of habits are central to human existence. All action and deliberation depend on prior habits that we acquire during our individual development. For example, much deliberative thought is dependent on, as well as being coloured by, acquired habits of language. In addition, to make sense of the world, we have to acquire habits of classification and habitually associated meanings. To act in and adapt to the world, our complex nervous system has to be developed and rehearsed. Habit is a crucial and neglected element in cognition, deliberation and reason.

As long as we can explain how institutional structures give rise to new or changed habits, then we have a possible and acceptable mechanism of reconstitutive downward causation. Of course, institutions may directly affect our intentions by providing incentives, sanctions or constraints. In contrast, a reconstitutive causal mechanism involves factors that are foundational to purposes, preferences and deliberation as a whole. This is where habits come in. By affecting habits, institutions can indirectly influence our intentions (Hodgson, 2004).

7 Conclusion

The model discussed in this chapter shows how a left/right traffic convention may emerge in an agent-based model. The main factor inhibiting this convergence is error. Also, in limited circumstances, agile avoidance behaviour can lead to recurrent, cycling patterns of behaviour with no emergent left/right convention. The simulation results show that increases in the 'strength of habit' of agents in the model when combined with evolutionary selection pressure can help to suppress both of these disturbing factors.

This simulation points to some of the deeper conceptual issues involved in the evolution of conventions, particularly the nature of rational decision-making and its reliance upon habit. Overall, the simulations show that the systemic convergence to a left/right convention is often improved and sustained by strength of habit. Accordingly, habit plays an important part alongside the 'intelligent' and calculative aspects of agent behaviour, particularly in cases where information is limited.

In contrast, the analyses of Stephen Jones (1984) and Ekkehart Schlicht (1998) maintain that conventions and customs emerge principally because individuals have a preference for them. In our simulations, this is not generally the case where information is limited. In these circumstances, habit is additionally and vitally important because it can often enhance stable behaviour and help to create stable outcomes.

The specification of habit in the model is redolent of the concept in the works of pragmatist philosophers such as Peirce and James. Habit acts in the model as if it were the foundation of a 'conviction' or firmly held 'belief'. This suggests that the evolution of conventions may depend not only on the rational calculations of actors but also on the widespread development of convictions or norms concerning appropriate behaviour.

This model also has implications for an understanding of the nature and role of habit. In the specification here, the conception of habit is clearly distinguished from serially correlated behaviour. This definition contrasts significantly with that in the work of Becker and others.

We also identify a mechanism of 'reconstitutive downward causation' among agents. Although each car has four inert 'instincts', the fifth variable concerning habituation changes as agent behaviour changes. As a left/right convention emerges among the population as a whole, this provides a channel of movement for every individual. Accordingly, individual habits reflect the emergent convention among the whole population. As a result, the formation of individual habits is guided by systemic conventions. This is tantamount to a change of preferences, and it results from a 'downwards' causal process from the emergent institution to the individual.

A possible criticism of this thesis could stem from a Beckerian approach where each agent has a meta-preference function with arguments representing all relevant temporal and other variables. We have shown that this approach comes up against the problem of computational limitations of agents required to deal with large and increasing amounts of information concerning their past. It makes more sense to treat preferences as partially endogenous and malleable. Furthermore, in contrast to the idea of a meta-preference function, the conception of habit defined here greatly reduces the number of variables that each agent has to take into account.

Given the powerful effect of habituation in our model, reconstitutive downward causation may provide a degree of durability and stability in institutional structure that is not explained adequately in standard models. The circular, positive feedback from institution to individuals and from individuals to institutions can help to enhance the durability of the institutional unit. There may be stable emergent properties that exist *not despite*, but *because of*, endogenous preference formation.

With the theoretical framework proposed here, it may also be possible to overcome the dilemma between methodological individualism and methodological collectivism. By acting not directly on individual decisions, but on habitual dispositions, institutions exert reconstitutive downward causation without reducing the role of individual agency. Upward causation, from individuals to institutions, is still possible, without assuming that the individual is given or immanently conceived. Explanations of socio-economic phenomena are reduced neither to individuals nor to institutions alone.

Notes

1. See, for example, Marimon et al. (1990) and Wärneryd (1990). Young (1996) provides an interesting historical account of the evolution of traffic conventions.
2. Despite the apparent simplicity of this monetary argument, analyses, experiments and simulations based upon it are extraordinarily complex (Marimon et al., 1990). Realizing this, we chose a simpler institution as the object of the present study in which each agent has a choice between only two behavioural options at any stage. Our intention was to illustrate the hypothesized results in the simplest possible institutional set-up.
3. For discussions of the limits of this approach see Field (1979), Hodgson (1998) and Aoki (2001).
4. See, for example, Becker and Murphy (1988), Alessie and Kapteyn (1991), Becker (1992).
5. The simulations described here were performed using Matlab software. All random numbers are generated from a multiseed generator with the theoretical lower limit of 2^{1492} before the number will repeat itself.

6. Earlier versions of this simulation included three 'inertia' parameters and an additional 'avoidance' variable applied to the area *two* zones ahead of the driver. The inertia parameters gave each driver a disposition to continue stubbornly with an inclination it has assumed in the recent past. We found that the effects of inertia are generally weaker than those of habit. The effect of the second 'avoidance' variable was at most marginal. Accordingly, the more parsimonious model was chosen, with the omission of these parameters.
7. The probability that a negative number will be drawn is extremely small ($7.43*10^{-6}$). An alternative method of selecting the first four parameters would be to draw them randomly from a uniform distribution in a specified interval. Instead, a normal distribution was selected because it was found that it reduced the death rates in the simulation. Selection along an interval will typically create a larger number of drivers with less fit parameters.
8. Experiments were performed using different habit functions, with similar but slightly weaker results. The chosen increments in the habit function in the present work decline at a rate that permits in principle the indefinite reversal of habituation from one extreme value to the other: no sign nor degree of habituation is ever irreversible.
9. Searches in parameter space confirmed that this was a global rather than a local maximum. However, the convergence optimization zone is almost flat, making accuracy to more than one decimal place superfluous.
10. Convergence to the left or right was monitored in all runs, confirming that the model had no bias towards one side of the road rather than the other.
11. More data from this set of simulation results are presented in Hodgson and Knudsen (2004).
12. Our article was published before we came across Epstein (2001), which also involves artificial agents driving around a circular ring. Epstein adopts a simpler decision-making algorithm, without habit, where a driver's horizon is reduced if there is no change in left/right decisions. He derives the robust and important result that the necessary horizon and degree of rational deliberation is inversely related to the strength of the reigning traffic convention. Epstein's work complements ours. Both studies emphasize that conventions are not only convenient outcomes for calculating agents, but also they help to reduce their computational and deliberational requirements.
13. On the concept of emergent properties and its history see Hodgson (2004).

References

Alessie, R. and Kapteyn, A. (1991) 'Habit Formation, Interdependent Preferences and Demographic Effects in the Almost Ideal Demand System', *Economic Journal*, vol. 101, no. 3, pp. 404–19.

Aoki, M. (2001) *Toward a Comparative Institutional Analysis* (Cambridge, MA: MIT Press).

Becker, G. S. (1992) 'Habits, Addictions and Traditions', *Kyklos*, vol. 45, pp. 327–46.

Becker, G. S. and Murphy, K. M. (1988) 'A Theory of Rational Addiction', *Journal of Political Economy*, vol. 96, no. 4, pp. 675–700.

Campbell, D. T. (1974) '"Downward Causation" in Hierarchically Organized Biological Systems', in Francisco J. Ayala and Theodosius Dobzhansky (eds) *Studies in the Philosophy of Biology* (London, Berkeley and Los Angeles: Macmillan and University of California Press), pp. 179–86.

Epstein, J. M. (2001) 'Learning to be Thoughtless: Social Norms and Individual Computation', *Computational Economics*, vol. 18, pp. 9–24.
Field, A. (1979) 'On the Explanation of Rules Using Rational Choice Models', *Journal of Economic Issues*, vol. 13, no. 1, pp. 49–72.
Hodgson, G. M. (1998) 'The Approach of Institutional Economics', *Journal of Economic Literature*, vol. 36, no. 1, pp. 166–92.
Hodgson, G. M. (2004) *The Evolution of Institutional Economics: Agency, Structure and Darwinism in American Institutionalism* (London and New York: Routledge).
Hodgson, G. M. and Knudsen, T. (2004) 'The Complex Evolution of a Simple Traffic Convention: the Functions and Implications of Habit', *Journal of Economic Behavior and Organization*, vol. 54, no. 1, pp. 19–47.
Jones, S. R. G. (1984) *The Economics of Conformism* (Oxford: Basil Blackwell).
Lane, D. A. (1993) 'Artificial Worlds and Economics', Parts I and II, *Journal of Evolutionary Economics*, vol. 3, nos. 2–3, pp. 89–107, 177–97.
Marimon, R. E., E. McGrattan and T. J. Sargent (1990) 'Money as a Medium of Exchange in an Economy with Artificially Intelligent Agents', *Journal of Economic Dynamics and Control*, vol. 14, pp. 329–73.
Mitchell, W. C. (1937) *The Backward Art of Spending Money and Other Essays* (New York: McGraw-Hill).
Radner, R. (1970) 'New Ideas in Pure Theory: Problems in the Theory of Markets under Uncertainty', *American Economic Review*, vol. 60, pp. 454–60.
Schlicht, E. (1998) *On Custom in the Economy* (Oxford and New York: Clarendon Press).
Sperry, R. W. (1991) 'In Defense of Mentalism and Emergent Interaction', *Journal of Mind and Behavior*, vol. 12, no. 2, pp. 221–46.
Sugden, R. (1986) *The Economics of Rights, Co-operation and Welfare* (Oxford: Basil Blackwell).
Wärneryd, K. (1990) *Economic Conventions: Essays in Institutional Economics* (Stockholm: Economic Research Institute).
Young, H. P. (1996) 'The Economics of Convention', *Journal of Economic Perspectives*, vol. 10, no. 2, pp. 105–22.

10
Implications of Behavioural Game Theory for Neoclassical Economic Theory*

Herbert Gintis
Santa Fe Institute, Unversity of Siena,
and Central European University

1 Introduction

Behavioural game theory is the application of game theory to the design and interpretation of laboratory experiments. Behavioural game theory aims to determine empirically how individuals make choices under conditions of uncertainty and strategic interaction, and to provide analytical models of the resulting behaviour. It is widely believed that experimental results of behavioural game theory undermine standard economic and game theory. This chapter suggests that experimental results present serious theoretical modelling challenges, but do not undermine a pillar of contemporary economic theory: the *rational actor model*, which holds that individual choice can be modelled as maximization of an objective function subject to informational and material constraints. However, we must abandon the notion that rationality implies self-regarding behaviour. The most recent stage in behavioural game theory research, rather than treating anomalous behaviour as flowing from faulty reasoning, builds analytical models premised upon the rational actor model, but with agents who systematically exhibit *other-regarding preferences*, i.e. they care about not only their own payoffs in a strategic interaction, but those of the other players and the process of play as well.

I address some general issues to which the research into other-regarding preferences has given rise, arguing the following points:

a. **The beliefs, preferences, and constraints model.** Recent experimental results support the 'thin' concept of rationality on which contemporary

* I would like to Samuel Bowles, Ernst Fehr and Jack Hirshleifer for their help and the John D. and Catherine T. MacArthur Foundation for financial support. This essay is dedicated to the memory of Jack Hirshleifer.

decision theory, game theory, and microeconomic theory are based. This concept assumes only that preferences are consistent over the appropriate choice space. Other-regarding preferences do, however, expand the content of the preference function beyond the traditional exclusive reliance on personal gain through consumption, leisure and asset portfolio enhancement. Moreover, the proper choice space must be empirically determined. For instance, according to prospect theory, the choice space privileges the agent's current position, and in hyperbolic discounting the choice space privileges the time at which choice is exercised. The term 'rational' is so connotation-laden that communication using the term 'rational actor model' is prone to inefficiency and misunderstanding. I therefore propose the term *beliefs, preferences and constraints* (BPC) model.

b. **Other-regarding preferences.** Several categories of other-regarding preferences need to be added to the standard model to capture human behaviour. These include strong reciprocity, inequality aversion and 'insider' bias. We define these as follows. A *social dilemma* is a game with two pure strategies, 'cooperate' and 'defect' in which all other players gain when a player cooperates, but a self-regarding player will always defect, giving no benefit to the group, whatever the other players do. *Strong reciprocity* is a predisposition to cooperate in a social dilemma, and to punish non-cooperators when possible, at a personal cost that cannot be recouped in later stages of the game. *Inequality aversion* is the predisposition to reduce the inequality in outcomes between oneself and other group members, even at personal cost. *Insider bias* in a game is the predisposition to identify other players who are 'like oneself' according to some payoff-irrelevant ascriptive marker (such as ethnicity or nationality) and behave altruistically on behalf of these 'insiders'. These categories are probably universal, but their content is culturally variable. *Character virtues* (honesty, trustworthiness, promise-keeping and the like) are norms of behaviour that are upheld for their own sake, even in the face of forgone material gains. They are supported by such psychological traits as the capacity to internalize social values, and the tendency to display such social emotions as empathy, shame, pride, and remorse.

c. **Complete and incomplete contracting.** A *complete contract* among a group of agents is an agreement specifying the rights and obligations of each party under all possible future states of affairs, costlessly written and enforced by third parties (e.g. the judiciary). In anonymous competitive market settings with complete contracting, individuals behave like the self-regarding actor of traditional economic theory. A *one-sided* incomplete contract is one in which one party to an exchange delivers a contractually enforceable quantity (e.g. money) in return for an unenforceable promise of delivery of services (e.g. work). Under conditions of competitive market exchange with one-sided incomplete contracting, other-regarding preferences (gift exchange, conditional cooperation and punishment) emerge. Such situations often attain a high level of allocational efficiency compared to the situation with self-regarding agents. These situations are characterized by non-clearing markets in which the agent on the short side of a contractual relationship, usually the party who is offering money, has power in some meaningful, quasi-political sense (e.g. employers, lenders, consumers) while agents on the long side enjoy rents (employees, borrowers, firms).

Section 2 explains why other-regarding preferences enrich rather than undermine the BPC model. The reason is that choice theory requires only that preferences be *consistent*, and is in principle agnostic to the *content* of preferences. This should be completely obvious to economists, but the epithet 'irrational' is so frequently applied in a manner inconsistent with its proper use in economic theory that formally addressing this issue appears to be in order. The upshot is that we can continue to affirm the principle that agents can be successfully modelled as maximizing a preference function subject to informational and material constraints.

Section 3 explores the implications of experimental economics for game theory. Since game theory provides the methodological foundations for experimental design and analysis in experimental economics, if the latter's empirical findings undermined game theory, they would thereby undermine their own validity – a situation demanding a serious, radical reconstruction of the general theory of strategic interaction. In fact, however, since the BPC model remains relevant, we can assume agents choose best responses in strategic interactions, and hence game theory is not undermined. Some experimental research, however, does suggest that game-theoretic predictions involving more than a few levels of backward induction on the part of agents generally predict very poorly, suggesting that agents do not choose best responses, and hence game theory itself is threatened. An important branch of game theory, known as *interactive decision theory*, often overlooked in methodological discussions of the implications of empirical research, indicates however that backward induction can be identified with choosing best responses *only under specialized conditions*, or only making questionable assumptions concerning the nature of logical and statistical inference (Fagin et al., 1995; Halpern, 2001; Aumann, 1995; and Aumann and Brandenburger, 1995). It follows that the experimental findings on backward induction do not threaten game theory, although they counsel against the indiscriminate use of backward induction arguments in parts of the game tree that cannot be reached by rational agents.

Additional support for traditional economic theory comes from the fact that when all aspects of market exchange are covered by complete contracts, agents behave as self-interested income maximizers, as suggested in traditional economic theory. Many experiments carried out by Vernon Smith and his co-workers support this generalization.

Many of the characteristics of modern market economies are the result of *incomplete contracting*. Herbert Gintis (1976) suggested that the major outlines of the employer–employee relationship (long-term contracts with supra-market-clearing wages, job ladders, and the use of promotion and dismissal as motivating devices) are due to the fact that in return for a wage, the worker cannot credibly guarantee any particular level of effort or care in the labour-time provided the employer. George Akerlof (1982) suggested that under such conditions the employer–employee relationship could be a 'gift exchange' situation, in which workers voluntarily supply a high level of effort when they believe that their employer is offering a fair wage and good working conditions. Samuel Bowles and Herbert Gintis (1993) introduced the notion of *short-side power* in the following terms: 'The short side of a market is the side for which the quantity of desired transactions is the least. Short-side agents include employers in labor markets with equilibrium unemployment, ... and lenders in capital markets with equilibrium credit rationing.' We asserted the following principle: 'competitive equilibrium ... allocates power to agents on the short side of non-clearing markets'. In particular, there tend to be both job rationing and credit rationing, in the sense that there are always more applicants for a job than job openings, and this excess supply does not lead to a bidding down of wages. Similarly, there are more applicants for loans than there are loanable funds, and this excess demand leads to strong collateral requirements rather than the bidding down of the interest rate. Gintis (1989) applied a similar argument to the relationship between consumers and firms that supply goods where contracts do not ensure the delivery of high-quality products. In this case, the supplying firm is on the long side of the market (sellers are quantity constrained), and price is higher than marginal cost, accounting for the fact that many firms in a capitalist economy see their task as 'selling their product', rather than maximizing profits with a given demand function.

Section 4 describes the achievement of Ernst Fehr, Simon Gächter and Georg Kirchsteiger (1997) in showing that Akerlof's gift exchange mechanism is strongly operative when the labour contract is incomplete. In a more elaborate setting, Martin Brown, Armin Falk and Ernst Fehr (2004) show that both gift exchange and threat of dismissal are operative in an incomplete contract setting. This experimental setting is especially interesting because it illustrates the coexistence of self- and other-regarding incentives in a single game. While doubtless at times self-regarding incentives 'crowd out' other-regarding motives, at least in the labour market the two probably coexist.

2 Rational choice theory and the BPC model

Rational choice theory models behaviour as agents maximizing a preference function subject to informational and material constraints. The term 'rational' is a misnomer, since the term appears to imply something about the ability of the agent to give reasons for actions, to act objectively, unmoved by capricious emotionality, and even to act self-interestedly. Yet, it has long been recognized that this connotational overlay is superfluous and misleading. Nothing has brought this fact home more clearly than the great success of the BPC model in explaining animal behaviour, despite the fact that no one believes that fruit flies and spiders do much in the way of cogitating (Alcock, 1993). The BPC model is the starting point for much of economic analysis, behavioural game theory, and is increasingly gaining credence with neuroscientists (Glimcher, 2003).

Formally, the assertion that consistent preferences are sufficient to model the individual as maximizing a preference ordering over a choice set A can be presented as follows. By a *preference ordering* $\succcurlyeq$ on a set A, we mean a binary relation, such that $x \succcurlyeq y$ may be either true or false for various pairs $x, y \in A$. When $x \succcurlyeq y$, we say 'x is weakly preferred to y'. We say $\succcurlyeq$ is *complete* if, for any $x, y \in A$, either $x \succcurlyeq y$ or $y \succcurlyeq x$. We say $\succcurlyeq$ is *transitive* if, for all $x, y, z \in A$, $x \succcurlyeq y$ and $y \succcurlyeq z$ imply $x \succcurlyeq z$. When these two conditions are satisfied, we say $\succcurlyeq$ is a *preference relation*. We say an agent *maximizes* $\succcurlyeq$ if, if from any subset $B \subset A$, the agent chooses one of the most preferred elements of B according to $\succcurlyeq$,

> **Theorem**: *If $\succcurlyeq$ is a preference relation on set A, and if an agent maximizes $\succcurlyeq$, then there always exists a utility function $u : A \rightarrow \mathbf{R}$ (where* **R** *are the real numbers) such that the agent behaves as if maximizing this utility function over A.*

The empirical evidence supports an even stronger notion of human rationality for such preferences as charitable giving and punitive retribution.

James Andreoni and John Miller (2002) have shown that one can apply standard choice theory, including the derivation of demand curves, plotting concave indifference curves, and finding price elasticities, in situations where individuals are faced with trade-offs between self-regarding and other-regarding payoffs. This is because individual preferences tend to satisfy the *Generalized Axiom of Revealed Preference*, which can be defined as follows. Suppose an agent chooses a commodity bundle $\{x_1, \ldots, x_n\}$ at prices $\{p_1, \ldots, p_n\}$ subject to the budget constraint $\Sigma_i \, p_i \, x_i = M$. Suppose $x^1, \ldots, x^m$ are any commodity bundles, so $x^j = (x^j_1, \cdots, x^j_n)$ for any $j = 1, \ldots, m$. Thus, x^j lies on the budget constraint if $\Sigma_i \, p_i \, x^j_i = M$. We say x^i is *directly revealed preferred* to x^j if x^j was in the choice set when x^i was chosen. We say x^1 is *indirectly revealed preferred* to x^n if there is some choice of $x^2, \ldots, x^{n-1}$ such that x^i is directly revealed preferred to x^{i+1} for $i = 1, \ldots, n - 1$. Finally, we say that the Generalized Axiom of Revealed Preference (GARP) is satisfied if, whenever x^i is indirectly preferred to x^j, then x^i violates the income constraint when x^j is chosen.

Andreoni and Miller used a modified version of the dictator game, in which the experimenter gives a subject an amount of money, with the instructions that he is to share the money with a second party, specified by the experimenter, in any proportions that he wishes. The recipient has no say in the matter. In the current experiment, the subject was given an amount of money m, of which he could keep an amount π_s of his choosing, the remainder, $m - \pi_s$, being divided by the 'price' p and given to the second party. It is easy to see that the 'commodity bundle' (π_s, π_o) satisfies the budget equation $\pi_s + p\pi_o = m$. The shape of the subject's preference ordering, and in particular whether it satisfies GARP, could be determined by varying the price p and the income m, and observing the subject's choices.

The experimenters found that 75 per cent of subjects exhibited some degree of other-regarding preferences (i.e. gave money to the second party), and 98 per cent of subjects made choices compatible with GARP. In some of the cases, p was chosen to be negative over some range, within which subjects maximize their own payoff by contributing *more* to the second party. Even in these cases GARP was generally satisfied, 23 per cent of subjects exhibiting *jealous* preferences, by making a non-personal-payoff-maximizing choice, the sole attraction of which is that it reduces the payment to the second party.

While much more experimentation of this sort remains to be carried out, at least at this point it appears that other-regarding preferences present no challenge to traditional consumer theory.

3 Backward induction and rationality

Game theory privileges subgame perfection as the proper equilibrium concept of rational agents (Selten, 1975). Subgame perfection, of course, is equivalent to the iterated elimination of weakly dominated strategies. It has long been known, however, that subjects in experimental games rarely engage in more that a few iterations of backward induction. In his ambitious overview of the current state of behavioural game theory Colin Camerer (2003) summarizes a large body of experimental evidence in the following way: 'Nearly all people use one step of iterated dominance ... However, at least 10 per cent of players seem to use each of two to four levels of iterated dominance, and the median number of steps of iterated dominance is two' (p. 202).

In this section, I outline the empirical basis for this assertion. Despite its importance, I want to stress that this empirical regularity does not in any way undermine the BPC model, since the interactive decision theoretic literature clearly shows that strong informational assumptions are necessary to justify the iterated elimination of (weakly or strongly) dominated strategies.

So-called 'beauty contests' are often used to determine the extent to which people backward induct. Suppose a group of subjects is told each should choose a whole number between zero and 100. The prize is $10 and the winner is the subject whose guess is closest to 2/3 of the average guess. One level of backward induction implies limiting one's choice to [0,67], since this is the greatest 2/3 of the average can be. But, if everyone uses one level of backward induction, a subject knows that the highest the average can be is 2/3 of 67, or about 44. With three levels of backward induction, the highest a bid can be is 29, and with four levels, 20. If all players backward induct all the way, we get to the unique Nash equilibrium of zero.

Rosemarie Nagel (1995) was the first to study this beauty contest, using a group of fourteen to sixteen subjects. She found the empirical results to be compatible with the assertion that 13 per cent of subjects used no backward induction, 44 per cent used one level, 37 per cent used two levels and less than 4 per cent use more than two levels of backward induction.

The failure of individuals to use backward induction is quite a shocker for classical game theorists, who tend to consider eliminating weakly dominated strategies a key element of rationality. However, assuming *common knowledge of rationality along the game path,* which means agents maximize their payoffs whenever it is their turn to play, given their conjectures as to the behaviour of the other players, Douglas Bernheim (1984) and David Pearce (1984) showed agents will only obey the iterated elimination of *strictly* dominated strategies. Such strategies are termed *rationalizable.* In a game such as the centipede game or the finitely repeated prisoner's dilemma, there are no strictly dominated strategies, so *any* strategy is rationalizable. If we were to accept rationalizability as the criterion of rationality, the observation that people engage in limited backward induction would not entail their irrationality.

Unfortunately, the concept of rationalizability embodies an excessively weak concept of rationality, since it assumes nothing concerning the behaviour of agents *off* the path of play. If a player moves at more than a single information set, backward induction in general eliminates *weakly* dominated strategies, so it is clear that even the simplest sort of incredible threats are rationalizable. Consider, for instance, the extensive form game in Figure 10.1. It is clear that a rational player 2 will not play l if he gets to move, but the normal form of this game, shown to the right in this figure, indicates that l is only weakly dominated by r, so both l and r are rationalizable for player 2, from which it follows that both L and R are rationalizable for player 1.

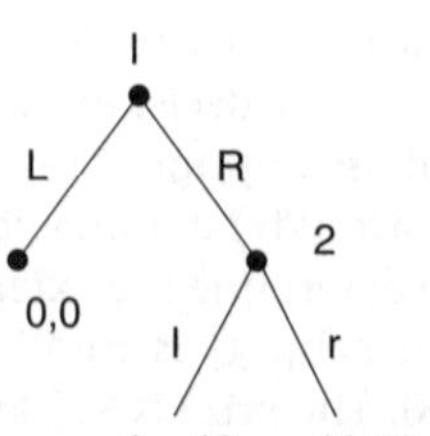

	l	r
L	0,0	0,0
R	−1, −10	10,10

Figure 10.1 A rationalizable incredible threat. The left pane is the extensive form game and the right pane its corresponding normal form game

By contrast, Aumann (1995) has shown that in generic games of perfect information (all information sets are singletons) if there is common knowledge of rationality both *on* and *off* the game tree, meaning that at each node, the player who moves acts to maximize his payoff in the subgame beginning at that node, then *only the backward induction solution remains.* To understand his argument, suppose there are players $i = 1, \ldots, n$ with strategy sets S_i for player i. Let Ω be the set of *states of the world.* For illustration purposes, suppose the game is that of Figure 10.1, where the most natural choice is $\Omega = \{Ll, Lr, Rl, Rr\}$, corresponding to the possible 'types' of the two players, Ll corresponding to a 'left-type player one' and a 'left type player 2', and similarly for the remaining three states. A *knowledge partition* for a player is a partition of Ω into non-overlapping subsets $\varepsilon_i = \{E_i^1, \ldots E_i^{ki}\}$, called *events,* with the interpretation that if the actual state is $\omega \in E_i^j$, then i knows only that the actual state is somewhere in E_i^j. For instance, in our example, if each player knows only his own type, then $\varepsilon_1 = \{\{Ll, Lr\}, \{Rl, Rr\}\}$ and $\varepsilon_2 = \{\{Ll, Rl\}, \{Lr, Rr\}\}$. Note that we assume that whatever else may be in a state of the world, the moves of the various players are among them. Aumann formalizes this by assuming that a knowledge system includes a map $\mathbf{s} : \Omega \to \times_i S_i$ such that $\mathbf{s}(\omega) = (\mathbf{s}(\omega)_1, \ldots, \mathbf{s}(\omega)_n)$ is the strategy that each player chooses in state ω. The informational assumption is formalized by requiring that for any player i and any $E_i^j \in \varepsilon_i$ and any $\omega, \omega' \in E_i^j$, we have $\mathbf{s}(\omega)_i = \mathbf{s}(\omega')_i$, i.e. a player must make the same move at all events in one of his knowledge partition sets.

Suppose E is any event (i.e. any non-empty subset of Ω). K_iE denotes the union of all elements of ε_i contained in E. We interpret K_iE as the event that i *knows* event E. We then write $KE = \cap_i K_iE$, which is the event that all players know event E. Finally, we write

$$C\,KE = KE \cap KKE \cap KKKE \cap \ldots$$

which is the event that E is *common knowledge.* For instance, in our example, the only event that is common knowledge is Ω itself. To see this, suppose K_1E includes $\{Ll, Lr\}$. Then K_2K_1E is either empty, or includes $\{Rl\}$ and $\{Rr\}$, in which case $E = \Omega$. A similar argument for the other partition elements shows that Ω is the only event that is common knowledge. We may also determine the event R_i that players i is rational, which is simply $R_1 = \{Ll, Rr\}$ and $R_2 = \{Lr, Rr\}$. Finally, we can identify the event that backward induction is used as being $I = \{Rr\}$.

Using this terminology, Aumann proves, under the stated conditions, that $CKR \subseteq I$, where R is the event that all players are rational, and I is the event that the backward induction solution is chosen. In the case of our example, there is no state at which there is common knowledge of rationality. However, let us expand the knowledge partitions to $\varepsilon_1 = \varepsilon_2 = \{\{Ll\}, \{Lr\}, \{Rl\}, \{Rr\}\}$, which says each player knows both his own and the other's type. Then $R = R_1 \cap R_2 = \{Rr\}$, so $CKR = KR = R = I$, which shows that common knowledge of rationality implies backward induction.

There are good reasons, however, to explore alternatives to Aumann's treatment of common knowledge. It is easy to show that $K_iE \subseteq E$ for any i and any E, which means that to know an event implies that it is true (i.e. to know that you are in one of a set of states implies that you *are* in one of those states). But, rationality off the game tree by player i includes rationality at nodes where i moves, but that could only be reached by i having previously behaved non-rationally!

Consider, for instance, the centipede game, depicted in Figure 10.2. Backward induction implies J will play D on the last round, awarding him 101 instead of 100. But to pre-empt this, M will play D on the next-to-last round, awarding him 101 instead of 98. Reasoning similarly, proceeding backward, we see that M will play D on the first round of play. Thus immediate defection (playing D) is the only subgame perfect Nash equilibrium to this game. Indeed, a little reflection will convince the reader that immediate defection is the only Nash equilibrium for both players.

However, backward induction on the last round makes sense only if J is rational there. But, to get there J must have been *irrational* in each of his last 49 moves! The only way this makes any sense at all is if we assume that players can make mistakes, and that both players have made almost 50 mistakes in a row. This is hardly a plausible assumption on which to base a justification of backward induction.

An alternative model of rationality allows individuals to change their assessment of an opponent's type when he has made an unexpected move. One such has been developed by Elchanan Ben-Porath (1997), which employs the concept of *certainty* in the place of *knowledge*, the difference being that *certainty* is a subjective state of assigning probability one to an event, even though the event may not contain the true state of the system. Rationality in this framework is defined as maximizing expected payoffs with a given set of expectations concerning the behaviour of the other player. For instance, two players of the 100-stage centipede game might hold common certainty of rationality, which implies the backward induction solution if it holds at all nodes, but if player one cooperates on the first round, player two then drops his assumption in favour of some other subjective probability distribution over how his opponent will act at later nodes in the game tree.

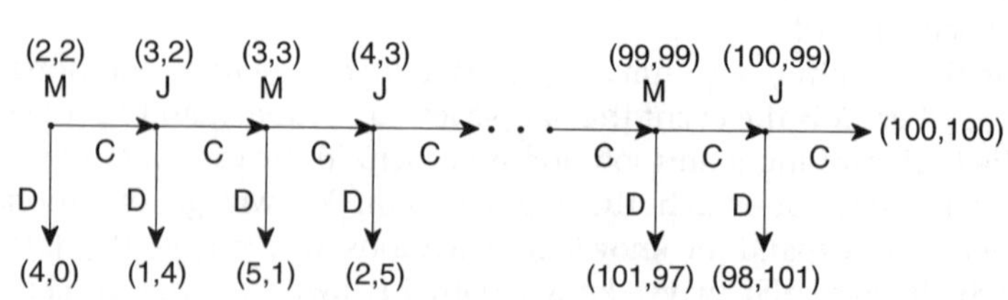

Figure 10.2 The hundred round centipede game

Ben-Porath shows that common certainty of rationality is equivalent to one round of elimination of weakly dominated strategies, followed by any number of rounds of elimination of strictly dominated strategies. Thus, in Figure 10.2, only the final two decision nodes can be eliminated by common certainty of rationality. This makes a good deal of sense. Both M and J may be rational in the sense of attempting to maximize their expected payoffs, and by playing C on his first move, M signals that he is not playing backward induction. In deciding how far to cooperate with M, J must have some probability distribution over where M will first defect, and choose a defection point that maximizes his payoff subject to this probability distribution. Experimental evidence (McKelvey and Palfrey, 1992) indicates that subjects generally cooperate until the last few rounds.

Nevertheless, in some cases the concept of rationalizability fails to encompass the bounds of rational behaviour. Consider, for instance, the following version G_n of Kaushik Basu's Traveller's Dilemma (1994). Two business executives pay bridge tolls while on a trip, but cannot get receipts. Their superior tells each of them to report an integral number of dollars between \$2 and n on their expense sheet. If they report the same number, each will receive this much back. If they report different numbers, they each get the smaller amount, plus the low reporter gets an additional \$2, and the high reporter loses \$2. The executives are not permitted to collude in deciding what to report.

Let s_k be the strategy 'report k'. It is then easy to show that $n > 3$, s_n in the game G_n is strictly dominated by a mixed strategy of $s_2, \ldots , s_{n-1}$. First, a glance at the normal form matrix for G_4 shows that s_4 is strictly dominated by a mixed strategy σ_4 using (i.e. weighting with positive probability) only s_2 and s_3. Second, it is easy to see that for any $n > 4$, if s_{n-1} is strictly dominated by a mixed strategy σ_{n-1} using only σ_{n-2} and s_2 in G_{n-1}, then s_n is strictly dominated by a mixed strategy σ_n using only σ_{n-1} and s_{n-1} in G_n. By the iterated elimination of strictly dominated strategies, this shows that the only rationalizable strategy of G_n is for both players to ask for \$2. This is also the only Nash equilibrium. Yet, it is clear that people will not generally play anything even approximating this equilibrium. Moreover, it is easy to see that this result does not depend on the size of the penalty! Any positive amount will do. In a beautiful experiment, Monica Capra, Jacob Goeree, Rosairo Gomez and Charles Holt (1999) show that for small penalties, players in G_{100} play near 100, while for large penalties, they play near the rationalizable/Nash equilibrium of the game, which is $k = 2$.

I have barely scratched the surface in the modelling of rationality in the interactive decision theory literature. However, I have presented enough to make it clear that the empirical evidence on limited nature of backward induction exhibited by human subjects does not call into question the rationality of human subjects.

4 Strong reciprocity in the labour market

Akerlof (1982) suggested that many puzzling facts about labour markets could be better understood if it were recognized that in many situations, employers pay their employees higher wages than necessary, in the expectation that workers will respond by providing higher effort than necessary. Fehr, Gächter and Kirchsteiger (1997) performed an experiment to validate this *gift exchange* model of the labour market.

The experimenters divided a group of 141 subjects (college students who had agreed to participate in order to earn money) into 'employers' and 'employees'. The rules of the game are as follows. If an employer hires an employee who provides effort e and receives a wage w, his profit is $\pi = 100e - w$. The wage must be between 1 and 100, and the effort is between 0.1 and 1. The payoff to the employee is then $u = w - c(e)$, where $c(e)$ is the 'cost of effort' function shown in Figure 10.3. All payoffs involve real money that the subjects are paid at the end of the experimental session. We call this the *experimental labour market game*.

The sequence of actions is as follows. The employer first offers a 'contract' specifying a wage w and a desired amount of effort e^*. A contract is made with the first employee who agrees to these terms. An employer can make a contract (w, e^*) with at most one employee. The employee who agrees to these terms receives the wage w and supplies an effort level e, which *need not equal the contracted effort*, e^*. In effect, there is no penalty if the employee does not keep his promise, so the employee can choose any effort level, $e \in [0.1, 1]$, with impunity. Although subjects may play this game several

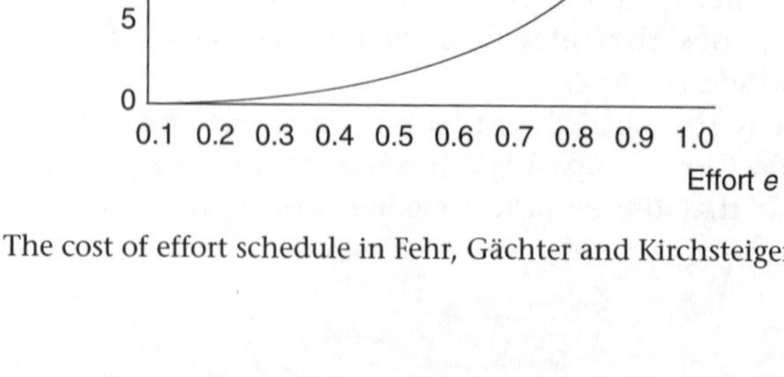

Figure 10.3 The cost of effort schedule in Fehr, Gächter and Kirchsteiger (1997)

times with different partners, each employer–employee interaction is a one-shot (non-repeated) event. Moreover, the identity of the interacting partners is never revealed.

If employees are self-regarding, they will choose the zero-cost effort level, $e = 0.1$, no matter what wage is offered them. Knowing this, employers will never pay more than the minimum necessary to get the employee to accept a contract, which is 1 (assuming only integral wage offers are permitted). The employee will accept this offer, and will set $e = 0.1$. Since $c(0.1) = 0$, the employee's payoff is $u = 1$. The employer's payoff is $\pi = 0.1 \times 100 - 1 = 9$.

In fact, however, this self-regarding outcome rarely occurred in this experiment. The average net payoff to employees was $u = 35$, and the more generous the employer's wage offer to the employee, the higher the effort provided. In effect, employers presumed the strong reciprocity predispositions of the employees, making quite generous wage offers and receiving higher effort, as a means to increase both their own and the employee's payoff, as depicted in Figure 10.4.

Figure 10.4 also shows that, though most employees are strong reciprocators, at any wage rate there still is a significant gap between the amount of effort agreed upon and the amount actually delivered. This is not because there are a few 'bad apples' among the set of employees, but because only 26 per cent of employees delivered the level of effort they promised! We conclude that

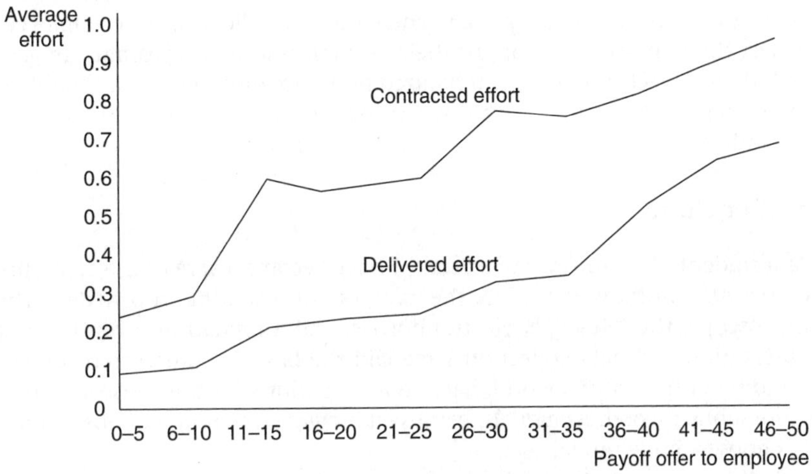

Figure 10.4 Relation of contracted and delivered effort to worker payoff (141 subjects). From Fehr, Gächter, and Kirchsteiger (1997)

strong reciprocators are inclined to compromise their morality to some extent.

To see if employers are also strong reciprocators, the authors extended the game by allowing the employers to respond reciprocally to the *actual effort choices* of their workers. At a cost of 1, an employer could *increase* or *decrease* his employee's payoff by 2.5. If employers were self-regarding, they would of course do neither, since they would not (knowingly) interact with the same worker a second time. However, 68 per cent of the time, employers punished employees that did not fulfil their contracts, and 70 per cent of the time, employers rewarded employees who overfulfilled their contracts. Indeed, employers rewarded 41 per cent of employees who *exactly* fulfilled their contracts. Moreover, employees *expected* this behaviour on the part of their employers, as shown by the fact that their effort levels *increased significantly* when their bosses gained the power to punish and reward them. Underfulfilling contracts dropped from 83 per cent to 26 per cent of the exchanges, and overfulfilled contracts rose from 3 per cent to 38 per cent of the total. Finally, allowing employers to reward and punish led to a 40 per cent increase in the net payoffs to all subjects, even when the payoff reductions resulting from employer punishment of employees are taken into account.

We conclude from this study that the subjects who assume the role of 'employee' conform to internalized standards of reciprocity, even when they are certain there are no material repercussions from behaving in a self-regarding manner. Moreover, subjects who assume the role of employer expect this behaviour and are rewarded for acting accordingly. Finally, employers reward good and punish bad behaviour when they are allowed, and employees expect this behaviour and adjust their own effort levels accordingly. In general, then subjects follow an internalized norm not only because it is prudent or useful to do so, or because they will suffer some material loss if they do not, but rather because they desire to do so *for its own sake*.

5 Conclusion

As a student of the history of science, I have become aware of the centrality of *scientific instrumentation* in the progress of scientific knowledge. The microscope, the telescope, electrophoresis, and a myriad of other tools of observation and data collection have laid the basis for our current understanding of the natural world. Each new tool allows for the construction of more subtle theoretical models, because it increases the power of observation to choose among models.

Behavioural game theory is simply one among a number of new scientific techniques that allow us to build better models of human behaviour, and to move the discourse concerning human nature from the realm of political philosophy, where there has been little progress since the eighteenth century, to the laboratory and the field, where stunning progress has, and doubtless will continue to be made. It is not too much to suggest that, with the addition of tools such as behavioural game theory, neuroscientific instruments for assessing brain function, and agent-based computer simulation of life processes, the behavioural sciences may one day be put on the footing now enjoyed by the natural sciences.

References

Akerlof, G. (1982) 'Labor Contracts as Partial Gift Exchange,' *Quarterly Journal of Economics,* vol. 97, pp. 543–69.

Alcock, J. (1993) *Animal Behavior: an Evolutionary Approach* (Sunderland, Mass.: Sinauer).

Andreoni, J. and J. Miller (2002) 'Giving According to GARP: an Experimental Test of the Consistency of Preferences for Altruism', *Econometrica,* vol. 70, pp. 737–53.

Aumann, R. (1995) 'Backward Induction and Common Knowledge of Rationality', *Games and Economic Behavior,* vol. 8, pp. 6–19.

Aumann, R. and A. Brandenburger (1995) 'Epistemic Conditions for Nash Equilibrium', *Econometrica,* vol. 65, pp. 1161–80.

Basu, K. (1994) 'The Traveler's Dilemma: Paradoxes of Rationality in Game Theory', *American Economic Review,* vol. 84, pp. 391–5.

Ben-Porath, E. (1997) 'Rationality, Nash Equilibrium and Backward Induction in Perfect-Information Games', *Review of Economic Studies,* vol. 64, pp. 23–46.

Bernheim, D. (1984) 'Rationalizable Strategic Behavior', *Econometrica,* vol. 52, pp. 1007–28.

Bowles, S. and H. Gintis (1993) 'The Revenge of Homo Economicus: Contested Exchange and the Revival of Political Economy', *Journal of Economic Perspectives,* vol. 7, pp. 83–102.

Brown, M., A. Falk and E. Fehr (2004) 'Relational Contracts and the Nature of Market Interactions', *Econometrica,* vol. 72, pp. 747–80.

Camerer, C. (2003) *Behavioral Game Theory: Experiments in Strategic Interaction* (Princeton, NJ: Princeton University Press).

Capra, C., J. Goeree, R. Gomez and C. Holt (1999) 'Anomalous Behavior in a Traveler's Dilemma', *American Economic Review,* vol. 89, pp. 678–90.

Fagin, R., J. Halpern, Y. Moses and M. Vardi (1995) *Reasoning about Knowledge* (Cambridge, Mass.: MIT Press).

Fehr, E., S. Gächter and G. Kirchsteiger (1997) 'Reciprocity as a Contract Enforcement Device: Experimental Evidence', *Econometrica,* vol. 65, pp. 833–60.

Gintis, H. (1976) 'The Nature of the Labor Exchange and the Theory of Capitalist Production', *Review of Radical Political Economics,* vol. 8, pp. 36–54.

Gintis, H. (1989) 'The Power to Switch: On the Political Economy of Consumer Sovereignty', in S. Bowles, R. Edwards and W. Shepherd (eds), *Unconventional Wisdom: Essays in Honor of John Kenneth Galbraith* (New York: Houghton-Mifflin).

Glimcher, P. (2003) *Decisions, Uncertainty and the Brain: the Science of Neuroeconomics* (Cambridge, Mass.: MIT Press).

Halpern, J. (2001) 'Substantive Rationality and Backward Induction', *Games and Economic Behavior,* vol. 37, pp. 425–35.

McKelvey, R. and Palfrey, T. (1992) 'An Experimental Study of the Centipede Game', *Econometrica,* vol. 60, pp. 803–36.
Nagel, R. (1995) 'Unravelling in Guessing Games: an Experimental Study', *American Economic Review,* vol. 85, pp. 1313–26.
Pearce, D. (1984) 'Rationalizable Strategic Behavior and the Problem of Perfection', *Econometrica,* vol. 52, pp. 1029–50.
Selton, R. (1975) 'Re-examination of the Perfectness Concept for Equilibrium Points in Extensive Games', *International Journal of Game Theory,* vol. 4, pp. 25–55.

Index